KEEPING FAITH AT PRINCETON

KEEPING FAITH AT PRINCETON

*A Brief History of Religious Pluralism
at Princeton and Other Universities*

FREDERICK HOUK BORSCH

PRINCETON UNIVERSITY PRESS

Princeton and Oxford

COPYRIGHT © 2012 BY PRINCETON UNIVERSITY PRESS
PUBLISHED BY PRINCETON UNIVERSITY PRESS, 41 WILLIAM
STREET, PRINCETON, NEW JERSEY 08540
IN THE UNITED KINGDOM: PRINCETON UNIVERSITY PRESS, 6
OXFORD STREET, WOODSTOCK, OXFORDSHIRE OX20 1TW
PRESS.PRINCETON.EDU
LIBRARY OF CONGRESS CATALOGING-IN-PUBLICATION DATA
BORSCH, FREDERICK HOUK.
KEEPING FAITH AT PRINCETON : A BRIEF HISTORY OF
RELIGIOUS PLURALISM AT PRINCETON AND OTHER
UNIVERSITIES / FREDERICK HOUK BORSCH.
P. CM.
INCLUDES BIBLIOGRAPHICAL REFERENCES AND INDEX.
ISBN 978-0-691-14573-0 (HARDBACK : ALK. PAPER)   1. PRINCETON
UNIVERSITY—RELIGION—HISTORY.   2. RELIGIOUS PLURALISM—
NEW JERSEY—PRINCETON—HISTORY.   3. UNIVERSITIES AND
COLLEGES—UNITED STATES—RELIGION—
HISTORY.   4. RELIGIOUS PLURALISM—UNITED STATES—
HISTORY.   I. TITLE.
BR561.P75B67 2012
261.2071'174—DC23   2011023646
BRITISH LIBRARY CATALOGING-IN-PUBLICATION
DATA IS AVAILABLE
THIS BOOK HAS BEEN COMPOSED IN
ITC NEW BASKERVILLE AND SABON
PRINTED ON ACID-FREE PAPER. ∞
PRINTED IN THE UNITED STATES OF AMERICA
1 3 5 7 9 10 8 6 4 2

CONTENTS

KEEPING FAITH AT PRINCETON

Introduction

O n the highest ground in town, center campus, neighbor to the
Firestone Library, stands the Princeton University Chapel.
On sunny days its stained glass windows are radiant with
biblical stories along with glimpses of heroes of literature,
philosophy, science, and education. The great south window pictures
Christ the Teacher. The building can accommodate two thousand people
and is the site for major university ceremonies and services. On Sundays
a Protestant ecumenical community, then, later in the day Catholics, followed by Episcopalians, gather for worship. When not in use for weekday services, weddings, funerals, concerts, or plays, often one finds a scattering of individuals listening to an organ practice, quietly praying or
reflecting. In times of crisis, tragedy, or concerned protest, it has been the
site on campus to come together. Every campus tour includes the chapel.

The fourth of the buildings used for worship and assembly at
Princeton,[1] the chapel stands as sign and symbol of Princeton's religious
heritage. By the 1970s, two and a quarter centuries after the school's
founding, the chapel—together with the Office of Dean of the Chapel—
had, however, also become sign and symbol for questions as to the role of
religion at Princeton. Furthered by the demographic shifts created by
World War II, moderate changes in the composition of the university had
been taking place since the dedication of the chapel and the establishment
of its deanship in 1928, but the pace of that change picked up rapidly
from the 1960s through the '70s. When I was an undergraduate in the
mid-1950s, the student body was all male. There were but one or two
black undergraduate students and few "others." Jewish students strove
largely to assimilate as Princetonians and Americans or they could expe-

---

[1] On other Princeton worship spaces and as the definitive book on the present building,
see Richard Stillwell, *The Chapel of Princeton University* (Princeton, NJ: Princeton University Press, 1971). Or one can go to the website of Princeton's Office of Religious Life
and then to "History of the Chapel" to find links to a self-guided tour and an extensive
audio tour.

rience either a subtle to overt anti-Jewish prejudice that was also part of
Princeton's heritage. Although growing in numbers, even Roman Catholics were another distinct Princeton minority.

By the late 1970s the student body at Princeton was edging toward
being half female. While racism was still a significant issue, African Americans, Asian Americans, and other "minority" groups were noticeably
represented in the classroom and many undergraduate programs and activities. With this diversification had also come changes in the religious
make-up of the campus. In the 1950s, more than three out of four students were active or nominal Protestant Christians, mostly affiliated with
"mainline" denominations, largely Episcopalian and Presbyterian, then
Methodist, Congregationalist, and Baptist, fairly much in that order.
There were the Catholic and Jewish minorities with a few Unitarians,
those of other denominations, and 3 percent or so who declared no religion. By 1979 the mild post–World War II religious revival of the 1950s
that had seemed to strengthen mainline Protestantism in America had
faded. There were now more Jewish and Catholic students and more
from "evangelical" Christian groups and predominantly black churches.
At that time it was largely the international graduate students, with a
scattering of international undergraduates, who brought their Muslim,
Buddhist, Hindu, or other faith traditions with them. Perhaps just as significantly, a number of students were less formally religious. They, with
their parents, had passed through the Vietnam War and its "pro" and
"anti" movements, some exposure to "death of God" debates, and an era
of challenging authority and established views. New modes of contraception had contributed to the questioning of traditional teaching regarding
sexual standards and morality and the very purposes of human sexuality.
"Going to church," and particularly to mainline Protestant churches, in
order to belong in American society was less important socially and intellectually. A growing sense of individual rights and decision-making autonomy (often encouraged by Protestant thought) made religious faith
and church attendance, especially among the educated classes, more a
matter of choice than a norm. While some family religious background
was still part of the lives of a majority of students, they might describe
themselves as more "spiritual" in their values and beliefs. If pressed further, a number of students might say they were "questing" as far as any
religious belief and practice were concerned, though such a quest was not
necessarily high on their youthful agendas. Some would claim agnosti-
cism; a few would admit that they leaned toward atheism.

What was true for the student body as far as religion was concerned was more evident with regard to the faculty. While Princeton's administrative and particularly its service staff had long been more ethnically, racially, and religiously diverse than the rest of the university, the faculty of the 1950s had looked a lot like an older version of the student body. Although less likely to profess any active faith, they often had a Protestant background if not practice. A number of the younger ones had served in the military or allied public service during World War II, and there were foreign refugees from that conflict, a small number of them at the Institute for Advanced Studies. While slower to change than the student body in terms of race and gender, the faculty of the late 1970s now had considerably more Jewish members, a few representatives of faiths other than Christian or Jewish, and a yet larger number of members who might describe themselves as spiritual and/or secular and nonreligious.

For over two hundred years the College of New Jersey and then Princeton University had been seen as providing encouragement for the beliefs and values of a form of Protestant Christianity. Although having a complex relationship with the Presbyterian Church, every president of Princeton until 1972 was either a Presbyterian clergyman or the son of one. Christian students who matriculated at Princeton could find an officially welcoming environment for their faith aspirations along with the opportunity to put their values into practice in service and worship. Were it requested, pastoral care in terms of counseling about faith questions or personal matters could be provided.

If, however, Princeton—heading into the 1980s and beyond—was to be a welcoming and supportive community for a more diverse religious, spiritual, and secular student body and faculty, how could it best do this? After providing a historical context for the role of religion at Princeton in chapter 1, chapters 2 and 3 of *Keeping Faith at Princeton: A Brief History of Religious Pluralism at Princeton and Other Universities* tell the story of the changes that took place at Princeton and why. What, we shall ask, were some of the opposing arguments? Then how were they responded to in institutional, ethical, and even theological terms? How were the new policies implemented and received through the next decade? In a final chapter we shall look at religion and religions at Princeton today.

While this is a narrative of institutional policies and religious beliefs and issues, it is also—to use a religious term—an incarnate story as well. It is about buildings and money, and it is particularly about people and their personalities, cultural attitudes, beliefs, and aspirations. In this perspective important parts of the story can be told firsthand because I was there at Princeton, first as an undergraduate and then as the dean of the chapel through much of the 1980s. Later I served as a trustee of the university, chair of the trustees' Student Life Committee, on the advisory board for the Center for the Study of Religion, and even returned for a short stint as interim dean of religious life and the chapel in 2007. I have been privileged to know, work, and sometimes pray with five presidents of the university and two previous deans of the chapel and my successors in that position. I have also been able to discuss significant issues with other figures involved in the decision-making and implementation process—faculty, students, trustees, and university staff—and to talk with a number of them about this study.

This story of the role of religions at Princeton is one microcosm of religion in America. But Princeton has hardly been alone among institutions of higher education in the passage from determined and hope-filled Christian beginnings—fully entwined with enthusiasm for the values of education—through years of Protestant hegemony, then the changes brought about by the influx of new immigrants to America, wars and economic cycles, and growing forms of secularism in this yet (in terms of numbers of professed believers and public rhetoric) quite religious society. With permutations due to particular histories, geography, personalities, and institutional mission, many colleges and universities experienced the shifting forces of demography, new knowledge, economics, and societal and pedagogical values that caused presidents and other administrators—trustees and faculty, too—to wonder and sometimes ask questions about the roles religious belief and practice could best have in their institutions. In times of growing religious pluralism—in a country in which religions have the power both to divide and sometimes link people together in a sense of common society[2]—how best, they may well ask, can our school provide for the religious and spiritual needs and aspirations of students while also protecting the rights and integrity of many in the campus community with little or no religious faith? Although more militant forms of secularism may lead some administers to want to exclude religion from the academy, more inclusive academic thinkers may also ask how the school could be a setting for learning and understanding among religions and philosophies of life for students who are to be citizens in a religiously

---

[2] This is the theme and thesis of the comprehensive overview of Robert D. Putnam and David E. Campbell, *American Grace: How Religion Divides and Unites Us* (New York: Simon and Schuster, 2010).

pluralistic society and world? How in these matters do we represent ourselves to prospective students, alumni, and other constituencies?

One can, for instance, see Yale University beginning to think about questions of pluralism and the place of religion in response to William Buckley's youthful diatribe *God and Man at Yale*, and then to William Sloane Coffin's prophetic ministry during the turmoil of the 1960s. Harvard had to negotiate President Nathan Pusey's 1950s efforts to give faith a greater role, while an early '70s committee charged to answer the question, "How can Harvard provide appropriate recognition to the diverse religious needs of its community while still maintaining the vitality of the traditions and programs associated with Memorial Church?" disbanded, frustrated by "the sharp divisions of opinion that exist throughout the Harvard community concerning the questions under review."[3] Decades later it may seem surprising to many that there should be controversy regarding a university's support of any particular religious beliefs, but there were thorny questions and some soul searching, and echoes of these concerns continue to be heard.

The questions had and have no ready-made answers, and, in some cases, the best response may have seemed a kind of institutional drift with the changing circumstances and times—not always an unwise response with issues that can be as volatile and, on occasion, hard fully to understand as those of religion. In other cases, however, while necessarily keeping an eye on their competitors for students, faculty, and funding, colleges and universities have been more deliberate in making alterations or more far-reaching changes in their support for religion as it has moved from once being at the core of the school's mission to be regarded more as a voluntary curricular matter and an extracurricular service offered to its community of students and scholars.

Thus, while Princeton provides the paradigm for this study, there is occasion in the trajectory of its story to note something of the changes that have taken place at peer institutions in America. In chapter 4 overviews are provided that focus on seven private universities selected because of Princeton's and my own interaction with them. Incarnate with their own personalities, buildings, and constituencies, these briefer narratives offer context and perspective for the Princeton story while being of interest and instructive in themselves. In their similar and different ways each institution has become not only a window on religion and

[3] See chapter 4.

religions in America today but also a significant setting where people of different faiths, little or none, can learn from and about one another. We are still discovering whether that learning and sharing can help lead to better understanding among religions and can foster cooperation and service in a nation and a world that greatly need such understanding and informed care.

ONE

The Protestant Heritage

"Curious about . . . interested in religion," was how I could have described myself during my undergraduate years in the mid-1950s at Princeton. I grew up attending a middle-of-the-road Episcopal Church in a well-to-do suburb of Chicago. I was an indifferent choir boy and then a reasonably diligent acolyte. I took an interest in the liturgical year and the story it tells and became intrigued by the prophetic and ethical pronouncements of the Bible and especially the person and parables of Jesus. I wanted to know more but was still learning how to frame and probe my questions.

I did not, however, want to think of myself as pious or just a "do-gooder," the put-down epithet of the time. I thought it important to "goof off" and shot hoops and played football, pool, and Ping-pong. I spent too much time at the bridge table, learned to drink beer and other "adult beverages," became a class officer, and dated girls in the summer or when I could figure out how to manage it while at Princeton. As a young man from a midwestern public school at an all-male college in central New Jersey, it was not easy to meet young women unless one wanted to spend a lot of time at it and what seemed like quite a bit of money. Although we talked of women and sex, it was—at least during the academic year—largely a theoretical subject for many of us. In that era it may have been a good thing. Certainly there was more time for study and for conversation and reflection on academic subjects—not least on long weekends.

Late in my senior year in high school, then through my freshmen year at Princeton—becoming worse in the following fall—I would sometimes cough up bright blood. It would happen when I exercised vigorously or even when I coughed or laughed too hard. The doctors could not find the cause. They probed my sinuses and throat and then lungs. It should heal itself, they hoped. But it did not, and it was finally determined that the problem looked to be in a lower lobe of my right lung. The offending portion was excised in a major lung operation during the first semester of my sophomore year, and I was cured. Somehow—in what the doctors described as a one-in-a-million circumstance—a piece of cellulose (from popcorn or a pine needle or something else) had become imbedded in a blood vessel. Once removed, I had only a rather lengthy scar on my back.

It had, however, been a sometimes-frightening experience. I had thought about dying young—strangling in my own blood. I found it not difficult to imagine myself a John Keats coming to an untimely end or to put myself in the sanitarium with the young Hans Castorp in Thomas Mann's novel *The Magic Mountain*. I wrote a short novel that dramatically employed as an epigram words from the dedication of Cervantes's last work: "With one foot already in the stirrup and with the agony of death upon me, great Lord, I write to you."[1] In whatever time was allotted to me, I wanted to find out more about "the meaning or significance of life," if there were any. Was there any "basis" for it? I was not expecting to find some definitive answer at Princeton but wanted to discover some direction in which it could be explored.

Princeton faculty members were understandably modest in response to any questions put too directly along these lines. Liberal arts courses engaged in historical overviews, surveys of knowledge and ideas, and then some closer reading of texts and sometimes-critical analysis of theories and methods of interpretation. I shall always be grateful to Princeton faculty for helping me learn how to read carefully and critically, while I also learned that questions about meaning or purpose in life had to be posed indirectly if they were to be heard at all. We could have some discussion of values and virtues in life as long as one did not press too hard for an understanding of a basis or rationale for these values and virtues.

I considered majoring in the Department of Religion, where I had already taken a course. The department had its beginning in a faculty study of 1935 that recognized that more was then being done with courses in religion in the general curriculum at a number of other colleges and universities. By the time of George F. Thomas's appointment in 1940 as the university's Professor of Religious Thought, followed by his chairmanship and development of the department, Princeton could be seen to have taken a rather pioneering step. At a 1957 luncheon honoring Princeton's then retiring President Harold Dodds, Harvard's President Nathan Pusey (him-

---

[1] See now in Celia Richmond Weller and Clark A. Colahan's modern translation of, Miguel de Cervantes Saavedra, *The Trials of Persiles and Sigismunda: A Northern Story* (Indianapolis, IN: Hackett Publishing, 2009), 365.

self much interested in the place of religion in a university) praised Dodds and Princeton for, "because of a blindness which has infected much modern education," being almost alone in "blazing a new trail when she set out in 1940 to build a strong Department of Religion."[2] By 1955 the department had a faculty of two full professors, three assistant professors, and three instructors and was beginning a graduate program. Over seven hundred students had taken at least one course in a department that also had twenty-eight concentrators or majors.[3] Most of the courses focused on or related to Christianity and the Bible. Prophetic and Wisdom Literature of the Hebrews was sometimes taught from a Jewish perspective, and there was another course called Religions of the Far East. Although not alone in having a religion department, Princeton's reputation encouraged emulation in a number of other college and universities.

The development of the department, however, had critics. From a longer perspective it could be seen as part of a decades-long process in which the once central teaching of the Bible, religious philosophy, and ethics had been minimized and then largely removed from the curriculum. Now, in the eyes of critics, it was relegated to a smallish department for those who happened to be interested in religion or who might want to gain some knowledge of the Bible for historical understanding and literary appreciation or to take a religion course for cross-disciplinary reasons. Other Princeton faculty members were now freer, some would argue, to ignore religious questions, including ethical and value issues that might be raised from a religious perspective. The majority of students would learn little or nothing of religion from their curricular studies.

From a different angle, there was concern as to whether "religion" could be properly defined and departmentalized as an academic subject and whether it would be taught with the rigor and critical objectivity that was expected of courses in a modern university curriculum. Perhaps the phenomenon of religion was best studied in history, anthropology, sociology, and philosophy courses and the Bible read in literature or "great

---

[2] In Nathan M. Pusey, "Harold Dodds," *Princeton Alumni Weekly* (*PAW*), May 10, 1957, 3–6, on 5.

[3] Philip Ashby, "Religion, the Department of," in *A Princeton Companion*, ed. Alexander Leitch (Princeton, NJ: Princeton University Press. 1978), 404. Further on the development of Princeton's department and religious studies and departments of religion more generally, see the introduction and essays in Paul Ramsey and John F. Wilson, eds., *The Study of Religion in Colleges and Universities* (Princeton, NJ: Princeton University Press, 1970), and D. G. Hart, *The University Gets Religion: Religious Studies in American Higher Education* (Baltimore: Johns Hopkins University Press, 1999).

books" courses. And what would the departmental faculty, most who came from a liberal Protestant background, do with their own faith perspectives in the classroom? Paul Ramsey, after all, taught and wrote about Christian ethics. George Thomas was known to speak to church groups in town and to Christian fellowship groups on campus. He had helped to found the intercollegiate Faculty Christian Fellowship and wrote for *The Christian Scholar*, which had as part of its raison d'être the proposition that faith and intellectual thought, though in "constant tension," were also "complementary."[4] Thomas promoted the study of religion as an integrating factor in the curriculum, a means of helping to overcome a tendency to impart knowledge without meaning, and a way of overcoming too much relativism. To a public lecture titled "Religion in the Universities," he gave the subtitle "Since World War II, There Has Been a Renewed Concern for Spiritual Values and Christian Faith."[5]

Yet Professor Thomas and other faculty—in a department that wanted to be seen as having a place in a research university—were aware of the need to defend their teaching as properly academic and critical. Some faculty wanted to talk of the "scientific" study of the Bible and religion, although the young faculty member Van Austin Harvey probably put it better when he taught and would later write about weighing the preponderance of evidence, as though in a civil court trial, in questions of historical interpretation.[6] Thomas knew full well that he was teaching in a largely secular environment. In the introduction to Thomas's inaugural lecture "Religion in an Age of Secularism," President Dodds had spoken of "three distinctive ways of approach to religion" that were available to students at Princeton: worship in chapel, opportunities for "applied religion" through practical service, and the "intellectual approach through courses in the curriculum."[7] Thomas understood that this third approach was his department's primary work even if not everyone agreed on how it was best defined.

[4] In "About the Journal: The Editor's Preface" of the newly renamed journal. *The Christian Scholar* 36 (1953): 3–6, on 4.

[5] The lecture was adapted for the *PAW*, January 28, 1955, 10–12.

[6] See his influential *The Historian and the Believer: The Morality of Historical Knowledge and Christian Belief* (New York: Macmillan, 1966); new ed., (Urbana: University of Illinois Press, 1996).

[7] The 1940 inaugural lecture of Thomas with Dodd's "Introduction" is in pamphlet form in the Spear Library of the Princeton Theological Seminary. This broad perspective on religion's role enabled, it seems likely, the university to use funds donated for the chaplaincy, the chapel, and its programs to help establish the Department of Religion.

Students were in a sense connoisseurs of all this—interested to see what role, if any, personal faith might play in the classroom, while making judgments as to whether departmental faculty were being sufficiently objective and critical or bending over backward in their efforts to appear so. While many a scientific course and some of the arts invited participation for their understanding and appreciation, we recognized that religion—perhaps because it could be such a personal and emotive subject—had in the classroom to be presented apart from any direct participation in its practices. Prayer, contemplation, worship, fasting, almsgiving, acts of service—even sacred music and much of theology—might be read about if they had some historical interest but were otherwise pretty much off the table and out of the syllabus. While a student with personal religious questions could find an open faculty door, the counsel would generally be in terms of a book to be read and/or a campus chaplain to visit.

I began to realize, however, what I was learning from George Thomas—in no small part because of his evident care and patience with students. He helped me to recognize some of the problems with reductionist forms of positivism and to recognize that teaching without any form of presupposition was an illusion. If the apparent gulf between faith and knowledge was to be bridged, one had to come to understand that there were different ways of knowing—to think of epistemology in terms of a more encompassing rationality: "perception of truth [that] not only employed reason and sense perception, but also intuition, imagination and feeling."[8]

One of the more popular faculty members in the Religion Department was a young instructor who came to Princeton in 1953 as he was finishing his doctoral thesis at Columbia. Malcolm Diamond was Jewish, a budding social activist, and, it seemed to us, refreshingly irreverent. He was assigned to teach the Literature of the Hebrews course but also knew a lot about Buber and Kierkegaard and was ready to entertain all manner of existential questions and even questions about the teaching of professors for whose lecture courses he led preceptorials of eight or so students.

Adding spice to an interest in religion at Princeton at this time were the opinions of the conservative, witty, and at times incorrigible Catholic chaplain, the Dominican Hugh Halton. Halton, who surely had read and

[8] George F. Thomas, "The Meaning of Truth," *The Christian Scholar* 36 (1953): 174–75. Quoted by P. C. Kemeny, *Princeton in the Nation's Service: Religious Ideals and Educational Practice, 1868–1928* (New York: Oxford University Press, 1998), 226.

digested William Buckley's *God and Man at Yale*,[9] and perhaps knew of Jesuit Chaplain Leonard Feeney's earlier denouncement of Harvard's secularism,[10] launched an attack on Princeton's "dogmatic secularism."[11] In a series of five sermons he criticized Princeton and its Stuart Professor of Philosophy, Walter Stace, for many "factual errors" in his teaching and particularly for his article "Man against Darkness: Has Religion Lost Its Power?," in which Stace wrote, among other things, that the world "is not ruled by a spiritual being but by blind forces."[12] Halton also faulted the Religion Department for having no one on its faculty as well trained in Roman Catholicism "as an eighth-grader at St. Paul's School"[13] (a local Catholic school). It was well reported to us that Halton had counseled Catholic students not to take any courses in the department—once referring to them as a "formal education in heresy."[14] A classmate (and later Harvard PhD and longtime professor of religion at Wells College) recalls one such conversation. Arthur Bellinzoni, then a devout Roman Catholic, nevertheless did major in religion and through courses like George Thomas's Major Problems in Religious Thought became for a time, as he put it, "a member of the Church of Total Confusion."[15]

In a way, Halton had a point about diversity. In a 1952 letter offering his understanding of the Religion Department's diversity, Thomas noted that the then five-member staff represented "different fields of specialization and different approaches. Though we are all Protestant, we belong to different churches and come from different seminaries. We have felt that it is important to have a diversity of interest, approach and point of

[9] William F. Buckley Jr., *God and Man at Yale: The Superstitions of "Academic Freedom"* (Chicago: Henry Regnery, 1951).

[10] See Kemeny, *Nation's Service*, 225, and John M. Cudahy, *No Offense: Civil Religion and Protestant Taste* (New York: Seabury, 1978), 49–64.

[11] See Hugh Halton, Letter to the Editor (a paid advertisement), *DP*, March 22, 1956, 4.

[12] Stace's article first appeared in the September 1948 issue of *Atlantic Monthly* and later as the lead chapter in W. T. Stace, *Man against Darkness and Other Essays* (Pittsburgh: University of Pittsburgh Press, 1967), 3–17, quotation on 3. Among the many commentaries on the Halton controversy, see *Time*, "God and Man at Princeton," October 7, 1957, 47. Also notable are the four anti-Halton and anti-Catholic pamphlets of Princeton Professor of Art and Archaeology Emeritus George W. Elderkin, *The Roman Catholic Controversy at Princeton University* (n.p., 1955–58). Many articles, editorials, and letters pertaining to the controversy are in a file in "Office of the Dean of Religious Life and the Chapel Records," (AC 144, Box 33) in Princeton's Mudd Manuscript Library.

[13] Halton, "God and Man at Princeton."

[14] In Robert A. Sklar, "Priest Sees Faith in Jeopardy," *DP*, October 1, 1956, 1.

[15] Arthur J. Bellinzoni, *The Future of Christianity: Can It Survive?* (Amherst, NY: Prometheus Books, 2006), 8–9.

view in a liberal university like Princeton."[16] Moreover, while Thomas wanted the courses to be taught with appropriate academic objectivity, he saw it as part of his work to present the Christian faith as intellectually respectable. Indeed, this was no doubt a major reason why Harvard's Pusey had praised the department's formation. Yet for Halton this high-minded, liberal Protestant view of Christianity was a bland, watered-down version of the Christian faith and an implied criticism of Catholicism. He viewed civic Protestantism as the established religion and culture of Princeton, which in turn responded to him that the day for having a Roman Catholic person teach religion at Princeton would come only when that person could be "free enough from ecclesiastical discipline to devote himself whole-heartedly to the community of teachers and scholars that is Princeton University."[17] Indeed, a number of the Christian faculty likely felt themselves more comfortable with liberal Jewish theology than with Catholic doctrine.

Chaplain Halton's theological and political conservatism led him also, however, to strongly critique the contemporary Catholic theologian Jacques Maritain, then residing and teaching in Princeton, and to forbid the distinguished Catholic historian and philosopher Etienne Gilson a Catholic forum. This criticism, of course, made some of us want to read them all the more, especially Maritain who strove to take the sciences and arts into his Thomistic and Aristotelian worldview. When a student organization invited Alger Hiss (recently released from jail after his sentence as a perjurer and still under suspicion by some as having been a communist spy) to speak at the university, Halton escalated his rhetoric and summed up his view of Princeton as a hotbed of "moral and political subversion."[18] In fact, President Dodds and others in the administration had leaned on the students to have the invitation rescinded,[19] but Halton felt they had just shown their weak-kneed liberalism. After several Catholic faculty members raised concerns about Halton's views and tactics (Senator Joseph McCarthy's methods would have been on many

[16] In a letter to Professor Frank J. E. Turner at the University of British Columbia, April 29, 1952. In Box 1, George F. Thomas Papers, Rare Books and Manuscript Division, Firestone Library, Princeton University Libraries.

[17] E. Harris Harbison in Letter to the Editor, *DP*, October 11, 1955, 3.

[18] In "God and Man at Princeton."

[19] Dean Jeremiah Finch later denied that there was any such pressure (*PAW*, Februry 23 and March 9, 1981, 8), but my classmate, Bruce Bringgold, president of the Whig-Cliosophic Society, and others felt it. See John D. Fox, letter to *PAW*, February 22, 1982, 8, 10, and letter by W. A. Pusey, September 26, 2007, 6.

a mind), even professor of chemistry and dean of the Graduate School, Hugh Stott Taylor (who, as a Fellow of the Royal Society, Knight Commander of the Order of the British Empire, and named by Pius XII Knight Commander of the Order of St. Gregory the Great, seemed as close to royalty and Catholic piety as anyone at Princeton could get) was not immune from Halton's disdain with regard to his knowledge of Catholic teaching, and Thomas Aquinas in particular ("incompetent"), and the character of his faith.

Nor did Halton think much of the philosophical or theological competence of Professor Gregory Vlastos (even though Vlastos had invited him to offer a lecture on Aquinas in one of his courses), and he continued to question President Dodds's veracity and integrity.[20] His politicized rhetoric and personal attacks on individuals at Princeton would by the fall of 1957 lead Robert Goheen (then the new president of Princeton and encouraged in this by retiring President Dodds) to suspend Chaplain Halton's privileges as a chaplain on campus. Goheen, who had a Catholic wife and six children being raised as Catholics, carefully distinguished, however, between Halton himself and the welcome the university continued to give to the Aquinas Foundation, the center for the Catholic chaplaincy at Princeton.

One reason I knew as much as I did about religion, and particularly the Religion Department at Princeton and its critics and supporters, was that my roommate was majoring in religion. David Sofield and I were roommates for three years within several larger configurations of classmates. Having been in several courses together, we were also complementary in our academic and intellectual interests. David, an agnostic with his concentration in religion, had an informed interest in literature and poetry and would go on to have a long career as professor of English literature and a poet at Amherst. I would major in English literature before taking on theological studies. David was in several ways a mentor to me in literature, and, I suppose, I was to him in matters of religion. Sometimes together with other roommates we had many a discussion of books, courses, teachers, and ideas.

Our opinions of Chaplain Halton were not favorable. In this view we were sometimes joined by Catholic classmates within and outside our

[20] Reported in *DP*, February 25, 1957: "Halton Blasts Again, Hits Dodds, 'Prince,'" 3.

group of roommates. Our views may have lacked some sophistication, but we were sure that Halton did not fully appreciate the values and responsibilities of academic freedom and free inquiry. Nor did he understand the responsibility of members of the Department of Religion to teach critically about religion rather than to try to teach religious faith from any doctrinal point of view. We might have wished, if only for argument's sake, that some of our professors could have been more open and personal about their religious views and the bases for their beliefs or nonbeliefs and values, but we thought we understood why this was generally not appropriate in the classroom.

As far as Professor Stace was concerned, he was one of the more respected "wise old men" at Princeton. He could take a bleak view of existence in a "purposeless and meaningless universe,"[21] but yet had developed an interest in mysticism. He was one of the few faculty members who would talk about such experience and who also brought non-Western religions into his perspective.[22] I do not recall our use of the phrase then, but in later years Walter Stace would likely have been described as a "spiritual person."

Walter Kaufmann was Stace's younger colleague in the Department of Philosophy who, if he was not in Chaplain Halton's sights, should have been. Raised a Lutheran who became for a time a kind of existentialist Jew, Kaufmann, an interpreter of Nietzsche, offered a sharp critique of all religious orthodoxies. Soon to be the author of *Critique of Religion and Philosophy* and *Faith of a Heretic*, he yet found a place for religious thought along with philosophy in the search for truth and the highest human values.

One figure about whose religious beliefs or nonbeliefs there was considerable speculation was Princeton's most famous resident. I was one among a number of students who caught glimpses of Albert Einstein on his morning walks from his Mercer Street house. I remember the day he died in the spring of our sophomore year. I was with my classmate Johnny (R. W.) Apple shortly after he broke the news in the *Daily Princetonian*. Apple then further showed his mettle as a journalist (he soon flunked out of Princeton for spending too much time being one) by looking in the Yellow Pages for the telephone numbers of two Trenton crematoriums and calling to find out the date and time of "Mr. Einstein's" cremation and then putting that out to the *New York Times*.

[21] Stace, *Man against Darkness*, 13.
[22] See his *Mysticism and Philosophy* (Philadelphia: J. B. Lippincott, 1960).

What happened to Einstein's mind and spirit at death? Did Einstein's great insights into the form and matter of the universe help him to believe in God? His sometimes-gnomic statements often left people wondering and even debating. We came to understand that Einstein did not have faith in any traditional manner in a "personal" God, but that he lived with a sense of awe and mystery he once put this way:

> The most beautiful emotion we can experience is the mysterious. It is the fundamental emotion that stands at the cradle of all true art and science. He to whom this emotion is a stranger, who can no longer wonder and stand rapt in awe, is as good as dead, a snuffed out candle. To sense that behind anything that can be experienced there is something that our minds cannot grasp, whose beauty and sublimity reaches us only indirectly: this is religiousness. In this sense, and in this sense only, I am a devoutly religious man.[23]

During those 1950s years there were also opportunities to learn about religious faith and practice outside the curriculum. In addition to the Catholic and Jewish Hillel chaplains, there was an Episcopalian and several other Christian chaplains, some offering opportunities for worship as well as evening fellowships, often a meal and opportunities for conversation and occasional talks or meetings with visiting theologians, clergy, or other religious leaders who would speak about aspects of faith and/or their commitments to ethical causes.

In part because we would regularly pass it on our way to the library, the chapel loomed large. A tour of its windows was a course in the Bible. In addition to the biblical figures, here, too, was homage given to philosophers and astronomers, scientists, theologians, and poets. While a pair of binoculars was helpful to spot them all, the iconography was a paean in stained glass to the harmony of faith and all knowledge. Attendance at Sunday worship in the chapel or at some other weekend religious service was still required for underclassmen at Princeton, though this had been modified to once every two weeks, and one suspected the obligation was on its way out entirely as was true at peer universities. This was the subject of editorializing and commentary in the *Daily Princetonian*, which would sometimes take the high ground by arguing that only voluntary

---

[23] From Einstein's 1930 "What I Believe," and quoted now in larger perspective in the chapter "Einstein's God," in Walter Issacson's *Einstein: His Life and Universe* (New York: Simon and Schuster, 2007), 387.

rather than required worship could lead to a mature faith.[24] My room-mate, David, would, from time to time, attend the Friday night Jewish services in order to keep his weekend free for study or other adventures. Others of us might go to a denominational service and some to local churches in town where we could get credit for chapel attendance. Certainly there were Presbyterian students who preferred the virtually on-campus First Presbyterian Church—a major town congregation where a number of the university and seminary faculty worshipped. One student from the class of 1953 who went into the Episcopal ministry later told me that he found the chapel services uninspiring, while the rector at Trinity Church, John Vernon Butler, preached the best sermons he had ever heard, and I learned that a coterie of faculty were members there as well. I sometimes followed them in Trinity's direction, but on a few Sundays went to the official eleven in the morning chapel services. There we were invited to sing hymns familiar to some of us. Our student choir, under Carl Weinrich's direction, sang anthems and other music, though we heard little that could be considered contemporary. One could become more involved by joining the choir or by becoming a chapel deacon, which meant opportunities to usher, read lessons, and have meetings with the dean or the assistant dean in Murray-Dodge Hall. It was evident that the dean or assistant dean had put considerable effort into the preparation of the Sunday sermons, often enough attempting to make contact with the academic reading, circumstances, and questions of undergraduates. From time to time distinguished visiting clergy ascended the high pulpit for these semi-ecumenical, Presbyterian-influenced liturgies. It was the only place in the university where a black person in a leadership position might address us.

It did not help the general Sunday morning atmosphere that freshman and sophomore attendance was still required. The president regularly came, as did Dean Jeremiah Finch, several other deans, and quite a few alumni and some townsfolk. But there were few faculty members in attendance and not many graduate students, which made it seem more like a formality that we were there. While one might exaggerate the deliberate expressions of undergraduate indifference, they were certainly present as well, especially among those who sat up in the balcony—books open in the lap, shuffled newspapers, and students appearing bored or asleep or yawning conspicuously. We heard rumors of years past when students

---

[24] E.g., Joseph Nye, "And Furthermore . . ."; J. S. Nye, *DP*, April 24, 1957, 2.

broke out in concerted coughing fits, and once several members of my class tried, rather half-heartedly, to emulate them.

The dean of the chapel during our first two undergraduate years was Donald Aldrich, a former Charter Trustee and resigned Episcopal bishop who, I was told, had health problems because of the war. He had been a US Navy chaplain and served less than a year as bishop before his doctors advised retirement from that position. Aldrich evidently had been an effective university chaplain, perhaps especially with the veterans returning to their studies. He had noticed increased attendance at chapel services and interest in the Student Christian Association. "The present day undergraduate," he was quoted as saying to the *New York Times* in 1948, "to a greater degree that his pre-war counterpart, has a readiness to identify himself with religion."[25] Perhaps, as some of these young participants or witnesses of war hoped, a renewed faith and commitment to God's ways—even of trying to love one's enemies—might help avoid the horrors of future wars. By 1953, however, Aldrich was coming to the end of his energy and tenure. I recall speaking to him but once or twice and thinking him a well-meaning man, but few of those in my class knew or remembered him well.

Things changed in the chapel in the fall of 1955. Ernest Gordon was a vigorous Scotsman in his forties who had already been the Presbyterian chaplain at Princeton the previous year. With his burr and Presbyterian convictions, he must have seemed to some like a modern-day version of Princeton presidents John Witherspoon and James McCosh, who had brought the same to Princeton in the two earlier centuries. Gordon also brought with him his dramatic stories of having been a captive of the Japanese for nearly four years and of his conversion through the caring of brother Christians amid the wretched circumstances of a prisoner-of-war camp. Although aware of the powerful forces of secularism throughout the campus, Gordon was all the more determined to offer to others the opportunity for a lively and living faith. The English evangelist Bryan Green and the youthful Billy Graham were invited to Princeton for conferences that were virtual preaching missions and opportunities for renewal. I recall Graham telling a small group of us that while he might or might not be able to bring individuals to Christ at Princeton, he could create an interest that others would follow up on. And Gordon strove through his own preaching and that of other invited speakers to

[25] *New York Times*, November 25, 1948, 29.

make Christian faith a matter of passion and courage as well as service to others.

There is no doubt that Ernest Gordon made his mark, and it says something about the significance of Christianity at Princeton (perhaps particularly for President Dodds) that he was chosen in 1955 to be dean of the chapel. Still, a number of us had the feeling that he was swimming upstream or was at least swimming out of the mainstream of the university. If asked about Princeton's overall commitment to the importance of religion at this time, many of us as undergraduates would likely have said that it seemed "official" and not insincere but mostly on the periphery. In the university ceremonies at the beginning and end of our time at Princeton (Opening Exercises and Baccalaureate), God was prayed to and occasionally referred to in addresses. The figure of Jesus could, as it were, be given honorable mention, and there was a place for the Lord's Prayer, hymns, and anthems. We knew that the motto on the university's seal (under a depiction of the two testaments—the *vetus* or *old* name, of course, pejorative to Jews) was *Dei Sub Numine Viget*, most often translated as "under God she flourishes," and we may have known that prayers were said at the beginning of trustee and faculty meetings. Moreover, some of us were aware that there were significant faculty figures who were known for their belief and Christian service, E. Harris Harbison, with his strong historical sense of what it meant to be a Christian scholar, being among the foremost.[26] Yet with regard to any vibrant religious faith at Princeton, all of this came across to many of us as mostly secondary and not at the heart of what the university was about. It translated, if and when we were paying attention, into the rhetoric of a dedication to learning, virtues of truth, courage, and service but lightly tethered to Princeton's Christian heritage. Princetonians ought to be men of character—in Princeton's case young men of honor adhering to the student-enjoined honor code. Because the university was a school of learning, dependent on honest and open inquiry, men of integrity always told the truth. The major goal of life was service—usually broadly defined, while particular lives of service could serve as illustrations. In our years Adlai Stevenson (Princeton 1922) was often mentioned. Woodrow Wilson's name was regularly in the background; therefore, it was particularly service to the nation, although sometimes, more parochially, service to Princeton. The

[26] His book *The Christian Scholar in the Age of the Reformation* (New York: Scribner's, 1956) was published during this period and influenced Yale's Jaroslav Pelikan in his writing of *The Christian Intellectual* (New York: Harper and Row, 1965).

Orange Key, through which student guides provided hospitality tours to visitors to campus and through which bus tours were arranged to sports events or to bring young women to campus dances, was described as the "University's principal undergraduate service organization."[27] Because we were privileged to attend Princeton, we were sometimes told, lives of value and purpose would be expected of us.

Although one might ask more about specificities of these values and virtues, it was hard not to agree in principle. That principle applied, first of all, to the discipline of our learning at Princeton and then to our choices with regard to vocation and life's service. Although I do not recall variants on the phraseology being used then, it was not difficult to gain a sense that we could, in years to come, "do well while doing good" or "do good while doing well," indeed, that we might well "do good by doing well" were we to gain the wealth to help others out of our bounty—education and Princeton in particular to be one recipient of our gratitude and care. Meanwhile, if one was looking for such while in college, there were opportunities for extracurricular service through local YMCAs, tutoring, or other such activities in Princeton or Trenton through the Student Volunteers Council. One could work for the Campus Fund Drive or devote eight weeks to counseling at the Princeton Summer Camp. While the Campus Fund Drive had become a separate program in 1952, the Volunteers Council and the Summer Camp were activities under the umbrella of the Student Christian Association, the successor to the earlier YMCA-like Philadelphian Society.

It must have been a problem for some students of that time that this advocacy of character and service would be given a Protestant Christian flavor with regard to its rationale. I imagine, as far as any nonbelievers or nontheists were concerned, that the flavoring might be regarded as but part of a no longer highly relevant heritage that was culturally theirs as well. But what if one's faith was not Protestant Christian, and, in this respect, what if one was somewhat different from the rest of the student body? Were Roman Catholics a second-class group at Princeton? Their numbers at Princeton (then about 10 percent) were certainly lower than their percentage in the population at large. For many of them Princeton must have seemed an Anglo-Saxon Protestant community into which they were welcomed as Christians but which was still not entirely theirs. Some of them might also have been aware of a longer cultural and reli-

---

[27] The *Bric-A-Brac 1954*. The 76th edition of Princeton's annual yearbook. Princeton, NJ, 100.

gious antipathy of Protestant America toward largely immigrant Roman Catholics—many of them Irish, Italian, Polish—although almost all of the Catholic classmates at Princeton seemed to be of northern European stock (English, Irish, some Germanic). One of the Catholic students' more important assignments at Princeton was to fit in as Princetonians and Americans, and among other things to show (as John F. Kennedy would need to do in 1960) that they thoroughly supported democracy and the separation of church and state. Devoted and even proud as they could be of their Catholicism, this should not cause them to be too distinctive. This was probably one of the tendencies that most bothered Halton, who wanted Catholics to be distinctive in their values and moral thinking. In retrospect one might understand Chaplain Halton's challenges to some of the programs and teachings of the university as much culturally as theologically driven. Relatively few of the Catholic students would appreciate Chaplain Halton's protests, but, that being said, Catholics of the time had yet been schooled to understand that they were definitely not Protestant. One of my Catholic classmates, the class president at the time, told me of an invitation he received to become a chapel deacon. He was honored, but that was one thing, he understood, he should definitely not do.

One could magnify a desire on the part of many Jewish students to fit in as Princetonians. Family and congregation wished them to do well at Princeton and in America. Often the most effective way to do this at a university long known for prejudice toward Jews was to assimilate as best they felt they could. A number of them did so, making little of their religion or culture while at the university. Others found it harder to do this easily, especially if they were thought to look particularly Jewish. Henry Morgenthau III relates a 1935 Princeton anecdote about which other Princeton students over the years could tell variations. Returning to his freshmen dormitory one evening, this lad, whose father was President Roosevelt's secretary of the treasury and thought of himself as largely assimilated, found a note under his door: "Despite your ham-eating propensity, you have something you cannot conceal."[28] Years later Morgenthau reflected on "uncomfortable memories of what it meant to be a member of a small, somewhat unevenly tolerated minority at that time. The pain was intensified by my own negative and poorly defined sense of Jewish identity."[29]

[28] Morgenthau quoted in Van Wallach's description of the relatively new Center for Jewish Life, "A Community to Turn To," *PAW*, April 19, 1995, 12–18, at 16.
[29] Henry Morgenthau in a *PAW* letter to the editor (May 18, 1981, 3) expressing grati-

Annually the issue of anti-Jewishness at Princeton became notorious when, during the spring of sophomore year, students entered the process known as "bicker" in order to be selected for membership by one of Princeton's seventeen eating clubs. From even before the days of F. Scott Fitzgerald, these clubs, with their reputations for pecking orders and various ones taking only "certain kinds of guys" (from socially prominent families, class officers and leaders, "jocks," the more artistically inclined), had fed into the Princeton image of elitism, social snobbery, and escape from the rigors of academic life. A few students might opt out of the bicker process, but this tended to make those who did so seem socially inept or otherwise unable to "fit in." For a good number of students bicker was a time of considerable anxiety. For some it was a cause of social anguish.[30]

While the number of Jewish students at Princeton continued to grow after World War II, and there were many indications of welcome in the classroom, their full acceptance was less so at the social level—particularly with the eating clubs. During the decade from 1948 to 1958 a group of sophomore class leaders, out of some human sympathy and not wanting to be the bearers of an anti-Jewish reputation, banded the class together into a covenant not to join any club unless all those who bickered were selected by at least one of the clubs. The Interclub Committee (made up of presidents of the seventeen clubs) responded with the "100 percent principle," a guarantee that all students who wanted to join a club would be admitted to some club. In most years this was, however, a painful process with forty or so students, more than half of them Jewish, regularly left out until the very end. Most of the clubs had accepted a few Jewish students—usually in a kind of pecking order with respect to the more well to do and/or socially acceptable. But no club wanted to become a "Jewish club" or "too Jewish." Nor did the Jewish students want that to happen, but there was a tendency in that direction with four clubs taking

---

tude to Princeton for the changes that had taken place, in particular that a student who was president of Yavneh, the student association of Orthodox Jews, and active in Hillel, had been honored with Princeton's prestigious Pyne Prize. Reflecting on his undergraduate days, he also wrote: "For some of us, assimilation had progressed to the point where we had lost all positive sense of Jewish identity." *Mostly Morgenthaus: A Family History* (New York: Ticknor and Fields, 1991), 278.

[30] See *Mostly Morgenthaus*, 278–80, and just as painful are the memories of Richard Cummings (formerly Cohen), class of 1959: "Looking Back in Regret," *PAW*, May 4, 1981, 58. On how others could feel about bicker as well, see the reflections of my classmate Edward Said, *Out of Place* (New York: Vintage, 2000), 274–75.

the most, Prospect Club being most open and in the eyes of many therefore, least selective. Finally, on the last night and on into the early next morning of the two-week process, after personal embarrassment, maneuvering, and pressure, the goal of full membership in the clubs was ostensibly achieved. I was class president during our sophomore year of bicker, and while as classmates we found some sense of accomplishment, it was a lesson in the cruelties of prejudice never to be forgotten. As my classmate (to-become-rabbi), Arnold Fink, later observed: "Few Jewish Princetonians who wore their Jewishness proudly rather than assimilate emerged from the 1950s without some pain."[31]

Black students posed no such problem for bicker then. Most classes had none or one. For two hundred years of Princeton's history there had been not a single black student until a group of four came through the navy's V-12 program in 1945. The story some of us were told at the time was that Princeton did not want to trouble or offend its constituency of southern students (e.g., Mississippi senator John Stennis's son, in my class) by admitting any "Negroes." In 1955 there were no blacks anywhere near the senior administration, or, to our knowledge, on the faculty. It is hard to imagine what it could have been like to "bicker" with even a tiny group of black classmates. Nor, at that time, would there have been any need to be concerned about meeting their religious interests or pastoral needs.

Were members of my class shocked or even much concerned with Princeton's prejudice and bigotry? Some of us did talk about it. Although the percentage of Jewish students had nearly tripled from Princeton's earlier decades, there was still scuttlebutt that a reason for an ongoing "informal" quota on Jewish students was that many of them were so bright and well motivated that they would otherwise win too many of the top honors and prizes in the university. This was true enough, although with opportunities for peer education with classmates like Arthur Gold in the English Department, I would say that their presence and any competition was much to the benefit of the rest of us. In any event, it did not seem to occur to us that we could do much to effect change within the university. I found out later that Norman Thomas (Princeton 1905, former Presbyterian minister and regularly a Socialist candidate for president, whom a small group in our class loved to cheer when he came to reunions) had tried to start a campaign as early as 1940 to begin to do something about

[31] In letter to *PAW*, February 22, 1982, 4.

Princeton's discriminatory policies toward, as they then were called, Negroes. Herbert "Bill" Lucas (class of 1950) tells of being called into President Dodds's office after he had coauthored an article for a liberal student publication arguing that it was past time that Princeton admitted some qualified African American students. Dodds, at first politely, told him that it was not yet the time actively to pursue this at Princeton as it could turn off some important donors. When Lucas had the temerity to persist, Dodds grew testy and compared Lucas (oddly if interestingly) to the bushy-browed and controversial president of the United Mine Workers, John L. Lewis.[32] But there was little public talk like that on campus in the 1950s. My among-the-elite eating club was content with the smallest amount of diversity, having accepted just several Jewish students and taking a chagrined pride in having as its Hispanic member the son of the Cuban dictator who on special occasions shared his splendid cigars and told us that he was already the president of the Cuban national railways. This was what came to be labeled as "the silent '50s"—the quiet before the turmoil and changes of the next decades. As my classmate and fellow Episcopalian, Hodding Carter (a southerner, later to become known for his civil-rights advocacy), described us, "Silent or not, we weren't inclined to rattle a lot of cages."[33]

Coming from a public high school (in an exclusive suburb, though less so a school district), I had had some exposure to students of other races and ethnicities, if mostly through athletic programs, but also (obviously a rather political young man) as president of a group of high school student councils and even governor of Illinois Boys' State, and so a representative to Boy's Nation where I (ironically to me given my later peace advocacies) became secretary of defense for a day, sitting behind Robert Lovett's desk in the Pentagon. I had expected that in going to Princeton I was entering a wider world. I was disappointed to find the still somewhat preppy feeling (mine was the first class to have a slight majority of public school students), all-white guy, southern culture tinged Princeton, set in a well-to-do exurban community. One might well ask why I did not know

---

[32] In relating the story to me Lucas notes that his Jewish coauthor, Don Rosenthal, was not called onto the carpet with him. The article, "The Negro at Princeton," was written for the "New Century," a short-lived publication of Princeton's Liberal Union that had for several years been advocating for some inclusion of African American students.

[33] See Merrill Noden, "The (Un)Silent Generation Speaks Again: Reflections from the Class of 1957, Half a Century after Essays Drew Attention to the Values of a Generation," *PAW*, July 18, 2007, 25–29. Carter quotation, 27.

better, but I was a little-traveled midwestern lad and had received practically no college counseling. I missed the SAT examinations the first time around because of illness and only belatedly sat for them because a brother-in-law, then a senior at Princeton, thought I should go there.

I took out some of my disappointment by working at the Princeton Summer Camp for underprivileged youngsters, some of whom I came to know and work with through the YMCA in their section of Princeton.[34] One summer, after camp concluded, I brought to Chicago, and then to a canoe trip with college friends in Canada, a black junior counselor from the camp. He may have been the first African American to portage and paddle deep into Canada's Quetico Provincial Park and was certainly the first black person to stay overnight in our suburban home. My father was only reasonably gracious about it, while the young man's participation in the trip caused the Louisville parents of another Princeton student to refuse to let him go on the adventure with us.

I realize how rather noblesse oblige this can sound: white Princeton student spends a little time befriending a black teenager. It was not doing much to change racial discrimination in America or at Princeton. Some years later my friend was involved in a homicide in a bar brawl and spent a number of years in jail. My class's ideas of service did not at that time include service to the nation and Princeton by working for fundamental changes in social, economic, and institutional circumstances. Yet volunteering at the Princeton Summer Camp was part of the Princeton experience I shared with several of my classmates. I was also hearing Christian leaders calling for transformation of the social and economic order— voices that were becoming an influence on my interest in religion and vocational path. In these and related philosophical matters I had come to view myself as a somewhat of a "contrarian." I pondered how the life and words of Jesus had inspired an Albert Schweitzer and Dietrich Bonhoeffer. Perhaps, as I had begun to hope, the life and teaching of that contrarian field preacher from Galilee long ago might provide leverage. I had also noticed that the neighboring Princeton Theological Seminary, even with its conservative theological reputation, was admitting and actually recruiting black students. Change was not on the near horizon at the university, but it seemed possible.

[34] One of Princeton's first African American students, Robert W. Rivers Jr. (class of 1953), later a vascular surgeon and university trustee, had grown up in Princeton and was earlier among the first black campers at the Princeton Summer Camp.

1746–1955

As an undergraduate I had only a general idea of the earlier history of religion's role at Princeton and other universities. Over the years I have found it instructive to survey the previous two centuries in order to place in context and better to understand what took place subsequently. In *The Soul of The American University: From Protestant Establishment to Established Non-Belief,* George W. Marsden studied a number of universities that were founded during a period of Protestant hegemony in the United States.[35] Each institution Marsden takes into account in his overview has, of course, its distinctive characteristics—its own denominational beginnings or religious connections, its own early constituencies, its geographical and cultural setting, and its later development. But there are also significant similarities. At each college education was a cherished value and motivation that the founders ardently believed would form Christian character and give students the knowledge and skills that would help build up the church and society.

While a number of the early colleges, Princeton included, viewed training for church ministries as a vital if not foremost purposes of their schools, the vision soon broadened to include other vocations important for the life and economy of the colonies and then the newly independent nation. At several of the colleges the development of a divinity school for the education of ministers allowed the rest of the institution to engage in a broader curriculum and to draw a wider constituency of students. Princeton (then the College of New Jersey, founded in 1746) took a somewhat different turn with the establishment in 1812 of the separate, although for many years closely related (through sharing or exchange of trustees, faculty, facilities, and classes), Princeton Theological Seminary. One of the agreements in the separation was that the college would no longer teach theology, as that would belong to the provenance of the seminary.

Tension between denominational "orthodoxy" and a spirit of nonsectarianism would be a theme running through the histories of a number of American colleges over the years. Periods (sometimes thought of as times of "renewal") that stressed more orthodox beliefs were followed by years of change that allowed colleges to take account of new knowledge and broaden their constituencies. While the stories of the older

---

[35] George W. Marsden, *The Soul of The American University: From Protestant Establishment to Established Non-Belief* (New York: Oxford University Press, 1994).

colleges (joined by newer colleges and universities after the Civil War) played themselves out with many a permutation through the nineteenth century, one may notice three recurring issues of concern in the debates about orthodoxy versus more liberal standards: the authority of the Bible, the divinity of Jesus, and Christian morals, with the morality and behavior of students (and occasionally faculty) at various times a concern of administrators and trustees, sometimes being linked with issues of biblical authority.

The greatest challenge to those who saw the Christian character of their colleges threatened by lack of orthodox rigor had been set in the early years by what may be called the "Jeffersonian" understanding of nonsectarianism. For Thomas Jefferson nonsectarianism meant, first and foremost, an avoidance of sectarian skirmishes over precisely such issues as the authority and interpretations of the Bible and the nature or "natures" of Jesus. In his ideal college, religious groups would be free to promote their views. It might be best if each sect even had its own divinity school, but the college itself would not be bound by or need to promulgate any particular set of dogmas or teachings about religion. Jefferson, of course, had also in mind his understanding of the neutral role of government as far as religion or religions were concerned, along with his confidence that reason should triumph over all forms of prejudice. "By bringing the sects together," he believed, "and mixing them with the mass of other students: we shall soften their asperities, liberalize and neutralize their prejudice, and make the general religion a religion of peace, reason and morality."[36]

Jefferson's musings about a general religion had led him to view Jesus as one of the world's great moral teachers. The Bible was a guide (more than authority) for this morality once reason had excised from the Bible all that was mythological, miraculous, and other-worldly, along with any teaching that contradicted the morality (affirmed by reason) that the human Jesus was understood to have actually taught. Others, with their prejudices and absent a reasonable religion, were free to believe and teach otherwise, but that should not be the official position of the college. What could be taught, in the words of Timothy Cutler (become an Anglican and then forced out of Yale's rectorship), "was not the peculiar tenets of any particular sect of Christians." Rather than impose these upon the

[36] Jefferson writing to Thomas Cooper on November 2, 1822. See Robert M. Healey, *Jefferson on Religion in Public Education* (New Haven, CT: Yale University Press, 1962), 224.

young scholars, the college should "inculcate upon their tender minds, the great principles of Christianity and morality in which true Christians in each denomination are generally agreed."[37] Moreover, in the view of Jefferson and those who thought as he did, such a "neutrality" could be joined with the spirit and attitudes that served the new democracy. Dr. Benjamin Rush, a Princeton graduate and supporter as well as friend of Jefferson's, set forth these themes patriotically and ardently:

> A Christian cannot fail of being a republican, for every precept of the Gospel inculcates those degrees of humility, self-denial and brotherly kindness, which are directly opposed to the price of monarchy and the pageantry of a court. A Christian cannot fail of being useful to the republic, for his religion teacheth him, that no man "liveth to himself." And lastly, a Christian cannot fail of being wholly inoffensive, for his religion teacheth him, in all things to do to others what he would wish, in like circumstances, they should do to him.[38]

Rush had been a student of Princeton's President John Witherspoon, a Scottish philosopher and theologian become American patriot and the single clergyman to sign the Declaration of Independence. So also had been James Madison, so responsible for the writing of the US Constitution and its Bill of Rights that set forth the American principle of religious freedom. One can imagine that the understandings of the role of religion in the college and in the nation of all three of them were influenced by the nonsectarian spirit of the Preamble to the Charter of 1748 for the College of New Jersey, which held that Princeton was to be open to students of "every religious Denomination [who] may have free and equal Liberty and Advantage of Education in the said College, notwithstanding any different sentiments in Religion."[39] The founders of the college were so-called New Lights or New Side Presbyterians who espoused an outgoing, evangelical faith that regarded too much concern with doctrinal conformity, especially in matters involving ordination, to be not sufficiently evangelical. Their stance was an illustration of the tension existing from

---

[37] Quoted in Marsden, *Soul*, 58.

[38] Rush quoted by Marsden, *Soul*, 56, from Richard Hofstadter and Wilson Smith, eds., *American Higher Education: A Documentary History* (Chicago: University of Chicago Press, 1961), 171.

[39] From the Preamble to the Charter of Princeton University. On Princeton's nonsectarian founding and early history, see also Mark A. Noll, *Princeton and the Republic, 1768–1822: The Search for Christian Enlightenment in the Era of Samuel Stanhope Smith* (Princeton, NJ: Princeton University Press, 1989).

the early days of Christianity in America between the desire to be free to practice one's faith while recognizing, if sometimes grudgingly, that this freedom called for a tolerance of the religion of others as well.[40]

As time went on, however, a number of Presbyterian leaders found dangers in Jeffersonian views. Placing human reason, even if regarded as God-given, over all forms of revelation and divine authority, eventually, if not sooner, led to rationalization and turning away from divine guidance. Although far from all Presbyterians were opposed to or deeply concerned about slavery, there were some who were already eager to point out the Jeffersonian forms of rationalization on this profoundly moral issue.

One can read the subsequent century and a half at many a US college and university as a sometimes overt and more often subtle struggle between Jeffersonian views of the role of religion in higher education (often presented as a form of Protestant liberalism) and the orthodoxies of versions of a more evangelical Protestant establishmentarianism. While the influence of the Jeffersonian ideal of a tolerant, nonsectarian and non-dogmatic Christian moralism as a kind of general civil religion for the academy was never silenced, the voices of orthodoxy tended to be stronger through the early part of the nineteenth century. It should also be noted, however, that not everyone who taught at or attended these institutions was exercised by such matters. Still, from time to time, were someone to challenge an orthodox tenet in an unacceptable manner, a faculty member might need to be disciplined, and the orthodox establishment would reassert itself and so, in some critics' minds, would a spirit of sectarianism again win out.

Viewed over the longer period and on into the twentieth century, any institutional victories of the conservative Protestant establishment can, however, be viewed as largely holding actions. New understandings and societal and institutional forces were at work that would weaken or liberalize its orthodoxies and rhetoric and replace them with a less dogmatic, more "enlightened" version of Christianity. This religion might be summarized in terms of the Fatherhood of God, the brotherhood of men,

---

[40] In *America and the Challenges of Religious Diversity* (Princeton, NJ: Princeton University Press, 2005), Robert Wuthnow offers a number of illustrations of how this tension between a belief in the superiority of one's own religion (at times together with a theology of exclusivism) and a civic code of pluralism (not least so that one can be free to practice one's own religion) has remained a constant in religious life in America and plays itself out today.

and a basic morality that focused on the attributes of good character, charitable acts, and service. Toward the close of the nineteenth century this enlightened and liberalized view of religion and its role in the college and university seemed well on its way to becoming the new establishment in a number of leading institutions of higher education.

Hand in hand with this liberalization, those who employed scientific methodologies and critical methods of historical inquiry grew in confidence. Literal readings of the Bible, its stories of miracles, and historical accuracy were all brought into question. Some of the biblical stories could now be regarded as myth or legend. The Bible was composed and put together by human beings trying to interpret what was believed to be happening in their lives in times very different from the contemporary Enlightenment era. Significant parts of the Bible could be regarded as inspiring and offering wisdom and guidance for contemporary society, but any sense of the absolute or history-transcending authority of the Bible was mitigated by the primacy of reason and reasonableness in interpretation. Humanity might never fully understand the person of Jesus, but to the extent reason could do so, he was best seen as a wise teacher of morality. He might well have been inspired by God and be thought to have some of the attributes of divinity, but his message was best heard apart from biblical legend and claims to divine status that had been attributed to him by later stages of biblical development. Jesus could continue to be revered, while reasonableness interpreted what was most to be valued in his teaching and example.

There were, of course, debates and days of conservative revival, but as the nineteenth century moved to a close, the liberalized interpretations of Christianity and its moral values had also come to fit with the several broadening constituencies of the colleges and universities. A major constituency was the growing number of students attending college—still heavily Protestant, but more now from a variety of denominations and a good number with little formal religion in their background. To encourage their attendance it became more and more politic to have a curriculum that would offer little that might be regarded as strongly sectarian or that could seem exclusive.

A second important constituency was the public and leaders of society, most particularly in the general demographic area the institution served. Although riven by a civil war and experiencing waves of immigration by "foreigners" who had become important to the labor force but took some time to "fit in," much of the public had again grown in the faith that they were building a new country and society. A good part of the purpose and rationale for an institution of higher education was that it was educating leaders who would further that development. Too much of what could be regarded as a sectarian spirit would not help. Many of the public institutions of higher education founded after the Morrill Act of 1862 were established for just these up-building purposes, and the older, private colleges, now becoming universities, recognized that they were in competition with the land grant institutions to demonstrate the value of their education for the greater society.

In order to fulfill their rationale the colleges and then universities needed money. In addition to tuition from a broadening student body, presidents and trustees began to look for donors who valued the public service being provided for the society, country, and economy by the college. This need could create tension. Some traditional sources of funding tended to be more supportive of a conservative and sectarian character for the college. On occasion, there could be objections from the denomination or denominationally oriented trustees if it seemed that monies from less traditionally orthodox Christian sources might come to influence the overall nature of the institution. On the other hand, it might be necessary to convince other donors or a foundation or government source that the institution was far more than denominational. It could be a tight balance, and academic leaders often had to be good at signaling to different groups what they hoped to hear about the future direction of the school. Yet always the funds were needed, and the pressures to broaden the constituency of donors tended also to broaden the nonsectarian character of the institution even if it retained some manner of Protestant affiliation.

George Marsden relates stories of the gyrations the Methodist clergyman who was chancellor of Syracuse College (1894–1922) went through as he attempted to retain Syracuse's ties to the Methodist Church while yet appealing to a larger pool of donors. Yes, Chancellor James Day maintained, Syracuse was Methodist, but it was "to be far more Christian than denominational."[41] Day was also widely known as a supporter and defender of big business in America. He was, therefore, not alone in finding that he also had to exercise caution as to which ethical reform movements of American Protestantism he would accept and commend. The most challenging of these, active in the late nineteenth and on into the

---

[41] Marsden, *Soul*, 284–87.

early twentieth century, was known as the Social Gospel movement. Walter Rauschenbusch and other leaders of the movement sought to apply Christian ethics to the problems of poverty, inequality, slums, weak labor unions, child labor, and poor schools and hygiene. Their fervent hope was to begin to bring to earth some measure of the kingdom of God. One can hear its ringing voice of reform and criticism of established business practices in this trenchant statement from the Episcopal bishops meeting in 1913 when they resolved:

> That the Church stands for the ideal of social justice, and that it demands the achievement of a social order in which the social cause of poverty and the gross human waste of the present order shall be eliminated, and in which every worker shall have a just return for that which he produces, a free opportunity for self-development, and a fair share of the gains of progress.[42]

Christian leaders of academic institutions, while they might personally feel supportive of the concerns and charitable goals of this reforming spirit, had, however, to be circumspect with regard to specifics—not least when it came to the needs and rights of workers. It seemed wise not to take sides in particular economic and political matters and certainly not to engage in what some would term "class warfare" or otherwise to offend the interests of those whose financial support seemed crucial for institutional development.[43]

Along with the three constituencies of students, the public and its leaders, and donors, faculty became a fourth constituency. The movement of a number of colleges toward becoming universities in the latter part of the nineteenth century and the need for more and better teachers, some of whom could teach scientific subjects, led to competition among institutions for the best faculty, resulting in less concern with a professor's theological beliefs, or, in some cases, even church attendance. Some of this competition came from the newer public universities that, while often encouraging and supportive of volunteer Christian groups and courses on campus, had perforce adopted the more Jeffersonian model of not

---

[42] *Journal of the General Convention of the Protestant Episcopal Church* (New York: Sherwood Press, 1913), 122.

[43] Perhaps somewhat surprisingly it was Harvard's President Eliot, so liberal minded in his religion, who yet seems to have been most opposed to the Social Gospel movement and also looked with great disfavor on labor unions—perhaps due as much to his utilitarian views and sense of social elitism as for any other reasons. See Laurence R. Veysey, *The Emergence of the American University* (Chicago: University of Chicago Press, 1965), 88.

being formally supportive of any religion and so being freer in faculty hiring policies. And faculty trained future faculty. More and more, the subject matter, whether in the hard or social sciences or in topics like history, was seen to demand free and open inquiry by enlightened minds that would not be caught up in any sectarian disputes or misgivings. A number of the newer faculty members had been educated in Germany or guided by the model of German universities. The older idea of the liberal arts college was designed to transmit knowledge. The modern university would now also create knowledge that need not be tied to past understandings and beliefs. Moreover, in this newer model learning was organized into fields or departments that did not need to have religious issues or concerns in their purview.[44]

Influenced by its constituencies and personalities, Princeton moved at its own pace along this general trajectory from the control and support of a more orthodox and evangelical Protestantism to a broader view of Christianity and its role in the institution. The college's central New Jersey location and Presbyterian roots and tradition kept it tethered to strong Presbyterian influences coming from Philadelphia and New York as well as more locally. The seminary and its constituencies continued to exert sway, and the First Presbyterian Church was virtually on the grounds of the small campus. John Witherspoon had served as its chief preacher for twenty-five years, and succeeding presidents of Princeton were expected to play roles in its worship and affairs. Also having its significant place in the community was the church's cemetery down and across Nassau Street where presidents, pastors, faculty, alumni, and townspeople were buried. Yet other theological, social, economic, and pedagogical forces were at work effecting movement toward a more liberal role for religion in the school. Two of Princeton's strongest and more memorable presidents were of particular significance in striving to guide and control this development.

The presidency of James McCosh (1869–88) brought to Princeton (still officially the College of New Jersey) the promise of renewal of its religious heritage and reform and progress. Coming from Scotland to

---

[44] See Jon. H Roberts and James Turner, *The Sacred and Secular University* (Princeton, NJ: Princeton University Press, 2000). The authors find this departmentalization of knowledge to be a leading factor in the exclusion of religion from a significant place in the curriculum of many universities.

Princeton exactly a century after John Witherspoon had done so, Mc-
Cosh was also an advocate of the philosophical movement known as
Scottish Realism and sometimes Scottish Common Sense Realism. This
broad and comprehensive philosophy was opposed to both idealism and
skepticism with regard to human knowing, affirming that rather than
knowing things only through ideas of them, human minds had been so
constituted by God as to be able to know things directly in a world
where reality was actual and observable. Stressing the unity of all knowledge and standing for a "common sense" belief in God and Christian
morals, McCosh's philosophical views were capable of holding together
support of a Newtonian worldview and the principles of scientific induc-
tion with a form of Calvinist orthodoxy. This comprehensiveness enabled
McCosh to deal with one of Christianity's greatest contemporary challenges by maintaining that the new Darwinian insights into biological
evolution were compatible with belief in an all-knowing, ingenious creator God. "We are not precluded from seeking discovery of a final cause,
because we have found a sufficient cause," McCosh held.[45] McCosh's
admirers regarded such "common sense" epistemology and theology as
teachable and preachable, and the broader constituencies viewed them as
a strong and helpful basis for supporting popular religion and social orthodoxy. It was reassuring at the Princeton Theological Seminary, where
Scottish Realism had long held sway, although battles over the authority
and inerrancy of scripture would continue there and sometimes threaten
to leach across Alexander Road to the college campus. There were also
some faculty members at both the college and seminary (including Francis Patton, who would be McCosh's successor) who were less willing to
accept Darwinian evolutionary theory. This was true of trustees of the
institution as well (a good number of them Presbyterian clergy, some of
who served on both boards), but McCosh's optimistic theology prevented
their doctrinal concerns from having much effect on the operation and
teaching of the college.

Scottish Realism had its critics, of course, and can be seen to have been
already fading as a respected intellectual philosophy, but it gave McCosh
the capacity to rise above unproductive debates about belief and wrong

[45] McCosh quoted by Jon H. Roberts in *Darwinism and the Divine in America: Protestant Intellectuals and Organic Evolution, 1859–1900*, new ed. (Notre Dame, IN: University
of Notre Dame Press, 2001), 19–20. Further on McCosh's philosophy and presidency, see J.
David Hoeveler Jr., *James McCosh and the Scottish Intellectual Tradition: From Glasgow
to Princeton* (Princeton, NJ: Princeton University Press, 1981).

belief. Immediately prior to and during the Civil War the College of New Jersey had been a rather moribund school, its resources further divided and depleted by that conflict, and it helped that McCosh had not been directly involved in that division. His faith in the power of education and the value of inductive and scientific methods enabled him to welcome the sciences and other new subjects into the curriculum. He brought new faculty into the still quite small school, strengthened the fabric of the college, and sought to raise academic standards and better discipline among the students. While enabling the college to continue in its sense of being fully a part of a Protestant establishment, McCosh was able to build-in foundation blocks for a modern university and to help the institution become more appreciated as an asset in service to the larger society, economy, and nation.

Worship and regular chapel attendance were, however, vital to McCosh's understanding of the college community, and he found the "old chapel" that seated 325 to be no longer adequate to accommodate the growing student body and faculty. One of McCosh's proudest achievements was the dedication in 1882 of the magnificent Marquand Chapel that could seat as many as a thousand for the Sunday worship services and daily morning chapel—at evening services, too, though under McCosh, vespers ceased to be required of the students.

In February of 1885, and again a year later, McCosh had met Harvard's president, Charles Eliot, in New York to debate first about curriculum and then about the place religion should have in a college. In the first debate McCosh argued against the free elective system that Eliot was instituting at Harvard. McCosh insisted that he, too, believed in progress and recognized the value of having some electives, but that the curriculum should yet have a core common for all students—foundational courses or "cardinal studies"—certainly some of the sciences but most assuredly classical studies and courses in the Bible, Christian philosophy, and ethics. Eliot's pedagogical views, however, extended to the role of religion. Not only should it, too, be elective in the curriculum, but Harvard had now also dropped all chapel requirements. Here McCosh again took the conservative position. It was as dangerous not to have compulsory chapel as to make elective the study of sacred subjects. Without this worship and common learning the value of a Christian education would be greatly lessened. More importantly still, the Christian character and morals that were a major goal of this education might otherwise never be properly formed. "Withdraw Christianity from our colleges, and we have then taken away one of the vital forces which have given life and body to our higher education."[46]

Eliot would not concede any higher ground to McCosh. He himself attended daily chapel at Harvard and upheld the value and role of religion in the society and the college and the importance of morality, but he disagreed as to how the knowledge and practice of religion were best inculcated. Religion was at its best when it was voluntary rather than compulsory. At heart, one can see, he and McCosh were being guided by major differences in their theologies and in their views of human nature. Eliot believed in a broadly conceived philosophical theism shaped by Unitarian teachings long dominant at Harvard. This religion he saw as more natural to human beings—rational and less dependent on any special revelation. It was, he believed, more inclusive and allowed for greater free inquiry as well as diversity in religious opinion. Moreover, in his view, college students were to be regarded as young men who could be expected to be rational and to live by a morality that was part of their nature.

McCosh saw such a liberal form of theism as not truly inclusive but rather as a minority view. The evangelical Protestantism that he and Princeton espoused was, he argued, the majority view and was, therefore, more capable of being inclusive. His Calvinistic and Augustinian views of human nature were also on display when he spoke of his students as "me boys" who were yet capable of much mischief and laxity and who were inclined toward selfishness rather than unselfish living if the requirements and parental roles of a college were slackened too early. It should also be noted of "Jimmy" McCosh, however, that along with his evangelistic understanding of Christianity, he could display a spirit of toleration and pastoral care for his students that might be thought prescient of how Princeton would one day show greater breadth of spirit in religion. "I have had under me," McCosh said on his retirement, "Catholics as well as Protestants of all denominations, Jews and heathens. I have religiously guarded the sacred right of conscience. I have never insisted on anyone attending religious service to which he conscientiously objected."[47]

---

[46] James McCosh, *Religion in College: What Place Should It Have? Being An Examination of President Eliot's Paper Read before the Nineteenth Century Club in New York, Feb. 3, 1986* (New York: A. C. Armstrong).

[47] McCosh quoted in Don Oberdorfer, *Princeton University: The First 250 Years* (For the Trustees of Princeton University, 1995), 78.

Many at Princeton were proud of McCosh's emphatic stances in the debates with Eliot. Even many students believed that he had upheld the college's strong Christian faith and morals against those of Harvard, which were weakened by Eliot's liberalism. Yet while debates regarding electives and core curricula would go on for generations—not least at Harvard, Eliot's views regarding the elective and voluntary place of religion in the curriculum and student's extracurricular lives would, over time, begin to win out at many schools, Princeton included. Among other factors, the relative prosperity of many Protestants in America had quietly undermined the Calvinist view of fallen human nature and begun to replace it with a faith in human progress that could be blessed by more benign forms of Christianity.

Woodrow Wilson was the first president of Princeton who was not a Presbyterian clergyman. But his father was, as was his maternal grandfather and father-in-law. A founder of the Southern Presbyterian Church that split from the northern Presbyterians at the beginning of the Civil War and a one-time slave owner, Wilson's father was an alumnus of the Princeton Seminary, a minister in Augusta, Georgia, and a seminary professor. Wilson, the son, cared devoutly about the moral life. He spoke often to the student Philadelphian Society, and though he had to pass much of the leadership of chapel services on to others, he still had a regular role in these services as a preacher and reader. Clearly his faith and commitment could make a deep impression on others. Years later—during my senior year at Princeton—renowned Judge Harold Medina (Princeton 1909) preached a sermon in the University Chapel in which he recalled Wilson's 1908 baccalaureate address. It was "the best address he ever delivered," Medina emotionally told the congregation. Wilson's virtual sermon was based on the text Romans 12:2: "And be not conformed to this world: but be ye transformed by the renewing of your mind, that ye may prove what is that good and acceptable and perfect will of God."[48]

Seeing himself in the tradition of Witherspoon and McCosh (McCosh had been his president while in college), Wilson believed that the renewal of the mind in the proving of God's will could best be developed through education, and he saw himself first and foremost as a reforming educator, interested in issues of governance and democracy and determined to raise the quality of teaching and learning at Princeton. Having joined the fac-

[48] Harold R. Medina's sermon, "Spiritual Strength Means Power," *The Evangel* (Winter 1957): 3–6, published by Faith At Work, 8 West 40th Street, New York, NY, 18.

ulty at Princeton in 1890, Wilson was again influenced by McCosh (who continued to teach philosophy at Princeton until his death in 1894), and he took on and then moved beyond the Scotsman's comprehensive spirit when it came to any specific matters of Christian theology or doctrine. The presidency of Francis Patton in the intervening years (1888–1902) no doubt strengthened Wilson's resolve in this regard because he had seen some of the problems created when the theologically conservative Patton, who once had insisted that he would "do what in me lies to keep the hand of ecclesiasticism from resting on Princeton University,"[49] nevertheless had waffled when it came to the nomination of the well-known but Unitarian historian Frederick Jackson Turner to the faculty. Wilson had previously tried to assure Turner that no religious tests were applied at Princeton. "The president and trustees are very anxious that every man they choose should be earnestly religious, but there are no doctrinal standards among us."[50] After the trustees turned down Turner's appointment, Wilson carried his anger and embarrassment over the incident into his presidency.

Problems and issues from Patton's time as president would influence Wilson in other ways. The student body more than doubled in size (600 to 1,300) while Patton was president and Princeton had officially become a university, but by 1902 it was also clear how much needed to be done to raise the academic standards of the undergraduate education and to develop a graduate school. Under the popular but administratively inattentive Patton, that doubling of the student body (still almost entirely Protestant with a rapidly growing number of Episcopalians and a high percentage of students from the better preparatory schools) had led to a wealthier student body, often more interested in their social and extracurricular lives than in their studies. Together with the increasing influence of the eating clubs, Princeton seemed on a path toward gaining a reputation as a country club for young gentlemen, a description Patton seemed rather to like. But not if Wilson could do anything about it, and in 1902, the trustees, who under Patton had grown less clerical and now included several educators and wealthy alumni business leaders, turned to the principled and scholarly Wilson to lift the academic standards for students and faculty as well.

[49] Patton in the *New York Herald*, January 21, 1898. On the incident involving Frederick Jackson Turner, and further on Patton's presidency, see Marsden, *Soul*, 221–22.
[50] Wilson writing to Frederick Jackson Turner on November 15, 1896, in Arthur S. Link, ed., *The Papers of Woodrow Wilson, 1986–1898*, vol. 10 (Princeton, NJ: Princeton University Press, 1971), 53.

One of Wilson's most cherished gifts to Princeton issued from his address "Princeton in the Nation's Service," delivered several years earlier at the school's three-day sesquicentennial celebration at which time the school officially became Princeton University. Wilson recalled the era of the revolutionary war and the presidency of John Witherspoon who had so well combined leadership in education and service for the making of the new nation. Witherspoon, because of the "generous union then established in the college between the life of philosophy and the life of the state,"[51] had encouraged a number of young Princeton men into such service.

"Princeton in the Nation's Service" (during his Princeton presidency Wilson more often spoke of "Princeton for the Nation's Service"), along with his companion word "duty," guided Wilson in the rhetoric of his leadership, and over time the phrase became a kind of unofficial motto for the university (expanded into "Princeton in the Nation's Service and the Service of All Nations" at the 250th anniversary in 1996). It is instructive to place the motto for service and the older motto *Dei Sub Numine Viget* on the same page or banner as they would later sometimes be at university ceremonies and celebrations. The Latin phrase, still honored in a form of civil religion but becoming more a part of the university's history and heritage as the years went on, can be seen and heard coming to have a lesser role in the rhetoric of Princeton's rationale and values. The motto extolling service and Princeton as a place where one learned service would come to greater prominence, not least in the addresses and public language of the university. The word *service* had the advantage of having a religious background that could become more pronounced by those who wished to reference it. The Christian life was often spoken of as a life of service. Service to others could also be service to God, and Jesus's words and example about a ministry of sacrificial service could be cited.[52] But service was also a general and encompassing virtue that Princeton's graduates might fulfill in a number of ways. Nor was it fully clear what was meant by the "nation," though for Wilson it was closely related to his ideas about service to democracy, freedom, and self-government by a people. The study of American history and politics at Princeton and then entering government or political service, or the teaching of these subjects, would certainly have been among Wilson's understandings of a life of service to the nation.

[51] Wilson in "Princeton in the Nation's Service," *Papers of WW*, vol. 10, 11–31, on 18.
[52] Mark 10:41–45

While imbuing the idea with his attractive moral seriousness, Wilson was far from alone among leading educators of the time in stressing the nation-serving character of colleges and universities.[53] With only 4 percent of age-eligible Americans gaining a college education at the time, service was an important justification for what seemed to others an elitist enterprise. Protestant Christianity provided significant moral force as it undergirded the rationale for service and the accompanying virtues of duty and responsibility, while Wilson, who tended to look askance at many of the sectarian concerns of theologically conservative Presbyterians, interpreted his faith quite liberally for his time. His understanding of its role in guiding the overall spirit of service found its place toward the midpoint of his "Princeton in the Nation's Service" address. After describing Princeton as having "always been a school of religion," he continued:

> Religion, conceive it but liberally enough, is the true salt wherewith to keep both duty and learning sweet against the taint of time and change; and it is a noble thing to have conceived it thus liberally, as Princeton's founders did . . . There is nothing that gives such pith to public service as religion. A God of truth is no mean prompter to the enlightened service of mankind; and character formed, as if in his eye, has always a fibre and sanction such as you shall not obtain for the ordinary man from the mild promptings of philosophy.[54]

Wilson's theological views allowed for a distinction between a covenant of divine grace and that of nature. The realm of the natural world, though also sacralized by God in different ways, could be studied by reason, enabling Wilson to keep special revelation and sectarian theological concerns distant from his educational philosophy and his views of the natural forces that shape the development of government. In time, many of the faculty, especially the newer ones, and trustees graduated to this worldview and perspective on the mission of the university. Under Wilson, required chapel attendance was reduced from two on Sunday, along with weekday services, to Sunday mornings and two weekday services (down to fifteen minutes and then ten) and later only half of the Sundays during the academic year. Early on he also eliminated the compulsory and elective biblical courses and abolished the Department of Biblical Literature, while then hiring a young man who could teach elective courses

---

[53] See D. G. Hart, *The University Gets Religion: Religious Studies in Higher Education* (Baltimore: Johns Hopkins University Press, 1999), 54.

[54] "Princeton in the Nation's Service," 20.

about the Bible and religion in a reasoned and reasonable manner. In all this, however, Wilson continued to insist that Princeton was thoroughly Christian in spirit while becoming a modern university with service as its public mission.

While harboring some concern that the sciences could breed "a contempt for the past" and a credulous hope for "success in every new thing,"[55] Wilson's practical piety and faith that God could be found in all phases of the Enlightenment enabled him to seek new faculty primarily for their knowledge of their fields and teaching ability. A 1906 Board of Trustees' Resolution again affirmed that Princeton was a "Non-Sectarian Institution," spelling this out by asserting that "no denominational test is imposed in the choice of trustees, officers or teachers, or in the admission of students, nor are distinctly denominational tenets or doctrines taught to the students."[56] This affirmation was no doubt issued with sincerity and with Wilson remembering the Frederick Jackson Turner incident, but it was also prompted by the growing influence of another constituency—by the insistence of Andrew Carnegie that his Endowment Fund and specifically its pension fund (the prototype for what would become TIAA-CREF) would only be available to institutions that did not hold any distinctly denominational tenets. The Trustee Minutes instructed that a copy of the resolution was to be sent to the president of the Carnegie Foundation of the Advancement of Teaching.

Wilson further dedicated himself to strengthening Princeton's academics, both requiring and encouraging students to become more devoted to their studies. Hopes for new undergraduate living and dining "quads" and his highly controversial and in the end failed opposition to the club system grew out of his concern that the clubs were nurturing an anti-intellectualism that was more interested in social activities and prominence than ideas and learning. His plans for a more open, democratic, and studious Princeton student body did not, however, extend much beyond Anglo-Saxon Protestant young men in the student body or faculty. Moreover, toward the end of his presidency, fully 78 percent of the student body was being admitted to Princeton from elite Protestant-populated preparatory schools.[57] A child of his southern culture, his noble views of service and democracy never escaped his inherited prejudices.

[55] So in ibid., 29.

[56] In Minutes of the Trustees of Princeton University, October 20, 1906, vol. 10, 732. Mudd Manuscript Library.

[57] Comparable figures were 65 percent at Yale, Harvard 47 percent, and Michigan 9 percent. See Kemeny, *Nation's Service*, 165.

Late into life he continued to defend some of the benefits of the institution of slavery and to find little place for African Americans in any roles of leadership or service other than subservience in America. Like other even moderately well-off families of the period, Woodrow and Ellen Wilson had household servants and felt themselves charitable toward blacks living in the area, but did not see them as able to profit from anything like a Princeton education. Although Wilson appointed the university's first Catholic faculty members and a Jewish faculty member (and would later elevate Louis Brandeis to the Supreme Court), he held, at least while he was at Princeton, generally prejudicial views toward Jewish people and probably Catholics as well—attitudes toward "foreign" and relatively new members of American society that were as much cultural as they were religious—that were shared by many others at Princeton. Along with his efforts to improve educational standards and his legacy of Princeton's service to the nation, these prejudices toward other races and religions would linger on as well in Princeton's traditions—a certain inbred sense of the superior stock of white Protestants when it comes to service to the nation—especially the service of leadership.[58]

Wilson's complex and at times conflicted personality further complicated the legacy he left Princeton in his sometimes tortured attitude toward wealth.[59] As president of the university he recognized the importance of money for making possible the new preceptorial program of teaching, his hopes for the building of his cherished "quad" system, and the new graduate school, but this son of a Calvinistic manse, who often worried about his own family finances, also resented the sense of privilege wealth could bring and efforts by wealthy trustees (among them one who became his enemy, the nominal Episcopalian Moses "Momo" Taylor Pyne) and others to control the direction and future of the university—especially when contrary to his presidential plans. In remarks he made in one of his last speeches while the university's president (to what was reported to be a stupefied audience of several trustees and Pittsburgh alumni), Wilson's lingering anger over his failure to change the club sys-

[58] On Wilson's prejudicial attitude and actions, see James Axtell, *The Making of Princeton University: From Woodrow Wilson to the Present* (Princeton, NJ: Princeton University Press, 2006), 8–9, but also more generally and appreciatively on Wilson's role in setting Princeton on a path to become an institution of academic excellence and a true university.

[59] "Contradiction in his character, so perplexing to every biographer" is an often-illustrated theme for W. Barksdale Maynard in *Woodrow Wilson: Princeton to the Presidency* (New Haven, CT: Yale University Press, 2009), xi, passim.

tem and fresh anger over his impending loss in the struggle regarding the placement of the new graduate college flashed forth. This was hardly the first time that Wilson signaled his ambivalence toward "monied interests" and large donors,[60] but now (indicative of his ongoing attention to church life and ethics) he started out with the Protestant churches who were, he believed, more interested in serving the classes than the masses. "It is the same with the universities," he continued, making it clear that he was thinking of Princeton in particular. "We look for the support of the wealthy and neglect our opportunities to serve the people."[61]

Wilson's biographers debate the degree to which Wilson, who had never taken his eyes off the possibility of a political career, was now making up his mind to commit himself to a more populist appeal against the rich and monied interests in American society. The evidence suggests he was again ambivalent and trying to think this through for himself. But the decision to depart the highly respected Princeton presidency to become governor of New Jersey and then likely candidate for the country's presidency would be interpreted in Princeton's lore as a victory for those who favored a college and university less democratic and academically rigorous and more "clubby" and susceptible to F. Scott Fitzgerald's soon-to-be-notorious caricature of Princeton as a place of lazy affluence, "the pleasantest country club in America."[62]

The graduate college that Wilson had wanted to locate in the central campus would be dedicated three years later on the "golf links" west of the rest of the university. Designed in the collegiate gothic that dean of the Graduate College and Wilson's nemesis, Andrew West, espoused and that was becoming the dominant architectural style of Princeton, it reflected the Anglophilic homage that other faculty and trustees (Wilson very much among them) had come to have for Cambridge and Oxford. West, while reminding the university's main architect, Ralph Adams Cram, that the Proctor Hall refectory was a secular and not an ecclesiastical room, saw to it that scenes from the Bible and those imaging Christian education in the great west window of the refectory were underlined with

---

[60] For another example, see his letter to Moses Taylor Pyne on the subject in August Heckscher, *Woodrow Wilson: A Biography* (New York: Charles Scribner's Sons, 1991), 191.

[61] Wilson's widely reported remarks and the longer story of the struggle over the placement of the graduate college building are presented in *The Princeton Graduate School: A History* by Willard Thorp, Minor Myers Jr., and Jeremiah Stanton Finch with a new chapter by James Axtell and edited by Patricia H. Marks (Princeton, NJ: Association of Princeton Graduate Alumni, 2000), 107–58.

[62] F. Scott Fitzgerald, *This Side of Paradise* (New York: Scribner's Sons, 1921), 40.

the words *Nec vocemini magister quia magister vester unus est Christus* (Neither be ye called masters: for one is your Master, even Christ).

West was another son of a Presbyterian minister, but one would have to ask for how many on the faculty of the university, if not for West himself, the window's message seemed as much a form of sentiment as practicing belief. Princeton's educational programs had in reality become quite secular. The faculty, a number of whom Wilson had brought to Princeton as part of the new preceptorial program, tended in their professional lives to align themselves with their discipline, its "scientific" methods of study, and the systemization of knowledge and scholarship. On the eve of the first great world war, how one understands and learns was coming to be viewed largely apart from religious beliefs and assumptions. Although a number of university presidents and faculty would continue warmly to espouse liberal Protestant beliefs and see education and the imparting of objective truth as sacred tasks, without a secure place in any of the departments, Christianity had come to play a much lesser and then, especially after the Great War, a still smaller role in the curriculum of this twentieth-century university.[63]

Wilson's concept of service to the nation took on sharper focus and often-sacrificial specificity for Princetonians during both the two world wars. Nor can one understand attitudes toward the role of religion at Princeton or at other universities in the second part of the twentieth century without taking those terrible wars into account. In the war periods, being in the nation's service meant for many young men being willing to fight and die for one's country or, at the least, to make sacrifices in the war efforts. During both wars Princeton offered the assistance of faculty and its facilities, along with the enlistment of its students and their lives. Indeed, President John Hibben and many members of the faculty exceeded Wilson in finding a high moral justification for the war against Germany along with a belief that it was democracy itself that was at stake. Both wars helped define the nation's service as a form of patriotism—for many a struggle for freedom and democracy and fighting its enemies in ways, not always easily specified, linked with Christian dedication.

[63] Again on this process of secularization, see Jon H. Roberts and James Turner, *The Sacred and the Secular University* (Princeton, NJ: Princeton University Press, 2000). The book, with an informative introduction by John F. Wilson, then of Princeton's Religion Department and dean of the Graduate School, resulted from a conference held as part of Princeton's 250th Anniversary Celebration.

Yet wars (and here one might also add in the harsh experiences of the intervening Great Depression in a nation still not fully recovered from the traumas of its Civil War) can be hard on religion, especially if one's view of the benefits of religious faith and practice are associated with ideas of human progress—of making life on earth better, more just, and with less suffering and evil. God's blessing and solace are frequently sought during wars, but such tragedies, with their millions of deaths and broken lives—the killing fields and fire bombings—are challenging to an understanding of God or God's ways, certainly of any easy understanding. Many prayers are offered, while so many deaths and horrors leave many wondering.

Clearly the faith of some can grow in dramatic ways in time of danger and tragedy, and commentators note the revival of religion in America after the Second World War in terms of more people attending churches. In retrospect, however, the revival of Protestant Christianity of the late 1940s and 1950s can be seen as rather short-lived and shallow. The questions linger and are deepened by so many civilian deaths, the Holocaust, and the use of atomic weapons followed by the fears of a nuclear war. Why? people ask. Or what good is God if God cannot or does not prevent such horrors? Woody Allen later gave voice to the agnostic anxiety when he observed of God "that basically He's an underachiever."[64] Or, as some returning veterans ruefully observed, God had been "missing in action"—begging the question of what is meant by or expected of divine actions.

Religious hope and practice does not cease. I recall being told as a young man the story of a chief rabbi who gathered together other leading rabbis after the Holocaust—the Shoah. Following devastating memories and theological agonizing, they decided that after what had happened, God could not exist. "We are agreed, then," concluded the chief rabbi, "there is no God. So now let us pray." People may try to forget or reinterpret the harshest experiences, or people of faith may continue to probe for a more profound understanding of God's presence and care and any meaning or significance for human life. There is the "and yet . . . and yet" in the sense of an edge of Presence in absence—a hope in *Logos* to undergird any reality for story, mathematics, logical reasoning, and being. Faith and religion go on, yet any academic setting is bound to continue to recall and to ask critical questions.

Such monumental tragedies also challenge both academics and reli-

[64] Woody Allen as Boris in his 1975 movie *Love and Death*.

gious people to think more critically and carefully about the values and benefits of education. Almost all of the institutions of higher education in the United States were founded and supported by religious people who believed that education was a way of forming better, wiser, more thoughtful people who would contribute to the building up and bettering of the social order. Educators, whether or not religious, shared that faith or hope in education, and the rhetoric of service expresses this. Nor could a college or university long continue without belief in some form of human progress through education. But after war and so much human wrong, what does *better* mean? What values underlie definitions of *better*? On what rationale might they be based? How would they be defined or described in those universities that increasingly came to claim that they could teach objectively in "value free" classrooms?

Many educators began to find a more sure and optimistic perspective when they concentrated on the work being done in the sciences, technology, and engineering. The war efforts had shown how well the universities could serve the nation by engaging in research and educating future scientists and engineers. Now growing knowledge and expertise could also be used to improve health, sanitation, agriculture, transportation, information storage and transmission, and other aspects of human life. While without professional or business schools, Princeton could contribute considerably to research and education in and for these fields through the development of new ideas, understandings, and techniques in its undergraduate and graduate programs. The School of Engineering would be strengthened and expanded. Although value questions about who and how people would benefit from these forms of progress and some of the potential downsides and dangers of them remained, such questioning could stay on the periphery as long as the universities and the public believed that some form of progress was being made with or without the benefit of faith in God.

For some faculty members and administrators it was more challenging to promote the assured values of a liberal arts education. Critics, remembering how American institutions had been adaptively modeled on German universities, pointed to the failure of an educated German citizenry and to the savage manner in which the Allies had fought the wars. More knowledge by itself did not seem to make better people. Could the study of history, literature, the classics, and arts help shape good character and a spirit of service? A number of leaders of American education wanted to hope again that they could. Learning to think critically, to express oneself well, to appreciate beauty, to understand the lives and circumstances of others, and so to gain perspective on one's own life and times were surely, many wanted to continue to believe, well worth teaching and learning.[65]

Through the long presidencies of John Hibben (1910–32) and Harold Dodds (1932–57)—through the world wars, depression, and recovery—Princeton's makeup and constituencies changed more slowly than the rest of the population. More and more young Americans began attending college, and the Princeton that had some 1,300 students during Wilson's tenure grew to 2,000 (deliberately held there for a time) by the 1920s and then to nearly 3,000 undergraduates and some 500 graduate students by the 1950s. Through the half-century, however, Princeton undergraduates remained male, almost entirely white, and predominantly Protestant. Through much of this period those identifying themselves as Episcopalians and Presbyterians made up more than two-thirds of the student population. A Catholic Club was begun by Professors Hugh Stott Taylor and David McCabe in 1928, and on into the 1940s the percentage of Roman Catholic students held relatively steady at 7 percent to 8 percent, while the number of Jewish students, consistently being held down by discriminatory admissions practices and abetted by Princeton's exurban setting, hovered around 3 percent or 4 percent.[66] By the time my class graduated in 1957 the percentage of Catholics had risen only modestly to become a tenth of the undergraduate body, while the growing numbers of high school students had begun more rapidly to boost the number of Jewish students toward 15 percent—putting, as we have seen, pressure on the social system and bicker and, no doubt, a cause of the so-called Dirty Bicker of 1958. The Student Hebrew Association (soon to become the Princeton Hillel Foundation) held its first meeting in late 1947, facilitated by the assistant dean of the chapel and attended by one Albert Einstein. Its founding director, Irving Levy, became a well-respected figure on campus, although friends of the time tell me that quite a few Jewish students

---

[65] For a history of how morality was to be taught or informed in American universities both when and after religion played a major role, see Julia A. Reuben, *The Making of the Modern University: Intellectual Transformation and the Marginalization of Morality* (Chicago: University of Chicago Press, 1996).

[66] On these figures, see Nicholas A. Ulanov, "The New Pluralism: Varieties of Religious Experience on Campus Today," *PAW*, March 26, 1979, 15. On the ongoing story of the restriction of Jewish admissions to Princeton over the years, see Jerome Karabel, *The Chosen: The Hidden History of Admission and Exclusion at Harvard, Yale, and Princeton* (Boston: Houghton Mifflin, 2005).

either did not find or did not want to find Jewish observance to have a
significant presence at Princeton. Were they observant, a number of them
would be so mostly while at home.

The Protestant Christianity that influenced the lives of the majority of
students continued to be theologically broad and ethical in its interpretation. In the earlier years of the century, although more conservative
speakers were not absent from Princeton, well-known preachers like
Henry Emerson Fosdick would stress that Christians need only to be
committed to the great truths of religion. He and others saw a modern
Christianity as the only believable and practical option between a more
tradition-bound evangelical Christianity and atheism. While many students were but nominal in their religious practice, Christianity continued to be popular with a number of active students and student leaders.
By now all daily chapel requirements had been dropped and there were
few opportunities to study the Bible or religion in the curriculum, but
Hibben often praised the voluntary participation of students in their
Philadelphian Society with its well-attended Bible study classes and
other programs, among them sending missionaries abroad, particularly
to China.[67]

After the Great War, however, and as the 1920s wore on, concerns
grew regarding the student interest in religion. Studies were done, and
Henry Pitney Van Dusen (Princeton 1919 and soon to be a major figure
in American and international Protestantism as well as for thirty-four
years a trustee of the university) was not alone in commenting in 1928 on
the "poverty of the religious background of the average American student." The vital influence of home and school on young people's religion
was seen to have diminished. For many families with students in college
it was a time of more wealth, more individualism, and secularization.
Maintaining that student interest in religion did not change that much
over the generations, Van Dusen categorized students into three groups.
One out of ten was antagonistic toward religion; one out of ten was
deeply interested; while eight out of ten were only nominally interested or
indifferent. Other reports noted that while a number of students at major
colleges had a positive interest in religion, formal religious participation
had fallen away. At Princeton this included sporadic but continuing agita-
tion against required Sunday chapel attendance.[68]

[67] On Christianity on campus during this period, see Kemeny, *Nation's Service*,
162–63.
[68] See Dean R. Hoge, *Commitment on Campus: Changes in Religion and Values Over
Five Decades* (Philadelphia: Westminster Press, 1974), 134.

A controversy of that time arose, however, because of what seemed to be too much interest in a certain kind of religion and morality. When Samuel Shoemaker (class of 1916) went to China as a young missionary, he met Frank Buchman and became a disciple of Buchman's teaching and the four absolutes of purity, honesty, love, and unselfishness. When Shoemaker returned to Princeton to be the secretary of the Philadelphian Society, he brought Buchman's teaching and practice with him, and was then followed in the leadership of the society by Ray Purdy, another ardent disciple of what was being offered to students as a real, practicing, and even exciting religion—contrasting with the rather bland and undemanding Protestantism that they believed students otherwise experienced. The Buchmanite methods of personal evangelism and what seemed to some to be too much interest in sexual sins ("impurities" Buchman called them) and public confession made the Buchman followers and then the Philadelphian Society subjects of controversy on campus and in national magazines.[69] (While there were rumors about too much concern with autoeroticism, and that some of the group were homosexuals, for Buchman "purity" meant mainly less indulgence in heterosexual activity, even in marriage, in order that followers could concentrate on reforming the moral order of the world, and Buchman and his followers would insist that homosexuals were among their major opponents.) Although the numbers were never large, early participants included students leaders like Pitney Van Dusen (undergraduate president of the society, then graduate secretary), Eugene Carson Blake (who would go on to be stated clerk of the Presbyterian Church, president of the National Council of Churches, and general secretary of the World Council of Churches, and also a Princeton trustee), and John D. Rockefeller III. President Hibben, a Presbyterian clergyman and the last theologian to be Princeton's president, was among the Christian leaders who found this version of religion, however inspiring to some, unwelcome and unhealthy. Nor was it conducive to the reputation of good religion at Princeton. He told Shoemaker in 1922 that Buchman was not welcome on campus, stating again in 1926 that "there is no place in Princeton for 'Buchmanism.'"[70] The controversy boiled over with editorials in the *Daily Princetonian* denouncing the movement. President Hibben, who had been pleased to accept Purdy's

[69] On the Buchmanite movement and the controversy at Princeton, see Kemeny, *Nation's Service*, 202–4, 211–13, and Daniel Sack, *Moral Re-Armament: The Reinventions of an American Religious Movement* (New York: Palgrave Macmillan, 2009), 29–52. Sack's study is based on his doctoral dissertation in Princeton's Religion Department.

[70] In "If This Be Logic," *DP*, October 23, 1926, 2.

resignation, appointed a university-wide committee of inquiry into the work of the Philadelphian Society. The committee, in fact, exonerated the work of the society and made several recommendations about ways to strengthen religion on campus, although in a few more years the somewhat wounded society would become the Student-Faculty Association, later to become the Student Christian Association. Buchman's movement interpreted hostility as a sign that they were fulfilling their calling by doing unpopular evangelistic work, and with its vision of a reformed moral society went on to further missionary activity and controversy as the Oxford Group and Moral Rearmament. But this was Princeton's first brush with what seemed to Princeton's president and others at the university to be an unhealthy cultlike group. Years later, when I was dean of the chapel, a kindly older graduate from that decade, who I surmised might once have been a member of the Buchmanite movement, invited me to lunch and brought up the subject of his concern with the impurities of contemporary undergraduates.

If the Buchmanite movement was to be interpreted as too much of the wrong kind of religion at Princeton, the toppling of the statue known as *The Christian Student* by members of the graduating class of 1929 signaled to others the end of a Christian era and a new cynicism if not irreligion among students. The statue of an athletic-looking young man, half in football uniform, an academic gown draped off a shoulder, books crooked in his left arm, and eyes up in a visionary gaze, had been modeled on a photo of W. Earl Dodge of the class of 1879 and donated to Princeton by his brother after Earl died as a young man. Earl Dodge had been captain of the football team, president of the Philadelphian Society, and a leader in the formation of the Intercollegiate YMCA. On the pedestal were engraved the words, TO MARK THE BIRTH-PLACE OF THE WORLD-WIDE UNION OF CHRISTIAN STUDENTS IN WORK FOR CHRIST. The sculptor, Daniel Chester French, had also fashioned the figure of Lincoln for his memorial in Washington and John Harvard in Cambridge. Hibben, in accepting the statue for Princeton in 1913, declared that "the ideas set forth by this figure represent the heart and center of Princeton tradition and Princeton faith."[71]

[71] The story of the pulling down of the statue is told by John P. Read in *PAW*, May 4, 1981, 27–29.

Looking back years later, one of the culprits in the toppling interpreted that first felling of *The Christian Student* as more a beer-fueled prank than any intentional attack on Christianity. Yet it was, he realized, probably born of resentment against the moral paternalism his classmates felt they had endured as students—a moralism somehow represented in that "smug" and "hypocritical" all-too-good idealized figure. He was "too innocent" for the times and all the challenges and doubts the just-graduated students felt they had to face.[72]

The university had the statue remounted. When, however, it was again pulled down and dragged across campus in the fall of 1930, officials had to recognize that *The Christian Student* had become a target for student antiestablishment feelings. The statue was dispatched to a warehouse, then found a place in French's former studio, before finally being returned to Princeton in 1987 and given a safe haven in the lobby of Jadwin Gym where, without pedestal, it is dubbed *The Princeton Student*.

Yet despite controversy and what critics saw as high degrees of student indifference during this era, the university remained officially committed to its Christian heritage and the future of the faith on campus. The one-thousand-seat Marquand Chapel had burned down in 1920, and now a larger new cathedral-like center would again be able to accommodate almost the whole Princeton community. The dedication of the chapel in 1928 seemed to many a splendid monument to Princeton's Christian tradition and a promise for its future. Indeed, it was the stated hope of Hibben and the architect Ralph Adams Cram that the beauty of the building (for Cram, iconic of all higher human aspirations) would inspire such reverence for beauty and learning that students would want rather than feel required to make the chapel part of their life at Princeton. Even while many intellectuals and academics were growing uncertain about the roles of both religion and human reason, the soaring, columned space and the figures and stories presented in stone, carved wood, and stained glass testified to a confident harmony of faith and knowledge. With a remarkable ecumenicity of mind and spirit here were gathered Jewish and other pre-Christian patriarchs and philosophers, even a great Muslim figure and the skeptic David Hume. Lawyers and politicians, poets and scientists looked down in tribute to Western catholic civilization—including

[72] Ibid.

its Renaissance, Reformation (Luther and Calvin are seated side by side), and Enlightenment. In a structure built in romantic homage to the Anglican gothic tradition in particular, one could yet find faces of the dissidents Milton and Bunyan.

This was also the time when the position of dean of the chapel (one of the recommendations of the committee President Hibben had appointed to investigate the Philadelphian Society) was established and endowed. There were critics of the amount of money being devoted to the office of a chaplain and for a building that would not be in use much of the time when there was, in their minds, more need for laboratories, libraries, and faculty salaries. Others were concerned that the nurturing of the Christian faith, once a responsibility of the president and, in some sense, the whole university, was now being given over to a single individual, who, it was soon learned, would not be permitted by the faculty to teach in the regular curriculum. Yet President Hibben and the trustees were at pains to make it clear that this appointment did not represent any lessening of the president's or the university's commitment to the pastoral care and Christian faith of its students. To the contrary, given the president's other responsibilities, the new position of dean of the chapel (filled by a Congregational clergyman, Robert Russell Wicks, who had previously been chaplain at Mount Holyoke) would ensure the presence on campus of one who, on behalf of the president and the university, could be devoted full-time to these purposes.

Through the next decades, President Dodds would do his best to show his support and concern. The devout son of a professor of the Bible at the Presbyterian Grove City College in western Pennsylvania, Dodds would often note that Princeton was a Christian (occasionally even a "Presbyterian") university.[73] Yet he and "Bobby" Wicks had to recognize that their students were living in a time of increasing tension and confusion. The 1930s had seen some rise in student social activism, especially having to do with the economic order and to a lesser degree with antiwar sentiment, but there was no marked rise in serious religious commitment among students. Indeed, perhaps reflecting some of the moral and ethical confusion of the decade and the economic class of a number of the students, they several times voted Adolph Hitler to be the greatest living human being. Dodds, however, continued to set forth his faith in the rel-

[73] On President Dodds's describing Princeton as Presbyterian, see Ulanov in *PAW*, March 26, 1979, 15, citing an alumnus's memory.

evance of Christianity. Speaking at a campus Forum on Religion in which he, along with philosophy professor Theodore Greene, professor of chemistry Hugh Stott Taylor, Reinhold Niebuhr, and others, sought to explore such questions as "Is Religion Implied in a Liberal Education?" and "Is There a Fundamental Conflict between Science and Religion?" Dodds noted that science cannot prove the existence of God. God was, however, the most reasonable explanation of the universe, and he went on still more optimistically: "The idea of a moral and social obligation has spread, and the spread was started by the teaching of Jesus."[74] Niebuhr was less sure that Jesus's teaching and religion, for that matter, were going to have that much positive influence in the face of human sin. His neoorthodox theology and social and political realism were already becoming far less attuned to ideas of humanity's progress in its "moral and social obligation." The Forum on Religion had begun on the Sunday evening of December 7, 1941. During the next days, reports about the forum had to vie on the front pages of the *Daily Princetonian* with stories of the attack on Pearl Harbor and the declaration of war against the Japanese.

1955–1980

English literature became my major during my junior and senior years at Princeton. I decided that were I to go forward with my half-formed plans to study theology in graduate school, I would yet have good time for such further religious studies. In any case, I had found a love for literature— poetry and narrative. It was a way to explore life's motifs and their import in art and story form. At that time at Princeton one could be given a sense (a "gesture" as one of our teachers, R. P. Blackmur, would say) that this was a better way to reflect on life's significations and perhaps meanings than more directly though the study of religion and philosophy. Poets probe and explore (T. S. Eliot's "hints and guesses") what could be alluded to by metaphor and indirection. "Tell all the truth / But tell it slant / Success in circuit lies," hinted Emily Dickinson.[75] Narrative, by forms of reshaping and recreation of reality could, as with other forms of art, help readers glimpse truths about life they might otherwise never imagine. "Art does not reproduce the visible but makes visible," con-

---

[74] Dodds's remarks reported in *DP*, December 8, 1941, 1.
[75] From Emily Dickinson's "Tell All the Truth."

tended Paul Klee.[76] The novels of Virginia Woolf were the subject of my senior thesis. I was interested in her attempts with words to describe moments in the flux of time that through artistic endeavor might somehow be "caught" and endure in life's ongoing passage. I thought then, as I do now, that attempts at such alchemy are the primary motivating desire for much artistry.

I gained a life-long appreciation for the sometimes-mystical poetry of George Herbert. Willard Thorp, Carlos Baker, D. W. Robertson for Chaucer and Edmund Kelly for Milton were among my teachers. I found out that one could argue with as well as learn from them. I was able to meet Robert Frost and watch his puckish face as, in response to some question of mine, he provoked me to recite his ditty, "We dance round in a ring and suppose, / But the Secret sits in the middle and knows." I listened in as he and his future biographer and interpreter, Lawrence Thompson, were already engaging in tweaking each other. Some of us decided to call another of Thompson's books, *Melville's Quarrel with God*, "Thompson's Quarrel with God." My thesis advisor, Larry Holland, a staunch agnostic, wanted me to recognize that despite all the intriguing allusions and metaphors in Eliot's *Four Quartets*, Eliot's conversion to high-church Anglicanism along with his politics was lacking in intellectual integrity. I can still see him arching his eyebrows when he learned that I was thinking of an ordained ministry.

I also came to know the Episcopal chaplain, William "Bill" Eddy—an alumnus who had fought in World War II. He was a rather quiet, but steady-in-his-faith forty-year-old who encouraged those of us who met with him from time to time in our educational endeavors and spiritual explorations. With two Episcopalian roommates I became a member of the St. Paul's Society and attended some of its Wednesday evening suppers and conversations. Eddy organized a trip to a monastery where I tried to learn more about prayer and the contemplative life. What I think was most attracting me to consider a religious vocation was a heartfelt, though not very well thought out, hope that through faith practice and trying to follow the teachings of Jesus about loving and unselfishness one might help make better people (starting with myself) and a world less individualistically centered—communities and societies with fewer of the

[76] Paul Klee, *The Thinking Eye: Paul Klee Notebooks*, ed. J. Spiller (New York: George Wittenborn, 1961), 1: 76.

inequalities, the racial prejudice, the sufferings of poverty, and other of life's injustices and cruelties. I tried to imagine that a next step in the evolution of humanity would be for individuals and communities to become somewhat less competitive and assertive for themselves, their families and clans, and more caring for the needs and opportunities of all—especially those less fortunate in life. Or, at least I thought, it was important to try. I had written in my memory words of Franklin Roosevelt (an Episcopalian who some in the church I grew up in referred to as a "class traitor") when he maintained that "the test of our progress is not whether we add more to the abundance of those who have much; it is whether we provide enough for those who have too little."[77] As far as worship was concerned, I more often than not went to Episcopal chaplaincy services and tested from time to time my prayers and moments of solitude, trying to understand if I had enough faith experience to keep thinking about a vocation in the ministry.

In retrospect I realize that there must have been more of a rising interest in religious vocations than I was aware of at the time. The numbers of those attending theological seminaries had risen steadily during the 1950s. Indeed, the Episcopal chaplain at Harvard claimed that while in his Princeton 1932 class "not one man out of 700 went directly from college into ministry, in the Harvard class of '57 there are already twelve who have decided to go into the Episcopal ministry alone."[78] I knew of no such numbers at Princeton, but I did have a few friends who were thinking of going on to theological studies. I had the model of my friend John Robinson, who died in an auto accident before our graduation, and Coleman Brown in the class ahead of me, the depth of whose commitments and Christian maturity I admired.[79]

In my junior and senior years I did attend some of the University Chapel services and even became a somewhat half-hearted chapel deacon. I liked the music and, though he seemed a bit Scots and foreign, I thought Dean Ernest Gordon interesting, while finding his ways of presenting the Christian message and faith rather unsophisticated by my lights. It was perhaps too Presbyterian and seemingly "earnest" (the pun was one of

[77] In Roosevelt's Second Inaugural Address, January 20, 1937.

[78] See Hoge, *Commitment on Campus*, 141, quoting from a *Newsweek* article of April 12, 1957, 120.

[79] My admiration was well placed, for Coleman Brown went on to a vital life and ministry as chaplain and professor of religion and philosophy at Colgate.

our little jokes) and long-winded for me. It also did not have enough of
the questioning that I found to be integral to my faith endeavors and
those of my friends with whom I could talk about belief and trying to be
a follower of Jesus. Paul Tillich, Reinhold Niebuhr, and Rudolph Bult-
mann were, after all, the great theologians of our era. What did Ernest
Gordon really know, I thought to myself, about Kierkegaard and Buber,
much less Albert Camus? (A fair amount, I later realized.) Moreover, I
definitely did not want to talk like a "Christer" or be seen as too out-
wardly religious. When it suited me, I was glad to join with those who
referred to the chapel as the God Box or Firestone South or Princeton's
two-and-a-half-million-dollar witness against materialism.[80] At least, I
reasoned rather self-righteously, Princeton had had the decency not to
honor the "laundering" of the money of a plutocrat, if not a robber baron,
by naming the chapel after him. Still, I would ask myself, how could the
passion and radicality of genuine Christianity be presented in a structure
indebted to such wealth inequality in America?

I had underestimated the staying power and breadth of Dean Gordon's
faith. Encouraged to do so by Assistant Dean Carl Reimers,[81] in 1960 and
again in 1962 he invited Martin Luther King Jr. into the chapel pulpit,
and it was sad if a bit amusing to hear of the anger in the alumni mail that
ensued. Gordon supported the principles of the civil rights movement and
knowing the horrors of war was an understanding ear during the protests
against the Vietnam War and over the bombings in Cambodia. Now criticized by some as being too liberal while others thought him too conservative, Ernest Gordon had to look on as his ways of presenting Christianity
came to be seen more and more as a minority view within Princeton. His
Sunday morning congregation had become smaller as the number of students with mainline Protestant affiliation was declining,[82] and when the
last vestiges of required chapel attendance (only for freshmen by then)
were finally abolished in 1964, President Goheen (doubtless recalling all
those previous years when the university had tried to take some respon-

---

[80] I later learned that President Hibben had at the Chapel's dedication pronounced the
building to be Princeton's witness against materialism and for higher values.

[81] Tom Wright (Princeton 1962) remembers sitting on the floor in Reimer's University
Place home having lunch and listening to King following one of his sermons in the chapel.

[82] By 1970 the number of Episcopalians and Presbyterians, through much of the century
more than two-thirds of the student body, was nearer 20 percent.

sibility for the religious and spiritual lives of its students) offered the in-coming freshmen class "the belief that the majority of you will seek the chapel or the church of your choice more fully and sincerely and there-fore will gain the more from them."

"We," he continued (evidently speaking for the university), "hold that without a religious dimension there is no fullness of being." Having titled his address "The Library and the Chapel Stand Side by Side," he in-structed the new students that their time at Princeton should be "a moral quest as well as an intellectual one." Both were of equal importance, while yet "the maturing and shaping of the moral and spiritual structure of your lives must be largely your own affair."[83] The campus newspaper noted the passing of the requirement with quiet approval, and even the already small numbers at Rabbi Levy's Friday night services (at times added to by non-Jews fulfilling attendance requirements) dropped off further.[84] Dean Gordon maintained that the end of the requirement was an idea he had urged for some years. Far better to have a congregation of those who wanted to attend. There were reports that his congregations did grow for a time, but as the decade wore on more with townspeople than students.

The turmoil of the late 1960s was a confusing time for students. Their support of the civil rights movement and for an end to the war in Viet-nam was driven by a moral earnestness that had some of the characteris-tics of a religious revival, though they were often unsure whether to re-gard forms of organized religion as their allies or just another part of the establishment. At Princeton and elsewhere a number of denominational chaplains joined the students in protest against establishment ways in government and religion—sometimes distancing themselves from de-nominational support in doing so. Princeton had its own chapter of the Students for a Democratic Society (SDS), and questions were sharply raised about the financial and scientific/engineering/technological links that some students believed made universities part of the military-

[83] Quotation from September 20, 1964, Opening Exerciese address, pages 4–6 in Mudd Manuscript Library, Office of the President Records, Robert F. Goheen Subgroup, Subseries 8E, Speeches, Statements, and Writings, Box 315. The next day the *New York Times* (September 21, 1964, 33) reported his address under the headline, "Goheen Stresses Moral Maturity."

[84] Chaplain Edward Feld told me he believed this was a major reason that Rabbi Levy left Princeton in 1965. My one-time colleague in Los Angeles, Rabbi Lennard Thal (Princeton 1964) remembers that Hillel during this period "functioned at a minimum level, with few active students." In "A Community to Turn To," *PAW*, April 19, 1993, 12–18, on 16

industrial complex that President Eisenhower had warned against. Indeed, some of the moral energy was directed at the university itself, its modes of governance and moral authority or lack thereof. Four years after President Goheen had told incoming students that "the maturing and shaping of the moral and spiritual structure of your lives must be largely your own affair," a number of students seemed angry that the university and many of its faculty seemed to them unable or unwilling to help them in what Goheen had advised "should be a moral quest as well as an intellectual one." At a time when, along with a kind of disestablishment of authority in sexual mores, the arts, religion, and a sense of a curriculum was taking place, students were no longer sure that the university was on their side in trying to be responsible and rightly educated adults and citizens. The murders of Martin Luther King Jr. and Bobby Kennedy in the spring of 1968 contributed to a sense of loss of moral leadership in the face of the challenges.

For several of these years there was a rising interest in how religion might be a part of the motivation for demonstrations and political activity. From 1966 into 1973 the numbers of students taking religion courses swelled—not least in courses in Eastern religions and religion and the arts. In anger and tears students came to the chapel to pray after Dr. King's death and to try to rededicate themselves as they heard words and prayers from the pulpit where he had preached. They came again in protest against the Vietnam War. At one gathering more than two hundred students offered up their draft cards on the chapel's silver plates. (Note, however: not to be burned at Princeton. They were later handed back if the students so requested.) There was an evening after the invasion of Cambodia when the chapel was filled to overflowing, and students of the time remember President Goheen using the pulpit forcefully to call the angry but confused students to adopt peaceful and constructive forms of protest.

Numbers returning to the chapel on a Sunday morning, however, dwindled further. The interest in church involvement that increased among college students in the two decades after World War II at Princeton and elsewhere dropped off rather sharply.[85] The concerted attempts of the mainline Protestant churches and faculty associated with them to have a significant influence on American higher education were also coming to an end.[86] The Faculty Christian Fellowship and its *The Christian*

---

[85] See Hoge, *Commitment*, 59–60.

[86] This is an important part of Douglas Sloan's well-illustrated thesis in *Faith and Knowledge: Mainline Protestantism and American Higher Education* (Louisville: Westminster John Knox Press, 1994).

Scholar both went out of business. Princeton's Presbyterian campus ministry that involved over a hundred students in 1955 by 1970 was down to twenty.[87] The Student Christian Association, not knowing what direction to take in this time of uncertainty and shifting attitudes toward the importance and significance of belief in God and church membership, withered away leaving only the Student Volunteers Council, now given the advisory support of the dean of the chapel's office.

At my class of 1957 baccalaureate service, retiring President Harold Dodds, as part of his farewell to the university, offered a thoughtful and admonitory address—still remembered by several in the class. His theme was tolerance—for one another and for those with whom we would live and work in years to come. He called us to a wise respect for minority views while also maintaining that minorities should try to understand and respect the views of others, as "the hallmark of civilization is the acquired capacity of men to respect the convictions of others without compromising their own." He then rooted this tolerance in a respect for the equality of all before God which Jesus's teaching of love toward others had made "the basis of Christian ethics."[88] I am not sure all that President Dodds had in mind about empathy and understanding for those who differed from us. Given the lack of wider tolerance in the admissions program at Princeton at the time and certainly in its eating clubs, one might have said, "beginning here." Remembering the man, I like to believe that was what he was also thinking—wishing Princeton might have done more after World War II when the returning soldiers had become more aware of the different races and cultures and even religions in America and the world.

That 1957 baccalaureate liturgy was held on a Sunday morning in the chapel. There were Christian hymns and prayers. If I did not wonder then, I wonder now what Jewish, other non-Christian students, and even Catholics and their families thought if they felt themselves able to attend. Perhaps they recognized and were willing to accept the fact that they were at the ceremony of a university with a Protestant Christian heritage. President Dodd's remarks, however, did seem to be reaching out to be

---

[87] Figures from Kemeny, *Nation's Service*, 232.

[88] The manuscript of the address marked in his hand as he delivered it is in the Office of the President's Records in the Mudd Manuscript Library: Series 15, Harold W. Dodds Records, Subseries 2, Speeches, Box 171, Folder 1. Quotations pp. 6, 20. An extract was printed in *PAW*, July 5, 1957, 13.

more inclusive, offering the service and character-oriented rhetoric, with occasional references to a generic God, that many of us had come to recognize as the kind of semiestablished civil religion of the university and, in good measure, of the country itself.

This not unattractive and generally inoffensive form of civil religion, particularly useful in a university setting with its heritage of believing that all truth is God's truth to be explored without fear, had a rational, broadly Christian humanistic cast to it. It has been described and was meant to be moral and uplifting: there was more to life than making money, enjoying oneself, and looking out just for one's own. Moreover, this was primarily what religion, I think many believed at the time, was all about. Historians might well have then said that it was the more Jeffersonian view of "general religion's" role in the academy that had finally won out. A modern university like Princeton was first and foremost an institution dedicated to education and scholarship and so in service to the wider society and nation. Among its students and faculty there were a number of people of committed religious faith and practice, but to best do its work the university's stance regarding religion was not only nonsectarian but also had already become secular in the sense that it would take no particular theistic or theologically based ethical stances into account in its administrative policies or curriculum.

Glancing back over our shoulders, my graduating classmates of 1957 and I were surprised if also pleased to find that the trustees had selected our soon-to-be thirty-seven-year-old assistant professor of classics as Princeton's new president. In some ways it may have seemed radical to have chosen such a young man and perhaps a sign that the trustees, though proud of Harold Dodd's twenty-three-year tenure through depression and world war and their aftermath, now wanted change. From another perspective, however, Goheen's selection could have seemed a safe choice. He was an alumnus, a product of Princeton's graduate school, and yet another son (come to Princeton with considerable tuition help) of a Presbyterian minister as both of his parents were missionaries in India where he had been born and educated through the tenth grade. He was relatively inexperienced, certainly as an academic administrator. There was no reason to think he would do other than build on Princeton's traditions––not seriously alter them.

This latter assessment made sense. Goheen was by nature a cautious man who cared deeply about traditions and loyalty to what he saw as the best of Princeton. He was also a man almost instinctively guided by the values and virtues of his liberal faith and Christian humanism. The words *service* and *duty, humility* and *courage* became him in his roles of leadership and management. His sense of duty led him to have a vision for Princeton, growing in its academic strengths and resources, while being able to change gradually with the times in order to grow most effectively.

During his presidency (1957–72) the endowment, buildings, and the size of the faculty grew considerably—the undergraduate body very little until the addition of women after 1969. More rapidly was Princeton developing its numbers of students and faculty strengths as a graduate school—in the sciences and engineering as well as the humanities. The Woodrow Wilson School of Public Affairs had become one of the top-flight public affairs schools in the country. During Goheen's tenure the number of graduate students tripled from 500 to 1500—in part a response to the need for new faculty to teach the rapidly expanding numbers attending institutions of higher education in America. A growing percentage of these graduate students came from abroad, in some cases bringing with them their non-Western religious faith and practice. Guided by his war experience and sense of fairness, by some of his faculty, and then by the burgeoning civil rights movement, Goheen began to put more effort into recruiting "minority" and especially African American students. Progress toward such diversity was modest during the first decade of his administration. The entering freshmen class of 1966 was still 95 percent white with an estimated 2 percent black, 1.4 percent "Oriental," and 1.5 percent listed as "Other."[89] Sheldon Hackney (Princeton's provost from 1972 to 1975) observed to me that when he came to Princeton in 1965 it struck him that a significant majority of the undergraduates were still in their "uniforms" of khaki trousers and shirts with sleeves rolled up twice from the cuffs. Compared with what was beginning to happen at some of its peer schools, and in the eyes of many younger faculty members, Princeton still seemed rather stuck in its past as far as the composition of the student body was concerned.

The civil rights movement was, however, causing a number of Americans to look harder at the problem of institutional discrimination in America. Desegregation in public schools had been the law of the land for over a decade. The pressure for change in private as well as public schools of higher education began to pick up. Three Princeton alumni played lead

[89] Figures from Karabel, *The Chosen*, 320.

roles. The man who stood in the doorway at the University of Alabama was Deputy Attorney General Nicholas Katzenbach ('45). John Doar ('44) and my classmate, Harrison Jay Goldin, brought their personal support to James Meredith and escorted him to classes at the University of Mississippi. The homogeneity that Princeton had long prized no longer looked so respectable. The "well-rounded" freshmen classes no longer appeared well rounded. Nor was Princeton as competitive as it wanted to be for the best students of whatever race or background. Harvard and Yale were doing more. Now diversity could seem good—good for other students as well as for Princeton. The black students who had already been admitted were not satisfied with tokenism. Faculty voices and those of some Christian and Jewish leaders grew more insistent. One fermenting group that met on campus, with Episcopal Chaplain Rowland Cox as a key member, dubbed itself the "Wholly Nameless Society." Another of its members was the relatively new professor of religion, John Wilson, who tells me that President Goheen several times joined with them, listened, and often agreed. Not only should blacks and other minority students be admitted, they should be recruited. Moreover, Princeton must now try to see that they were fully welcomed on campus—perhaps the biggest challenge. And if Princeton were to do more than accept minority students from well-to-do families, where would more scholarship funds be found?

"Princeton was lowering its standards." "Princeton was turning its back on alumni children." "Princeton was changing too rapidly." "Princeton was trying to remake society," came the voices of alumni critics over the next years. Yet they were now themselves a kind of minority. Goheen hung tough, and pressure built up to put African Americans into leadership positions—certainly on the faculty, but also in the upper levels of the administration and as trustees—where, one could have argued, the change would best have started.

Embarrassed, too, by Princeton's anti-Jewish past, and aware that some of the top-flight Jewish students were choosing to go elsewhere, attempts were made to undercut this form of prejudice as well during Goheen's presidency, though the results were mixed. While by 1960 the percentage of Jewish undergraduate students was as high as 15 percent, it had receded to an estimated 12 percent in 1966.[90] The continuing social significance of the eating clubs at Princeton (over 90 percent of the soph-

---

[90] Figures from *The Chosen*, 320 and nn. 152, 624.

omore students joined one in 1966) and the exurban setting of Princeton were no doubt factors causing some of the best Jewish students to go elsewhere. But it would seem more subtle factors were still at work as well with Princeton continuing to strive for a "balanced" student body and the use of the more subjective nonacademic qualities of "leadership," "character," and "well-roundedness" in admission decisions, leading to an ongoing covert control of the numbers of Jewish students.

The percentage of Jewish undergraduates would, however, hold steady and then begin slowly to rise—particularly after William Bowen became president in 1972. It helped that there was now a group of more active Jewish alumni who wanted to join in the process of recruiting, interviewing, and recommending prospective students and who were donors or potential donors to the school. The number of Jewish faculty also continued to increase, and by the end of the 1970s some 18 percent to 20 percent of the entering classes were Jewish.

At first opposed to the admission of women (in part because of a worry that this might get in the way of other efforts for diversity), President Goheen overcame his concerns and saw Princeton through the beginnings of this momentous change, weathering no little criticism and second guessing for doing so. Some of the alumni who were at first objectors suddenly realized, however, that now there was a chance that their daughters and granddaughters might attend Princeton. Moreover, whatever the other merits in becoming coeducational, Princeton came to realize how much it had to lose by not taking into account half of the top students in the country for admission and also coming out on the short end with those young men who would no longer consider attending an all-male school.

Economics professor William G. Bowen had been Goheen's choice to be Princeton's all-but-first provost (1968–72) and became his collaborator and prodder on issues of gender and race diversity, and then Princeton's next president (1972–88). Goheen understood full well that Bowen's personal and institutional passion for equal opportunity for the brightest and best motivated of students meant advocacy for a still greater diversity, more emphasis on merit and on different gifts and promise in the admissions policies. The decision to admit women had also brought about another increase in the total number of Princeton students. As president, Bowen concerned himself with the kind of welcome women and students from different racial, ethnic, and cultural groups, including a growing number of international students, would find on campus. He knew that the understanding of their needs and opportunities meant more changes in the administration, the faculty, and the make-up of the trustees. With President Goheen he would appoint Princeton's first black senior administrator and later a Jewish man as dean of the faculty and a Jewish woman as dean of the college and, in 1983, the first black dean of students. By 1979 one could contend that Princeton still had a good ways to go in fully accepting and including diversity and pluralism, but it was a remarkably more diverse community than the one from which my class graduated in 1957. How could this welcome and full acceptance now be offered with respect to religion?

TWO

Opportunity and Challenge

In September of 1978, President Bowen, acting with the Executive Committee of Princeton's Board of Trustees, asked for the formation of a Faculty Committee and a Trustees' Committee that would engage in "full and careful consideration of the ways in which the Chapel may best continue to serve the needs of the university community."[1] The chapel was evidently understood as a kind of synecdoche for the work and ministry of the Office of Dean of the Chapel and the uses of the chapel building under the dean's direction.

An immediate catalyst for this study, noted at the beginning of both reports, was the impending retirement of Dean Ernest Gordon after nearly twenty-five years of service as the chapel's dean. Both reports, perhaps the Report of the Trustees in particular, were handsome in their appreciation of Dean Gordon's long tenure and ministry.

> All Princetonians of the quarter century who know the Chapel know it primarily for its witness under his leadership. His ministry has touched countless members of the University community—and beyond—as he has testified to the Gospel, which he has lived and preached. The way in which he has carried on the 'goodly heritage' of his predecessors has maintained the Chapel as a place of significance in the University and brought it to the threshold of a new chapter which we believe holds great promise.[2]

In that last sentence, and with the words "maintained" and "new chapter," one can hear indications of a desire for changes in the character and

---

[1] From the Report of the Trustees' Advisory Committee on the Roles of the Chapel and the Dean of the Chapel (Trustees' Report), 1, and the Report of the Faculty Committee on the Chapel (Faculty Report), 1. Both reports were published in the *Princeton Weekly Bulletin* (*PWB*): Faculty Report, June 7, 1979 and Trustees' Report, November 5, 1979, and the *PAW*: Faculty Report, June 25, 1979 and Trustees' Report, November 19, 1979, the latter without pagination. Page numbers herein are for the Faculty Report in *PAW* and the Trustees' Report in *PWB*.

[2] Trustees' Report, 1.

scope of the dean of the chapel's ministry. Ernest Gordon had made a number of efforts to reach out, not least pastorally, to those of other faiths and to those of different Christian denominations. But his understanding of the Christian faith and its place in the university, and his concerns with the secular functioning of the institution, made him seem, to some faculty and administrators toward the end of his tenure, too narrow in his vision of the ministry and made him seem to have become somewhat isolated in his relationship with the leadership of the university.

The changes that had taken place in the composition of the student body, particularly in the last decade of Gordon's ministry, were, however, far more significant. As both the faculty and trustee studies would report, there was considerable religious activity and interest in religion on campus, but it was now estimated that "probably less that half of the [student body] were Protestant."[3] In fact, something like 35 percent of the students were Protestant with now 22 percent Roman Catholic, 18 percent Jewish, 5 percent "other," and 20 percent students who indicated no religious affiliation.[4] While some of those who listed no religious affiliation were probably of a culturally Protestant background, this meant that the number of Catholics and Jewish students together was now as large as the Protestants, and, in terms of those in some way active in faith practice, likely greater in numbers. "Protestant" was also more of a catchall word since there were now a larger number of "evangelical" students at Princeton along with African Americans, some of whom brought with them the worship experiences and concerns of their churches. Princeton's first full-time, denominational Baptist chaplain had come in 1973, and "other" included Christian Orthodox as well as small numbers of Buddhists, Muslims, and Hindus. While there are no certain figures with regard to the faculty, I have heard estimates that during this period in Princeton's history, the percentage of faculty who were Jewish in religion and/or culturally was as high as the percentage of Jewish students. In some departments it was higher still.

Along with most of those who indicated no religious affiliation, the number of students with little religious education and knowledge of their traditions continued to increase. The denominational chaplains, as well as faculty in their classrooms, came to recognize that many contemporary students now had scant knowledge of the Bible. When teaching at Prince-

[3] Faculty Report, 2.

[4] Figures for 1977 from Nicholas A. Ulanov, "Religious Life on Campus," *PAW*, March 26, 1979, 15.

ton, I, and others, learned that we could not expect from the majority of students much if any familiarity with the story of the Exodus, Jesus's Last Supper with his disciples, or even a parable like that of the Good Samaritan. I remember about this time standing in a museum near two college-age young men looking at a painting of Lazarus rising from the dead and overhearing one student trying to explain to the other that the story came from somewhere in Shakespeare. On another occasion, I had just begun an educational tour of the chapel when a student pointed to the thirty-foot-tall sixteenth-century French pulpit. I started to explain its provenance until he asked me, "What's a pulpit?"

THE FACULTY REPORT

While the personal religious interests and concerns of the faculty were not a focus of either the report of the faculty or of the trustees, both recognized a faculty stake in wanting to represent a university where religion and religious ethical positions were not taught dogmatically or required of anyone—certainly not the belief systems of one particular religion. At the same time the Report of the Faculty Committee on the Chapel (hereafter Faculty Report and Faculty Committee) struggled with language to express a sense that "a liberal arts university is, by its very nature, based, 'however implicitly,' as one observer has put it, 'on the assumption of a transcending—even ultimate—unity of meaning and value, however elusive or ineffable that unity may be.' Religion, many people say, underlies and contributes to this sense of transcendence and 'wholeness' in such ways that the religious perspective—the perspective of faith—infuses the life of a modern liberal university."[5]

"Infuses" was unlikely to have been a description all faculty members would agree with, but as the report continued, "even those who are not religious seem to agree that the university should provide opportunities for persons who are concerned with things spiritual."[6] It is at this point in the Faculty Report that the words "spiritual" and "spiritual opportunities" first occur, significant words that here and elsewhere in the process and in years to come seem meant to be inclusive both of persons with a formal religious background and those who might prefer to see themselves open to exploration of religious themes and values or, more broadly

[5] Faculty Report, 2–3.
[6] Ibid., 3.

still, to some "unity of meaning and values, however elusive or ineffable that unity may be."

The Faculty Report recognized that some students might satisfy their spirit of inquiry and search for understanding through courses in the Religion Department, but that they and others may also want to do so through other activities in the company of those worshiping, praying, singing, discussing, or otherwise practicing and trying to live out a particular form of religion. (It might well also have been pointed out that for some this will happen with practices and expressions of faith that are closely linked with their particular cultures and languages; for example, familiar music, food, using some words of, say, Hebrew, Spanish, or Arabic.) Of express focus was the concern of the report that as an almost wholly residential community with care for the whole person, Princeton should offer opportunities for all students to find welcome and support for their religious needs and aspirations. In order best to do this, the report insisted, the university ought no longer have as part of its community any students who felt themselves to be "second-class citizens" when it came to their religion.[7] The report particularly noted how many Catholic and Jewish members of the community ("now probably the two largest religiously active denominations on the campus"[8]) had spoken to them about their concerns in this regard. More pointedly yet, while Catholics could have some sense that they could share in the Christian heritage of the university and make use of the chapel building, Jewish students had neither of these. Clearly (although not explicitly) a major motivating force within the faculty committee was a desire to overcome Princeton's past lack of concern with having Jewish students find themselves fully accepted at Princeton. They shared President Bowen's hope that all future Princetonians—whatever the character of their religious affiliation or background—would feel welcomed and supported by Princeton.[9]

The Faculty Committee that presented its report in May of 1979 had six faculty members joined by two members of the administration. The

[7] Ibid., 6.
[8] Ibid., 3.
[9] That the full acceptance of the religion and culture of Jewish members of the Princeton community was at that time the particular hope of President Bowen is affirmed in his *Lessons Learned: Reflections of a University President* (Princeton, NJ: Princeton University Press, 2010), 112–15.

dean of the faculty and professor of physics (Princeton PhD, 1954), Aaron Lemonick, and professor of classics, Froma Zeitlin, were Jewish. John Marks, professor of Near Eastern languages, was an active member of the chapel congregation and also an ordained Presbyterian minister who would serve as interim dean of the chapel immediately after Dean Gordon's retirement. Professor of politics, Paul Sigmund, was Roman Catholic. Arthur Link, professor of American history, was a Presbyterian, president of the Board of Trustees of the Westminster Foundation at Princeton, and chair of the Wesley-Westminster Joint Board that supervised a chaplain shared by Methodists and Presbyterians. Link was an admirer of Woodrow Wilson, and his major scholarly work at that time was as editor of The Papers of Woodrow Wilson housed at Princeton. As an American historian, Link was, of course, also familiar with Jefferson's ideas about the place and role of religion in the ideal academy. Another member of the committee and a younger leader of the faculty at that time was John Fleming (Princeton PhD, 1963), professor of English and an Episcopalian. His wife, Joan Fleming, would later be ordained as an Episcopal priest.

Of the two members of the committee from the administration, one was Thomas Wright (Princeton class of 1962), then general counsel and secretary of the university, who was serving on the Vestry of Trinity Episcopal Church, Wall Street, in New York, and who, as President Bowen liked to point out—as though to assure others of Tom's religious pedigree--was the son of an Episcopal bishop. Tom Wright could be seen as the president's personal liaison on the Faculty Committee and would later direct the process for the selection of the new dean of the chapel. He had a particular concern with the ways in which the report would describe the work and capabilities of the new dean. Wright and Marks acted as conveners of the committee.

Another member of the committee (and its secretary) was Frederic "Fred" or "Freddy" Fox. Fox is hard to describe in a few sentences. He was an ordained clergyman (United Church of Christ) who occasionally helped lead chapel services, and he was one of the editors of the hymnal then used in the chapel. He had been a congregational pastor, newspaper reporter, a liaison to volunteer groups in President Eisenhower's White House, and then the university's recording secretary. He also became the university's first and only "Keeper of Princetoniana," and his Nassau Hall office, across the hall from that of the president, was a vast store of

Princeton memorabilia—banners, buttons, songs, signs, symbols, and stories. Dedicated in his Christian faith, he yet loved to see himself as an outlier. "Anticlerical and a born dissenter," is how I, and I am sure others, heard him describe himself. He knew how to appeal to Bill Bowen's sense of humor, serving as a kind of court jester, and was immensely popular among students and alumni.

Because of his faith, his keen interest in the ministry of the chapel, and his position in Nassau Hall and on the Faculty Committee, Fred Fox played a pivotal role in the drafting of the Committee's Report, and he would have had a valuable role in the transition were it not for his untimely death early in 1981. One can hear something of the influence he had in Bill Bowen's remarks at his memorial service, held in a full chapel with the colorful and sometimes outrageous Princeton marching band present, looking only a little less scruffy than usual, and leading the congregation forth afterward to the tune of "When the Saints Go Marching In." "How hard he worked," Bowen noted, "to encourage . . . a broader conception of the role of religion in the life of the university, at the same time so faithful to his own beliefs as an ordained minister and devout Christian." "His sense of the university's religious traditions was secure enough and generous enough to infuse his views of the Chapel and its place on this campus with a broad perspective. . . . He was for me and so many others, a pastor."[10]

An important behind-the-scenes advisor on these matters was the provost of the university Neil Rudenstine, a close collaborator of the president and colleague to the members of the committee. Neil Rudenstine was an alumnus (class of 1956), himself a former chapel deacon who had been Princeton's dean of students and dean of the college before becoming provost. He knew Princeton and the role of religion—its opportunities and issues—well.

The Faculty Committee was industrious, meeting thirty-two times and consulting widely with university officers and departments, with Dean Gordon, the denominational chaplains, alumni members of the Chapel Advisory Council, the Chapel Council (made up of local community

[10] "Remembering Frederick E. Fox '39, Keeper of Princetoniana," William G. Bowen *'58, *PAW*, March 23, 1981, 23–25. The rumor that Fred Fox's ashes were privately interred beneath the chapel is true. He asked me to do so, and I did.

members who worshipped in the chapel), groups of students, and faculty. In response to the committee's requests, some of the denominational and other campus groups prepared written statements. The committee members attended a variety of worship services and met with students in student settings. They spoke with denominational governing boards, attended lectures and symposia, and "carried on a number of personal conversations related to our charge with people throughout the university."[11] Interest in the process and study was indicated by several reports in campus publications and the *Princeton Alumni Weekly*.

On behalf of the committee, Fred Fox wrote to a number of "religious leaders" (university chaplains or their equivalents) at a variety of colleges and universities inquiring about the role of religion and religions on their campuses. Listing them in good alphabetical order, he reported that helpful replies were received from Duke, Grinnell, Harvard, Lewis and Clark, Rollins, Smith, Stanford, Vanderbilt, Vassar, Wellesley, and Yale. All agree, he noted, that "'the day of pluralism and secularism has definitely arrived' (Wellesley). All use the popular words: pluralism, ecumenical, nonsectarian, diversity." Several of them indicated, but only in rather general terms, that they were considering how best to respond to this pluralism. Harvard had earlier considered a kind of triumvirate of a Protestant, Jew, and Catholic as university chaplains, although President Bok had found the idea to be unwieldy.[12]

The recommendations of the Faculty Report may be summarized under two headings: first regarding the official ceremonies of the university and then the character and work of the office of dean of the chapel. At that time the university officially sponsored four ceremonies in the chapel: Opening Exercises, Baccalaureate, and the services of Commemoration (for families and friends of faculty and staff who had died during the year previous) and Remembrance (held on Alumni Day to commemorate alumni who had died during the year before). All the services used biblical readings, prayers, and hymns, generally of a Christian character. The dean of the chapel regularly gave the sermon at the Service

[11] Faculty Report, 1.

[12] After Fred Fox's death, his files relating to the chapel study were collected in a box (hereafter Fox Files) now in Princeton's Mudd Manuscript Library (Call No. AC 144, Box 7). Fox's summary of what he had heard from the other schools is in these files and also in *PWB*, June 7, 1979, 6. Minutes of the Faculty Committee meetings, responses from other colleges and universities and from Princeton chaplains are in these files as well.

of Commemoration and an alumnus clergyman was chosen to offer a sermon or reflection at the Service of Remembrance. Opening Exercises and Baccalaureate were held in the chapel at eleven o'clock on a Sunday morning.

The usefulness and significance of the chapel building were recognized ("a meaningful symbol and a worthy and inspiring center for the University"[13]) with the recommendation that the official ceremonies continue to be held there. None of them, however, the Faculty Report contended, should be on Sunday mornings, and they should become "truly interfaith in character" rather than "modified versions of Christian services."[14]

The Faculty Report's recommendations regarding the office and work of the dean of the chapel were necessarily more detailed and reflected some differences of opinion or emphases. Their main thrust was strongly to recommend that the next and future deans would not be, or be seen to be, representatives of an established Protestant tradition on campus. Instead, the dean should be able to encourage and support all religious and spiritual activity, and this should be his (in a footnote there was recognition that the dean could be a woman) major ministry.

For this to be so there was a concern that the dean of the chapel no longer be primarily identified with the Sunday morning ecumenical Protestant service in the chapel. Were the next dean to be of a faith group or denomination other than Protestant Christian this would not be an issue. Otherwise, it was suggested that a Protestant dean might turn primary responsibility for this service over to another, perhaps to campus chaplains from Protestant denominations or to an assistant dean of the chapel. In any case, it was recommended that the Sunday congregation should provide financial support for its worship services and not be dependent on university funding, as this would privilege this group over other worshiping communities.

There were several caveats. Among the recommended qualifications of the new dean was that this "religious leader should possess a deep personal faith." "A person with a vital personal faith, even though it would inevitably differ from that of many religious people on campus, is distinctly preferable to someone of a bland stripe."[15] The Faculty Report

[13] Faculty Report, 7.
[14] Ibid., 4.
[15] Ibid., 6.

then recognized that such a person of faith would need a community with whom to share and express that faith. Moreover, the majority of those on the Faculty Committee and with whom they discussed the matter felt that "it would be highly desirable to have as Dean of the Chapel a minister who would carry on Princeton's tradition of great preaching" in the chapel's "highly visible pulpit"—a pulpit that could also attract other "extraordinary preachers far beyond the resources of the usual parish church or synagogue."[16] The report had to hint at a kind of "catch-22" here, for, if the new dean was a Protestant known for "great preaching" and inviting other great preachers (not all of whom, however, needed to be Protestant Christians), might not this encourage an ongoing sense that the person if not the Office of Dean of the Chapel still had the flavor of some preferential support for Protestant Christianity?

If the Sunday morning chapel congregation were to be independent, there were also potential issues regarding the provided worship space in the chapel (should expenses for heating and electricity and the sound system be reimbursed?) and music. The organ, its upkeep, the principal organist, and the Chapel Choir with its director, all were partly supported by endowments that had been given for these purposes. The Faculty Report tended to overlook these issues, or not to see them as contentious. The organ and the choir, after all, were valuable for the university ceremonies, sometimes for pastoral services (weddings and memorials or funerals), and many people appreciated the concerts held in the building. As to the space, the chapel was also used by other denominations, particularly Episcopalians and Roman Catholics. In addition, space in Murray-Dodge Hall (not far from the chapel, very much center campus and the site of the dean's office) was made available for the Hillel Jewish group and for several other Christian as well as other faith groups. The Office of Dean of the Chapel might also make available some funding support for the activities of these groups. The several denominational chaplains of the United Campus Ministries (UCM) had office space in Murray-Dodge, and the Faculty Report recommended further development of this cooperation and sense of shared ministry to the campus.

The impulse of both the recommendations and caveats was in the direction of more rather than less. Yes, the next dean, if a Protestant Christian, could have an important and visible role as a preacher and even

---

[16] Ibid., 7.

leader of worship, but that should be more of an addendum than the main ministry. It was suggested, for instance, that the pastoral care of members of the chapel's Sunday morning worshiping community who were not students be handed over to others. The "primary ministering role of the Dean of the Chapel should be directed toward the campus—chiefly to students . . . and, to a lesser degree, to members of the faculty and staff."[17] Without quite putting it in these terms, the Faculty Report seemed to suggest that it was in large measure a matter of time, energy, and visibility. The next dean of the chapel, as an officer of the university, should be seen to devote the great majority of the ministry's service to the support and encouragement of all campus religious groups and to ecumenical and interfaith spiritual programs, conversation, learning, and discussion.

On the question of whether the next dean should be a scholar and educator who would participate in the "academic programs of the University," the Faculty Committee heard differing views and itself seemed divided. Some thought it would enhance the role of the dean of the chapel "if he had academic standing." Others though the dean could be more effective if the position had a clearly different role. But all agreed that "the dean should have a good mind and be able to communicate effectively with the Princeton academic community."[18] In any event, it was clear that the new dean, while not in any sense a "mere administrator and bureaucrat," had also to have good administrative skills. The committee did not spell out all that was to be administered but was probably thinking, among other things, of the relationship with the other chaplains, a staff to supervise, a budget to oversee, and the care for the fabric and operation of the chapel building and Murray-Dodge Hall. The committee emphasized the qualities of a "cooperative, collegial and ecumenical style of leadership" that would fully support "the vigorous, pluralistic religious life of the campus" and treat "other persons and groups of other traditions as full and equal partners in the religious life of Princeton."[19] Such a style of leadership "would also be welcomed by other agencies of the university that touch on the overall well-being of students: the Office of Dean of Student Affairs, University Health Services, the Counseling Center, the Board of Advisers and the Resident Advisers."[20] Signaling

[17] Ibid.
[18] Ibid.
[19] Ibid., 6.
[20] Ibid., 6–7.

their view of the significance of the position in the university and an awareness of how the position had first been fashioned to take over some of the overall spiritual, pastoral, and religious roles of the president of the university, the committee held that the dean should report directly to the president.

In the final consideration of the "characteristics of the Dean" the report asked that the Office of the Dean continue to enhance effective leadership and support for "social service" on the campus, particularly in the work of the Student Volunteers Council. This student-led group, providing volunteers for tutoring programs and a number of other service activities, was nonsectarian and not specifically religious in character— open to all students whatever their interests and motivations, but would continue to be well served by support and encouragement from the chapel's office.

THE TRUSTEES' REPORT

The Report of the Trustees' Advisory Committee on the Roles of the Chapel and the Dean of the Chapel (hereafter Trustees' Committee and Trustees' Report) was submitted in September of 1979 and was significantly influenced by the Faculty Report that had been presented four months earlier. The Trustees' Committee members had consulted with a number of groups and individuals on campus as well as with the Executive Committee of the Alumni Council, and had received, as had the Faculty Committee, numerous communications from alumni—many recognizing that a new day had come but urging Princeton not to diminish its religious heritage.

Members of the Trustees' Committee were fulsome in their regard for the role of religion at Princeton. "We begin with the conviction that an understanding of the religious dimension of human experience—although interpreted in various ways and degrees by different people—is a[n] integral part of the purpose of a university." While recognizing that an interest in religion is not for everyone and should be imposed on no one, "that purpose," the Trustees' Report continued in a broad religious and humanistic spirit, "is carried out in a variety of ways."

The spirit of free and open inquiry which permeates the whole life of a community devoted to learning is probably the most important. The curricular offerings are another. Courses which deal with the human enterprise—whether specifically "religious" or not—and which touch on any aspect of our common humanity—intellectual, moral, spiritual—provide the raw material for the educational enterprise. In part also this task is carried out by opportunities given on the campus to explore and practice religious faith and values in a variety of traditions and communities of religious faith.[21]

The Trustees' Committee then went on to adopt the major recommendations of the Faculty Report, several times quoting from that document as they did so. A central argument of the Trustees' Report was that what was being proposed should be seen, not as any lessening of the religious spirit that guided Princeton's founding, but as an expansion of it. The report recalled how the founding of the College of New Jersey was occasioned in part by a clash within colonial Presbyterianism about ministerial qualifications—one party stressing doctrinal conformity in the terms of the Westminster Confession, while the other group (which included a number of the college's founders) wanted to emphasize conversion and regeneration over what they regarded as overly sectarian concerns. The college, the report contended, had over the years adapted and changed to take into account changing circumstances and needs. Now in 1979, when "religious commitment abounds at many levels among individuals and sub-communities of the campus," but in a more pluralistic manner, "the Trustees are called to define a policy concerning the Chapel which reflects the heritage of the institution and the need of the present and future University community. More specifically, we must devise a strategy which brings a *relatively* homogeneous Protestant past together with a more heterogeneous future in which that tradition stands as one among several important traditions in the framework of University religious life."[22]

The chair of the Trustees' Committee was John Coburn of the Princeton class of 1936. A bishop of the Episcopal Church, himself an educator and former head of the Episcopal Theological School, it is hard to imagine one better suited to the task—especially from Princeton's perspective. A respected charter trustee of the university, alumnus, and close friend and classmate of the chairman of the Trustees' Executive Committee,

---

[21] Trustees' Report, 1.
[22] Ibid., 2.

Manning Brown, Coburn brought experience, his Christian commitments, and a proven loyalty to Princeton to the work of the committee.

Other trustees signing the report included four other trustee alumni with their own religious interests and commitments. Among them was Eugene Lowe, also an Episcopal clergyman, a young (class of 1971) African American who would (in 1983) become dean of students at Princeton. Lowe was a student of American religion and was at the time writing his doctoral thesis on Richard T. Ely, an Episcopalian reformer and economist closely connected to the Social Gospel movement. Another trustee signer was Susan Speers, one of Princeton's first two women trustees and the spouse of an alumnus and prominent Presbyterian minister who himself was the son of another distinguished Presbyterian cleric.

The Trustees' Committee concurred with and expanded upon a recommendation in the Faculty Report for the creation of a University Committee on Religious Life, "with members drawn widely from within the University community." This committee, which also "should foster awareness of moral values and value conflicts," would have an advisory role in assisting the next dean of the chapel "in fulfilling the University-wide responsibilities of that position."[23]

The two major recommendations of the Trustees' Report closely tracked those made by the Faculty Committee: the four major university ceremonies should become fully interfaith in character, and the primary ministry of the dean of the chapel should now be "to serve the religious needs of the student body more fully" by "assuming oversight for all religious activities on the campus." The dean would do so by helping to see (here the Trustees' Report quoted the Faculty Report) that "all university-recognized religious groups should be accorded full and equal status on the campus." This, the trustees maintained, "and we do not say this lightly, [is] a God-given opportunity" that would continue "the Christian spirit which helped found and undergird the University." The committee thought it important to add, however, that this oversight by the dean of the chapel should "be done without in anyway prejudicing the autonomy of the different religious organizations."[24]

There were other significant nuances. The Trustees' Report recognized that with new circumstances and challenges, it would be the responsibility of the next dean to work out the details of the opportunities and du-

[23] Ibid.
[24] Ibid.

ties of the office: perhaps in particular the ways for the dean to be a person of faith and leadership, active in one tradition, while yet not being so identified with that one tradition as to give it preference since the primary ministry was to support all traditions and denominations. Leaving such "details" to the new dean, the Trustees' Committee concluded by urging the president to "initiate the search process for a new Dean of the Chapel at as early a date as convenient."[25]

REACTIONS AND RESPONSES

News of the Faculty and Trustee's Reports and their recommendations were largely welcomed on campus by those giving these matters attention. Most students and faculty who had thought about the issues seemed to regard the major recommendations with respect to the wider interfaith ministry of the dean of the chapel and the interfaith character of the four university ceremonies as an appropriate accommodation to the way things should be in a modern university whose student and faculty were both more pluralistic in religious faith and where many others were less identified with any particular religious practice. The new directions were especially appreciated by Jewish and Roman Catholic leaders who hoped they now would be recognized as full and equal members of a Princeton community that welcomed and supported their traditions. One can imagine that a more cautious sense of "let us see" came from those in other faith groups whose numbers were still to be found predominantly among graduate students.

Perhaps surprising to some was the warm approval that came from among the Protestant and other non-Roman-Catholic Christians. More conservative Christian groups, the Orthodox, and some Baptists had in recent years felt rather second class in their relationship with the semiestablished, mainline Protestantism of the chapel and its dean. The Episcopalian, Lutheran, and Methodist-Presbyterian and Baptist chaplains (with whom in latter years Dean Gordon had not always had an easy relationship) shared some of this resentment. All these denominational groups seemed to feel that the policies encouraging equality of opportunity on campus would give them a new sense of support for their

[25] Ibid., 4.

sometimes-competitive activities, while, at the same time, also allowing for more cooperation in a new even-handed relationship with the Office of the Chapel and its dean.

The reception among alumni, a number of whom had been following the process with interest, was more mixed. There had earlier been several hundred letters and other forms of communication—some welcoming a broader ecumenical (though usually as Christian) approach to religion on campus. The esteemed Eugene Carson Blake hoped that the religious faith of Princeton would not become "syncretistic," but rather remain "Christian, Protestant and Presbyterian," though, as he put it, fully ecumenically so and welcoming and in dialogue with those of other faiths.[26] Many of the letters had similarly urged that "the Christian witness of the Chapel be maintained" and emphasized the importance of "the committed Christianity of Princeton's founders," "spiritual guideposts," "moral values in a permissive society," and their hope that the new dean would be a "devout Christian," one "with a vital faith." Several stressed their concern that the new dean should teach the Bible and not "merely opinions." A few insisted that the Bible should be taught as the literal word of God.

The strongest criticism of the recommendations for the new ministries of the chapel and its dean came from self-styled conservatives, some of whom had objected to other changes at Princeton, including the admission of women. A young Philip F. Lawler, former managing editor of *Prospect*, the magazine of the Concerned Alumni of Princeton (CAP), though himself a Harvard graduate laid out his lament in a sharply written cover story for the *National Review*. His article, "Getting God out of Princeton," viewed the new policies as part of a plot that had been brewing for some time in a struggle between Dean Gordon, critical of the growing secular humanism of the campus, and President Bowen, spokesperson for this "paltry humanism" who "has no discernible religious affiliation."[27] (At the time Bowen became president in 1972, he had asked for and received the trustees' permission to become the first president of Princeton who would not regularly participate in the Sunday services of the chapel.) When "Dean Ernest Gordon, a Scottish Presbyterian in the

[26] February 15, 1979 letter of Eugene C. Blake in Fox Files along with nearly a hundred other letters, communications, and responses to them, often from Fred Fox, but also from other members of the Faculty and Trustees' Committees, President Bowen, and Tom Wright.

[27] "Getting God out of Princeton," *National Review*, October 3, 1980, 1192–93.

mold of John Witherspoon came to retirement age," Lawler wrote, "Bowen pounced on the opportunity." Bowen and the study committee he impaneled solicited ideas "from students and professors outside the Chapel precincts, including miscellaneous agnostics, as to how the Chapel might best serve their individual spiritual needs. Thus Bowen's committee pondered the possibility that one university official should care for the spiritual wants of all students, regardless of the variety (and incompatibility) of those assorted needs."[28]

"The strategy," Lawler concluded, "was (pardon the expression) devilishly effective."[29] Even the denominational chaplains (one of whom, Lawler wrote, "doubles as a sex therapist" and seemed to approve of homosexuality, and another who had recently returned from Iran where he had apologized for America's sins) had gone along. Although several of the chaplains were less liberal on political and theological issues, they were "understandably jealous of their own prerogatives. Since the Dean had been their overseer, they would naturally cooperate in any effort to decrease his power."[30] In effect, they had, Lawler maintained, colluded with President Bowen who was still "maneuvering to circumscribe the power of the new Dean."[31] Interestingly, Lawler, a conservative Roman Catholic, did not refer to the generally positive response of the Catholics at Princeton to the new arrangements.

Lawler, however, was not alone in his concerns. An article in *Christianity Today* ("Critics Charge Princeton Strays from Founders' Path") picked up on Lawler's observations and added those of Robert Connor, a Princeton graduate (class of 1978) who had been active as a Christian evangelical on campus. Moreover, Connor, elected by classmates to be a young member of the Board of Trustees, had served on the Trustees' Committee dealing with the ministries of the chapel and its dean and had refused to sign their report. Connor criticized the report's "universalistic perspective." The "original Christ-centeredness" of Princeton's founders had been distorted, and the "omission of the covenant relationship between the university and the Lord as embodied in *Dei Sub Numine Viget*" was "ominous."[32]

---

[28] Ibid., 1193.
[29] Ibid.
[30] Ibid.
[31] Ibid., 1194.
[32] *Christianity Today*, November 7, 1980, 69. See also "Trustee Won't Sign Chapel Report," *The Prospect Letter*, December 15, 1979, 1.

Prospect magazine, which, beginning with an earlier Lawler article, "The Great Chapel Debate," and commentary from concerned alumni,[33] had been keeping a close watch on the whole process, presented a student-authored article titled "'—— Sub Numine Viget' (fill in the blank)," picking up on Connor's concern for Christ-centeredness by criticizing the search process for its exclusion of Dean Gordon from any contribution to it and contending that no new dean could live with the tension inherent in the Trustees' Report, requiring that the dean be both a fair-minded administrator supportive of all religious activities and a vigorous witness to his own faith.

The Dean is not a component of the academic package with respect to those who pay tuition. He is not a relativistic umpire of denominational manifestations. He is not an element of public-relations convenience, a walking proof that spirituality is alive and well at Princeton University. He is, merely, the representative of Christ on campus, and his mission of service derives directly from this representation. If the University no longer needs this representation, it no longer needs a Dean of the Chapel.[34]

Fuel was added to this concerned fire when it was reported that a Jewish rabbi had participated in the Opening Exercises of September 1980, and that while music, readings, and prayers referred to God, Christ's name had not been mentioned. Moreover, "the administration had removed the cross from the altar."[35] In fact, a cross had been temporarily removed from its place behind the altar and placed in the dean's study by Acting Dean of the Chapel John Marks, who thought it best not to have it as the central symbol for an interfaith service in a chapel otherwise replete with Christian symbols. But for some, this removal of the cross from the chapel, even if only for a few hours, was highly symbolic of the loss of the role of Christian faith at Princeton.

More tempered alumni, among them clergy, also lamented that something of great worth was being lost—not only an important part of Princeton's heritage and tradition but also that which should continue to provide a basis and guidance for its values. "We are living in a material-

[33] *Prospect*, Spring 1979, 16–19.

[34] *Prospect*, Spring–Summer 1980, 14–18, by Simina Farcasiu '83.

[35] In *Christianity Today*, 69. See also "Neutrality in the Chapel," *The Prospect Letter*, November 1, 1980, 3, and David Canfield, "Religion by Committee," *Prospect*, Autumn 1980, 14–17.

istic age," wrote H. Russell Baker Jr. (class of 1920). "Religion is being consistently down-graded." He continued:

> Religion is a fundamental need of mankind. Without it we drift aimlessly in a sea of troubles. . . . There are many religions. Of them all, I as a Christian, or at least a would-be Christian, firmly believe that Christianity has the most to offer. All the good that exists in the world and counteracts the forces of evil has its roots in the life and teaching of Jesus Christ. Princeton was founded by Christians and although hospitable, as it should be, to other faiths has been primarily a Christian-oriented institution. . . . My very earnest plea is that we should not abandon but should rather maintain and strengthen the tradition under which we prospered and contributed so much to the world's benefit.[36]

A retired Presbyterian clergyman rued more succinctly to a fellow classmate, writing of his "heavy heart" and preference to give money to other causes than "an institution which long ago forgot its Christian nature and purpose."[37]

There were also comments and letters that either commended the recommendations of the Faculty and Trustee Reports or suggested that they did not go far enough. Several staunch Christians felt it would be better if university ceremonies that were not specifically Christian were held in some other venue than the chapel. In this, a few nonreligious alumni who did not want any religion to be part of the services joined them. A younger alumnus, who indicated that he was among those who "reject religious cosmology," was more concerned to contest any suggestion that morality came only from religion. "Morality may come from religion, but not from religion alone. Morality is everyone's business. But please, keep your religion to yourself."[38]

Several university figures involved in the process took it upon themselves to defend the new policies regarding the chapel and its dean. Fred Fox wrote to *Christianity Today*, noting errors in its article (picked up from Lawler's "Getting God out of Princeton"), and reminding the editor of

---

[36] In a letter to John Marks then published in *The Prospect Letter*, May 1, 1980, 2.

[37] Private correspondence of January 10, 1980, between 1926 Princeton classmates. Copy in my possession.

[38] Daniel Krimm (class of 1978), *PAW*, October 8, 1979, 12.

Princeton's nonsectarian character from its founding and that it was President Witherspoon's pupil, James Madison, who had "become the architect of the U.S. Constitution and its Bill of Rights establishing the American principle of religious freedom."[39]

Professor Arthur Link was more heated in a lengthy letter to the editor of the *National Review*. Not only were there errors in Lawler's article, there were slurs. Link rose indignantly to the defense of the character and spirit of Professor Froma Zeitlin and the Methodist-Presbyterian chaplain, Bill Kirby, whose ministry, which Link helped supervise, "has been a blessing to this campus."[40] Link vigorously upheld the thoughtfulness and openness of the process that President Bowen had called for. Far from diminishing the role of the dean of the chapel, it was actually being given a stronger and broader significance in the university. "I have talked with President Bowen many times about the religious life of this campus and the role that the Chapel could play in that life," Link went on. "[President Bowen] continues to support it with vigor and enthusiasm."[41]

In more irenic correspondence and conversation in response to the concerns of alumni, Fox, Link, Wright, Bowen, and others pointed to the carefulness of the process and the work of the study committees. With only the one dissent (that Bowen felt added to the credibility of the process[42]), the trustees had voted in support of both the process and the recommendations of the Trustees' Report. The concern was for the full inclusion and respect and support for the religion of all Princeton students. Yes, times had changed. Princeton had been among the last universities to give up all vestiges of required attendance at religious services, and Princeton was not and could not now be in the business of in loco parentis with regard to the religious and spiritual beliefs and practices of it students. But that did not mean it could not see that Princeton was a welcoming campus for all who sought support in their faith and practice or who wished to pursue faith and spiritual aspirations and understandings while at the university. The university would continue to devote resources to make that support and care possible, and the chapel would continue to be used mainly for Christian worship and as a house of prayer

[39] Fox letter to John Moust, editor of *Christianity Today*, November 14, 1980, 1. Unpublished in Fox Files.

[40] Arthur Link letter to the editor of the *National Review*, November 10, 1980, 2. Unpublished in Fox Files.

[41] Ibid.

[42] Bowen, *Lessons Learned*, 113.

open to everyone. The chapel would also continue to be used for official
university ceremonies in a manner that would seek to be welcoming to
all. In so doing, Princeton was acting in a conservative manner, attempting to carry forward the Christian spirit of its founders in a new day. In
those words of the Trustees' Report, this could be seen as an "expanded"
role for the chapel and its dean and a "God-given opportunity"[43] that
should be implemented with confidence and thanksgiving.

[43] Trustees' Report, 2.

THREE

Religions at Princeton: The 1980s

"Bill Bowen is a persuasive guy. His enthusiasm can rub off on you," University Counsel and Secretary Tom Wright, directing the search process for the new dean of the chapel, warned me. "While he will want others to interview and consult with you, the decision is his. The President appoints the deans here, and he is very enthusiastic for Princeton and this new position."

Tom Wright also knew why I would be an attractive candidate to Bill Bowen. I was an alumnus with a background in teaching and educational administration. I was a believing Christian with a PhD in theology coming from an ecumenical consortium of theological schools also engaged in forms of interfaith dialogue. John Coburn had evidently already weighed in on my behalf. As long as I saw value and opportunity in the new policies for the chapel and religions at Princeton, I would be able to offer some sense of continuity with the university's heritage and traditions while helping to put the new directions into effect. It did not hurt that I had once known Ernest Gordon and would want to consult with him as my predecessor. Tom Wright was right about Bill Bowen, and somewhat to my own surprise vocationally, I, who had otherwise only set foot in Princeton once since 1957, found myself and family heading across the country and "back," as Princetonians like to sing, "back to Nassau Hall."

A THEOLOGY FOR THE MINISTRY

First to guide my understandings and decisions and then to be able to articulate them in various ways to others, I recognized a need to think matters through. It seemed that a priority for helping to implement the new directions for religion and religions at Princeton should be a theological rationale. I do not believe I was under illusions about the now generally secular character of the university. For many years religion and

Christianity in particular had no longer played any required or central role in the curriculum and little more in the administration or overall community life of the school. Quite a number of faculty members and administrators did not have an active faith, and the guidance of Christianity in the university had, as I have noted, for many decades become more generalized into the significance of good character and service—sometimes also with reference to a compassion and wisdom that went beyond knowledge, information gathering, and creation. These virtues and values did not have to be thought of or presented blandly or even nonreligiously, but they were nonspecific when it came to the particulars of any one religion. In this perspective it could be seen that the university had its good reasons for the broadening of the ministry of the dean of the chapel and the four major university services into ceremonies with multi-faith characteristics that went beyond religious interests per se. In seeking to attract, offer a full sense of acceptance, and gain the loyalty of the best-qualified students from the broadest possible range of the population, and to be able to raise funds, government, foundational, and private, from as many sources as possible, Princeton wanted to be seen as a fully nonsectarian institution offensive to no one's religion or lack thereof. The president and the trustees, it was known, were about to engage in a major capital funds drive. Princeton was a private rather than a state educational institution, but its mission in the latter part of the twentieth century was to be in service to the greater public of all the nation and the wider world.

On the other hand, Princeton had not interpreted its secularity as hostility or indifference to religion, or its role of neutrality toward any particular religion, as meaning it could not offer support for the beliefs, faith practices, and explorations of members of its community. As a semipublic, nonsectarian institution, instead of following a First Amendment interpretation that meant it could aid no religion, Princeton had understood that it could offer some form of support and welcome to all religions as long as it did not preference one over another or establish or make any form of religious belief or practice a qualification for participation in the life of the university. Obviously, one could debate nuances in that interpretation and how well it was being carried out, but it could also be argued that in this Princeton was following what was essentially in the mind of its alumnus James Madison, well influenced by Jefferson, regarding the independence of religion and government. One could also understand that the last gift of the spirit of liberal Protestant Christianity in terms of any privileged relationship with the institution was to encourage Princeton in the full inclusion and acceptance of all its members, whatever their religious beliefs.

There were obvious gains for Christianity as well as for other faiths. While some observers might regard it as only ironic that Protestant Christians' support of freedom of and for religion had led to its own disestablishment and marginalization as but one among several forms of religion, Christians, while continuing to be supportive of many of the university's educational purposes, now no longer needed to feel constrained to regard the university's broad understanding of civil or civic religion and service as descriptive of all it could mean to revere and follow Jesus. Letting go of any sense of being members of a privileged religion within the university, Christians could feel freer to witness to faith in a Lord whose message and example were service rather than privilege, who came "not to be served but to serve."[1] Indeed, a number of Christians had learned that their faith could be at its best when it had no privilege and did not try to control or in any way dictate to the lives of others. Here, too, was an insight they might share with those of other faith groups.

Seeing themselves as equally welcomed by the university, Protestant and other Christians were also better able to enter into conversation with one another and members of other religions about matters of common concern and about their differences. In a society and world where better understanding of others—not least in matters of religion—was greatly needed, the setting of the university, with its standards for dialogue, learning, and respect, was a special and rare place for such exchange. In this context Christians and those of other faiths should also be better able to engage in cooperative programming and to remind themselves and the larger community of the privileges together experienced at Princeton and consequent responsibility to the many in the world who lived with much less and many fewer opportunities.

Two particular tenets seemed paramount in dialogue among faiths and denominations. The first was an appropriate modesty in theology, specifically with regard to claims to know and understand God and God's ways. When I first put forward this foundational theological view to colleagues at Princeton, several of them said to me, in effect, "Good luck with that!" They were recognizing the strong tendencies of religions to be exclusivist—claiming God to be "our God," that "God is on our side." Through their

---

[1] Mark 10:45.

scriptures, if not in their theology, many may believe they own an infal-
lible or far superior knowledge of God and God's claims upon humanity.
Traditionally, as has been particularly the case with Christians and Muslims, a main objective of their faith practice is to persuade or even try to
compel others to convert to the one true faith and obedience to God. For
Christians a central tenet may be Jesus's words, "No one comes to the
Father except through me."² While Muslims honor Abraham, Moses, and
Jesus, they also teach that the Qur'an has subsumed all previous pro-
phetic religion into one completed and universal faith.

These exclusivist characteristics of religion, while true in their way, are
not, however, descriptive of the whole theological spectrum or of much
religious experience. Within religions, often in their most profound theology and prayer life, there is regularly an intimation of the mystery of
Divine Life—even of the elusiveness of the God who is beyond all human
ideas or understanding about God. While I know this awareness best
within Christianity, in every religion there is a recognition that all human
analogies, naming, and ways of comprehending must fall short if God is
truly to be God.³ "No one has ever seen God," is a foundational theological statement of the Bible.⁴ When Moses requests the name of the Divinity that has made itself known in the burning bush, God responds in syl-
lables that might best be translated as "I will be who I will be."⁵ "My
thoughts are not your thoughts, nor are your ways my ways," says the
Lord of Israel through the prophet.⁶ A sense of the mystery of God's
presence—even in seeming absence—is plumbed in Hindu and Buddhist
mysticism, in Hasidism, Sufism, and Christian writings such as *The Cloud
of Unknowing*, but a measure of apophatic theology and sense of the dif-
ferentness of God to be God are not unique to any religion. "The tao that
can be told is not the eternal Tao," maintained Lao-tzu, known as the
founder of Taoism. "The name that can be named is not the eternal
Name."⁷ Only such a "Way" or "God" beyond human comprehensions
could be God who was "owned," as it were, by no religion or people, but
might be related to by all.

² John 14:6.

³ On this sense of the elusiveness of God and the inability of words to describe Deity at
the heart of theology, see N. Ross Reat and Edmund F. Perry, *A World Theology: The Central Spiritual Reality of Humankind* (Cambridge: Cambridge University Press, 1991).

⁴ So John 1:18 and I John 4:12.

⁵ See Exodus 3:1–15.

⁶ Isaiah 5:8.

⁷ Tao Te Ching, chapter 1 in the translation of Stephen Mitchell, *Tao Te Ching: A New
English Version* (New York: HarperCollins, 1988).

The mystery and elusiveness of God need not signify that God, "the Source of All Life," "That Which Lets All Life Be," will not graciously *inhabit* and reveal something of the Divine Life even through inadequate human ways of understanding. Yet this revelation evidently comes through story, sign, and sacrament—in worship and song, in service, and through the lives of others. In these there still is a need for human wonder and interpretation. In biblical narrative much of revelation comes in surprising ways—more often in the seemingly uneventful and in apparent weakness rather than might—in ways that cannot be demonstrated or proved. Biblical stories tell of a God who is at once challenging in holiness and the demand for righteousness and justice, yet, in seeming paradox, ever compassionate, forgiving, and merciful.

This modesty about knowing God and, if one will, honesty in theology, is also helpful in conversation and learning from those whose religions are polytheistic or who might describe themselves as agnostics or nontheists,[8] spiritual or humanistic, or who believe in some divine power or life force but not a personal God. All of these words and terms—not least "personal" (less than *personal?* far more than *personal?*) and the very word "God"—are begging of many questions as to their meaning and what one may infer from them, but that is the point of the conversation. Such modesty in dialogue may also better allow for the discovery of where and when there can be shared values and commitments among those who have differing beliefs and religious or spiritual understandings.

This profound awareness of the mystery of God need not mean that people of religion cannot be strong in their faith and sense of relationship with the Divine Life. I remember Gerson Cohen (then chancellor of the Jewish Theological Seminary and soon to be a member of our Chapel Advisory Council) saying that the last thing he wanted for interfaith relations and dialogue at Princeton was a bunch of people just being nice and not trying to live out their faith at its best and most demanding. There are, we both recognized, fundamental differences in religions and differences in the ways they are practiced and lived out. Some of those differences are deeply rooted in the cultures from which those religions have come and/or in which they now express themselves. Gerson noted, with a characteristic smile, the tendency still alive among those who either wanted to show their liberality or who had little practicing religion, to

---

[8] I had come to prefer *nontheist* as a descriptive term to *atheist*, since the latter is sometimes given negative connotations in our society and may sound antireligious when this is not necessarily intended, though one, of course, must leave it to others to best describe their understandings and positions.

suggest that there was a kind of Judeo-Christian religion for America. Genuine dialogue, we agreed, requires humility, learning, and careful listening, but among people knowledgeable about their faith and experienced in living out its precepts and commitments.

That requirement for learning and listening needed to apply very much to me. The study of other religions was not my scholarly field, and I had much to learn if I was to be helpful in facilitating discussions.[9] At that time there was a measure of romanticism about pluralism and diversity of religion in America, as though it could be enough just to celebrate that there was diversity. Some hoped to revive the earlier search for an essential religion of humankind. Analogies of one light source with many lamps or several paths to the top of the one mountain were used to suggest how religions could point or bring people to the one God. The analogies had their uses, and every analogy is inadequate, but I preferred to think in terms of farms of plants and trees, differently shaped by their cultures and many efforts to find values and meaning, but with deep roots reaching in hope toward the ultimate goodness of life and with the desire, through sorrow and tragedy, to share in the divine compassion for the human adventure.

For Christians this hope and faith is centered on Jesus as it was for the earliest disciples, especially after whatever happened to cause them to believe he was still living after his crucifixion. The heart of the Christian faith beats in the worship and following of Jesus as one who was human but who also shares in the life of God.[10] One of the easier theological *moves* for a Christian engaged in interfaith dialogue is to have a "low Christology"—one that primarily views Jesus as a good or great human being and teacher. Then Jesus can be presented as one of the prophets of God—his life and example, along with his sayings and stories, making him among the best of the guides and philosophers for good and right living, to be honored alongside other great teachers, perhaps on a plane with Moses, Buddha, Mohammed, and other "founders" of religions.

One had also to be aware that matters of Christology (the human and divine characteristics or natures of Jesus) had been regarded as major sectarian issues that many educators—not least Christian educators—

---

[9] Fortunately, I once had as a colleague Ninian Smart, one of the leading scholars of religions who through his writings had become something of a mentor to me; e.g., his early book *World Religions: A Dialogue* (Baltimore: Penguin Books, 1960).

[10] See Larry W. Hurtado, *Lord Jesus Christ: Devotion to Jesus in Earliest Christianity* (Grand Rapids, MI: Eerdmans, 2006).

had wanted to play down or avoid in years past. But in the context of interfaith dialogue, faith in Jesus could be presented, it seemed to me, not as concluded, divisive doctrine, but as the belief of a robust Christianity to be shared and explored.

Christology is, of course, a complex historical and theological subject, with its many nuances and gradations.[11] Having a Christology that concentrates on Jesus's humanity is a reasonable and understandable position, held in the past as well as in modernity. One understands the value of this way of seeing Jesus when in conversation with those of other faiths,[12] but it does not fully represent the faith of the many other Christians who have found in Jesus one through whom God has been and is present to fashion a new relationship between human and Divine Life. That being said, I have long valued the pithy insight that while Christ helps *define* God for Christians, nonetheless God is not *confined* to Christ.[13] The special or unique revelation of the divine Spirit in and through Jesus does not mean that this Spirit is not present in its own special ways in other religions. I have found that the better and more interesting interfaith conversations take place when Christians, honoring this presence of God's Spirit in other religions, also present the fullness of their faith as they believe, understand, and practice it. One asks for the same from others.

INTERFAITH CEREMONIES AND SERVICES

How best to configure a university-sponsored ceremony with interfaith (or perhaps better to speak of multifaith) characteristics in a cruciform

---

[11] While at Princeton I offered a short series of teaching sermons dealing with Christology, published as *Jesus: The Human Life of God* (Cincinnati: Forward Movement, 1987) and also as an audio book from the Episcopal Radio-TV Foundation (Atlanta, 1987).

[12] John Hick is a tough-minded theologian and advocate of interfaith understanding who at that time argued for the authenticity of such a nuanced view of Jesus and its place in dialogue with those of other faiths. See his *The Metaphor of God Incarnate: Christology in a Pluralistic Age* (Louisville: Westminster John Knox Press, 1993), and, among his many writings, *A Christian Theology of Religions* (Louisville: Westminster John Knox Press, 1995); also my "Other Faiths and Ours" in *Outrage and Hope: A Bishop's Reflections in Times of Change and Challenge* (Valley Forge, PA: Trinity Press International, 1996), 152–55.

[13] So J.A.T. Robinson in his book on Christ and other religions, *Truth Is Two-Eyed* (London: SCM Press, 1979), 129, quoting William Sloane Coffin, *Once to Every Man and Nation* (New York: Atheneum, 1973), 117, who traces the insight to his teacher Erich Dinkler, while similar thought is also found in Christian theology in India.

Gothic-styled chapel? The other chaplains and I did not find many helpful models at the time, but we had several principles to guide us. We
wanted to be inclusive, using themes, symbols, readings, and music from
several faith traditions. We did not, however, want anyone to feel unwelcome by asking them to say words or to assent to prayers that might
disconcert or offend—perhaps most obviously by asking non-Christians
to sing specifically Christian hymns or to pray in Jesus's name. Yet at the
same time I wanted people not just to sit there but also to be able to participate in parts of the service—to sing, if they wished, and join in the
prayers in one way or another. We were also keenly aware of the criticism
that multifaith worship would inevitably be eclectic without much integrity, and in striving to be inoffensive to all, cautious to the point of being
dull. We had some fun in the planning: Rabbi Feld wanted to be sure that
Jewish readings did not always precede Christian ones, as though from
the *Old* Testament, and Catholic Chaplain Charles Weiser suggested we
occasionally use "Catholic" music and not just Bach. Music was a saving
grace. Without words it can speak to the aspirations and longings of the
human spirit. "Music," suggested George Steiner, is "the unwritten language of theology."[14] Our organist played a good deal of Bach, some
Handel, Langlais. The choir sang anthems: Randall Thompson's "Alle-
luia," "Silent Devotion and Response," or "Benediction" from Ernest
Bloch's "Sacred Service." The choir sang or chanted psalms, and the people could join in: "Praise the Lord, O My Soul." We found that there were
hymns a number of us could sing together—beginning with "All People
That on Earth Do Dwell" or "The God of Abraham Praise." Other hymns
might be slightly adapted or we could write a new stanza for interfaith
purposes and/or to recognize the academic character and setting of the
occasion.

We learned as went along. Prayers for the interfaith services used
phrases and themes from several faith traditions, and we would regularly
have a form of litany in which the people could participate responsively.
With the change of just a few words the semiofficial Princeton prayer
could be said by all.

The readings also would come from several traditions. At times they
were composite; that is, making use of a sentence or two from the scriptures of several religions that could interweave with one another: words
of the prophets and from other scriptures, words of Jesus, sometimes

[14] George Steiner, *Real Presences* (Chicago: University of Chicago Press, 1989), 218.

from a philosopher. I wrote one of the readings we used. Or one might come from Martin Luther King Jr. or Gandhi or Wendell Berry.

At various times the Jewish rabbi, the Catholic chaplains, or others of the chaplains, in addition to being vested for the services would participate in the liturgy. Students of various faith traditions also participated, and in later years made their suggestions about the readings. By the fall of 1981 I was joined in the work of the Office of Dean of the Chapel by the chapel's first woman assistant (later associate) dean, the Reverend Sue Anne Steffey Morrow, a Methodist in her ordination, who would often participate in these university services and help make sure that their language was fully gender inclusive.

The first of these services included materials predominantly from Jewish and Christian traditions. This made sense as students and faculty from these traditions and backgrounds were by far the majority in the assembly. But we came to be yet more inclusive. As I am a bit of a Native American, and all Americans can also recognize this heritage and spirituality, we might read from Chief Seattle or quote from Black Elk or pick up the cadence of Native American chant. From Native American spirituality and the poetry and imagery of other religions we learned how such spirit language is "not elusive and far removed. On the contrary, it is intimate language."[15] And light and fire, a burning bush, fountain and stream of life, wind and breath are ways of alluding to the Spirit of God in all of life. When in the services we exchanged peace and said to one another: "Shalom. The peace of God be always with you," "And also with you," the gesture and words seemed to take on extra significance.

The annual Services of Remembrance for alumni and Memorial or Commemoration for recently deceased faculty and staff presented special challenges since these liturgies had pastoral dimensions, and the language of scripture and prayer had in the past been largely drawn from Christian resources. But we learned ways to be inclusive of all who came to mourn and give thanks for those they had loved and admired. The speakers at these services would, according to tradition, usually be an ordained alumnus at Remembrance and myself as the dean and university chaplain at the Commemoration service. But this could now vary. One year Edward Feld, the Hillel rabbi, was the speaker at Commemoration, and now the preacher at the Service of Remembrance could also be from another faith

---

[15] Diana Eck, *Encountering God: A Spiritual Journey from Bozeman to Banaras* (Boston: Beacon Press, 1993), 119.

as we as a university community strove to be sensitive to all in our words and thoughts. Since classes returning for major reunions often had their own memorial services in the chapel, we tried to be helpful to them in providing suggestions and materials that would show this same sensitivity and inclusiveness.

The speaker at Opening Exercises was regularly the president of the university. In the context of academic pomp and parade as well as multi-faith liturgy, his was an address of welcome and invitation to the adventure of higher education. President Bowen often used story, sometimes poetry, and occasionally humor in an invitation to the matriculating students to revel in that adventure while also asking them to commit to Princeton's tradition of learning, especially learning from others of the past or present who might be quite different in their insights and wisdom.[16]

Because by tradition Princeton has no speaker other than its president at commencement exercises, the baccalaureate speaker can seem partially to fulfill this graduation-time function. When Bill Bowen came to the presidency in 1972, he relinquished the opportunity to give the baccalaureate address (in part because Princeton's president also spoke to the graduates at Class Day and commencement), but then was careful to see that the first speakers to replace him were recognized religious figures. John Coburn; Notre Dame's President Theodore Hesburgh; Princeton Stuart Professor of Philosophy Gregory Vlastos (a scholar of Plato and a Christian); James McCord, president of the Princeton Theological Seminary; and then Gerson Cohen were among the speakers during the 1970s. Perhaps because of the welcoming, interfaith character of the ceremonies, the services came to be still more crowded after 1981, overflowing into rows of seats set up in the plaza in front of the chapel. As dean of the chapel, and in consultation with President Bowen and then with student input, I had a strong hand in the invitation to the baccalaureate pulpit, and the choice of figures with a clear religious connection continued with the Reverend Homer Ashby, Ira Silverman (president of the Reconstructionist Rabbinical College), George Rupp (Princeton class of 1964 and then president of Rice University, formerly dean of the Harvard Divinity School), and Andrew Young. There were also now more lay people: Senator Paul Sarbanes (Princeton class of 1954); Sisela Bok (lecturer on medical ethics at the Harvard Medical School); my classmate Tom Kean, then

[16] These and other addresses are collected in William G. Bowen, *Ever the Teacher: William G. Bowen's Writings as President of Princeton* (Princeton, NJ: Princeton University Press, 1988).

governor of New Jersey; and Patricia Schroeder, US representative from Colorado. As the years went by, and particularly as the students were given more say in selecting the baccalaureate speakers, others (from the arts and entertainment, educators and political figures, military leaders, a physician, business leaders) were chosen more for their distinguished careers and ability to speak to the students on humanistic and broadly spiritual themes than for any specific religious identification. After 1988 I was only occasionally present at baccalaureate, but when I would hear or sometimes read these baccalaureate addresses, I would often wonder what these speakers thought about giving an address in that context and from that high pulpit (fourteen steps up a narrow staircase). Sometimes, of course, they could not help remarking on their perch, while then often going on to make the audience laugh before referencing and illustrating the virtues of integrity, compassion, tolerance, courage, humility, and service they trusted were compatible with the prayers, readings, and music that also came with the ceremony.

But then in 1981, what should be done at these ceremonies with the lustrous brass cross that had its central place behind the altar and had been the source of earlier controversy? One could appreciate the sensitivity of acting Dean John Marks in removing the cross from its position for the Opening Exercises of the fall of 1980 and placing it temporarily in the adjacent dean's study. In reality it was only about three feet tall—in some ways not all that noticeable in so large a building and sanctuary, but symbols can stir up the greatest controversy. I asked my new colleague and friend, Hillel director and Rabbi Edward "Eddie" Feld, to help me understand the best approach to the issue. Eddie Feld told me that the great majority of Jewish faculty and students were not troubled with coming to the chapel for university-wide ceremonies. They respected the building for its place in Princeton's heritage and recognized that its size made it useful. Many of them would rather be in a building with a religious aura than in a secular hall. At the same time, in a cruciform building, otherwise full of Christian iconography, with Christ a major figure in the great east and west and transept windows, it did not seem to be expecting too much to ask that a cross no longer be so central a symbol at these services. For many Jews, who remembered persecution or discrimination and the Shoah, the cross signified to them something quite different from the depth and victory of God's love than it did for Christians.

I decided upon a strategy of more rather than less—addition rather than subtraction. In exploring the basement of Murray-Dodge Hall, I discovered eight attractive leaded glass doors that I later learned had once enclosed bookcases in the library in Prospect House when it had been the president's home. (Although heavy and unwieldy, they were so attractive that an official from University Facilities eventually insisted on having them back for some other project.) For the next year or so I put Carmelo Sapienza, the slight chapel sacristan, in charge of mounting the doors behind the altar. On the altar we placed a menorah, a chalice, a Qur'an, a loaf of bread, the Hebrew Scriptures, the New Testament, books of prayers, and symbols from other faiths. Candles, symbols of our common search for truth and light, reflected in the panes of glass. Mind you, some people could well (and a few did) complain that the cross of Christ, while not removed, was now hidden from view. Together with some further explanation and teaching as to the positive reasons for having university multifaith ceremonies in the chapel, the controversy, however, seemed to dissipate.[17]

After a year or so, we devised a less cumbersome and more lasting approach. (They were reclaiming my doors anyway!) John Sully, a city planner and spouse of a university administrator, was also a maker of church vestments. John, who had already designed and sewn several stoles and altar frontals for the chapel, created a large banner with a representation of the biblical burning bush out of which God spoke to Moses, a story found, too, in the Qur'an.[18] The symbol could also be interpreted as representing the tree of life found in the Genesis story and the Book of Revelation, and, for some, then, the tree of Jesus's passion as well. The banner can be carried in interfaith processions and is placed directly behind the altar at university ceremonies in the chapel to this day. It became for some of us a sign and symbol of our multifaith and interfaith ministries.

It should also be noted that the dean of the chapel was invited to say prayers at other university events, regularly at the first faculty meeting of the year and an opening prayer along with a benediction, at the commencement exercises. These prayers needed also to be crafted to be as inclusive as possible for all present.

[17] "Chapel Ceremony Improved, but Cross Screened from View," *The Prospect Letter*, October 15, 1981, 3–4, was partially complimentary.
[18] Exodus 3:1–12. Parts of the story are found in several places in the Qur'an; e.g., 20:11–19; 27:7–10; 28:30–31.

I was asked to write an article, "Worshiping Together in the University," for the *Princeton Alumni Weekly* offering a rationale for the new policies and developments with an example of an interfaith liturgy from one of the university ceremonies.[19] Although some correspondents and commentators responded by warning that Princeton was becoming "syncretistic" or "universalistic" or "making a hodge-podge" of religions, the majority of responses to the changes and other developments in the multifaith ministry of the Office of the Dean of the Chapel were appreciative. I was particularly pleased by a letter from Rabbi Arnold Fink, who wrote, "Jewish alumni can only smile at this new reality and although it may take time for old stereotypes to be broken, we believe the university as a whole will be greatly enriched."[20] Arnie Fink and I would for many years preside together at reunion memorial services for our deceased classmates, until the time came for me to remember and give thanks to God for his life and ministry.

A more regular correspondent and once conversationalist at that time was William H. Hudnut Jr., Princeton class of 1927, prominent Presbyterian clergyman, and father of six Princeton sons, two of them clergy and one also then the mayor of Indianapolis. Hudnut had written earlier to Fred Fox and the *Princeton Alumni Weekly* and continued to let me know of his concerns with regard to what Princeton was losing in this transition. At one point he instructed me that should the trustees begin to require that all the chapel services become interfaith then the "only course you could possibly adopt would be to resign. Even the suggestion of such a thing would, I think, bring the Trustees to their senses." I replied that I was glad to have all the free advice I was receiving in this new ministry. We laughed, and he showed a willingness to listen and to recognize what might be gained both for Protestant Christianity and for the place of other religions in the university. I reminded both of us that religious tolerance and not intolerance and the making and protecting of space for those of different religious beliefs and practices were also a vital part of our American heritage. In "On the Bright Side: The New Dean," *Prospect* magazine was even rather commendatory and seemed ready to move on to other issues,[21] although the young and brash Dinesh D'Souza, brought in to be what turned out to be *Prospect*'s last editor, later made a stab at trying to reopen some of the controversy with his views of my views on

---

[19] "Worshiping Together in the University," *PAW*, February 8, 1982, 7–9.
[20] Letter to the *PAW*, February 22, 1982, 6.
[21] *Prospect*, Winter 1981, 3–4.

women in ministry, sexist language, homosexuality, and biblical interpretation, and contrasting them with those of Dean Gordon.[22] It no doubt helped that I was a Christian, able to provide some sense of continuity in the Office of the Dean of the Chapel, and perhaps the best some conservative alumni thought they were going to get. I also had an opportunity to meet with Bob Connor, the young alumnus trustee who had dissented from the Trustees Report. Some of his deeper concerns were not allayed, but we had interesting and, I like to think, mutually beneficial conversations about theology, Christology, evangelism, and religion and religions in the university.

Advisory Councils and the United Campus Ministries

Both the Faculty and the Trustees' Reports had recommended a new University Committee on Religious Life, appointed by the president in consultation with the dean of the chapel, to meet with and advise the dean on policy and new directions. Its first members were from the Faculty Committee on the Chapel, but it was not difficult to find additional faculty willing to contribute. The eight-member board proved valuable in wide-ranging discussions about religion, the place of religion on a contemporary university campus, religious and spiritual values, and new programs and strategies. They were helpful, too, in that the other chaplains had the ear of one or more of them as a way of making criticism and suggestions if they had other ideas about the implementation of the new policies for the welcome and support of all faiths and denominations. These faculty members became, as well, a resource of friendship and encouragement to the new dean. Paul Sigmund continued to be a thoughtful advisor. Julian Wolpert at the Woodrow Wilson School and Professor of Jurisprudence and Politics Walter Murphy, best known at the time for his novels about a fictional pope, could both be counted on for shrewd insights and good humor. John Wilson, through some of those years chair of the Religion Department, became another friend who could offer counsel and perspective on the whole enterprise.

As with most other university departments, the chapel had an external advisory council that met to listen, advise, and make a report on the work of the department. This council, which through those first years met an-

---

[22] "A Tale of Two Chaplains," *Prospect*, June 1984, 7–9.

nually, included several alumni and was now expanded to incorporate representatives of other religions and traditions. Among them was Gerson Cohen who continued to cheer us on. Ira Silverman of the Rabbinical Reconstructionist College later joined him. Other members were Robert Johnson, director of the Cornell United Religions work; Professor Thomas Long from the Princeton Theological Seminary; Stanley Higgs, then with the Community Development Association of Wildwood, New Jersey; Sister and Professor Mary Boys, then teaching at Boston College; the Reverend Theodore Rutkowski, rector of St. Paul's Roman Catholic Seminary in Pittsburgh; the Reverend Helen Neinast with the Campus Ministry Section of the Methodist Board of Higher Education; Judge Henry Kennedy, (Princeton class of 1970) of the Superior Court, District of Columbia; and another alumnus, Frank Strasburger, who in 1987 would become the Episcopal chaplain at Princeton. Stanford's former dean of the chapel, Davie Napier, came from Yale to give his counsel. Later in the decade alums from the multifaith years, Susan Cohen, Ellen Sheehy, and Bradley Collins, joined in the conversations. We often had the other campus chaplains come to these meetings where we could reflect on what we had done in the year past and imagine new possibilities for the common enterprise.

Meetings of the United Campus Ministries (UCM) were a far more regular source of conversation, critique, ideas, program planning, and collegiality. The UCM had first been organized in 1967 as the United Christian Ministries and reorganized in 1973 with the leadership of Episcopal Chaplain Timothy Cogan as the United Campus Ministries and Rabbi Feld as a member. In 1981 it consisted of the full-time Protestant chaplains (at that time Baptist, combined Methodist-Presbyterian, and Episcopal), the rabbi director of Hillel, and the Catholic chaplain with sometimes his one or two associates. By all accounts, it had been an important contributor to meetings of the Faculty Committee on the Chapel and had a tradition of seeking to have its own voice and program activities within the university and meeting separately from the dean of the chapel. Indeed, one observer had described the relations between Dean Gordon and the denominational chaplains as "distant at best, hostile at worst."[23] I hoped that was something of an exaggeration, perhaps truer with the Protestant chaplains than others, as Eddie Feld told me he had

---

[23] Comment in Nicholas A. Ulanov, "Religious Life on Campus," *PAW*, March 26, 1979, 18.

had a helpful working relationship with Ernest Gordon. I invited the group to begin meeting with me on a twice-a-month basis during the academic year, with Assistant Dean Morrow soon joining us. There was at first a bit of suspicion and "wait and see" attitude while we learned to work together in a collegial and mutually supportive manner.

I also sensed some tension between the UCM chaplains and full-time chaplains from other Christian groups along with other part-time chaplains who had been given formal recognition by the university. While the UCM members believed that they ought to have a different status because of their full-time ordained ministries representing long-established denominations, some of the other chaplains did not want to feel as if they were in a second- or third-class category in their relationship with the Office of the Dean of the Chapel now that there was supposed to be encouragement and support for all recognized religious groups on campus. The tension was in some measure resolved when we invited all the chaplains and directors of religious groups to occasional larger meetings. They did not always come, and I continued to rely on meetings with the UCM for much of our common planning and ministry, but it proved useful to have a gathering of and a forum for those leading the many campus groups. Before long the Alpha-Omega cohort began using the Marquand Transept Chapel in the University Chapel for their Friday night services, and we were able to have conversations with Peter Muscato of the Campus Crusade for Christ. The insights and friendship of the Baptist Chaplain John Walsh assisted me in doing this. The staunchly dedicated Wayne Weaver and his Princeton Evangelical Fellowship continued to hold their noon prayers and Friday worship and fellowship in Murray-Dodge Hall, and, despite theological differences (not least about what we agreed to call "biblical hermeneutics") and a few rather stiff conversations, we established, I think, a reasonable relationship. Also helpful was an annual retreat of full-time campus chaplains, usually held at a bed and breakfast near the Jersey shore, where we had opportunity to eat, share our stories, pray, and develop a greater sense of shared ministry. We had time to talk together about some of the psychological and social aspects of young adults coming to college and perhaps leaving religion or testing, finding, exploring, sometimes changing faiths.

Recognized status as a campus religious group with a chaplaincy came officially from the president of the university on recommendation from the dean of the chapel. Guidelines for this acceptance involved conditions such as having a student-focused orientation and membership, financial responsibility, an advisory board that had significant faculty and/or university administrator membership, making an annual report, and recognizing the role of dean of the chapel in seeing that their activities were respectful of others. An Orthodox Christian Fellowship, with professor of chemistry and Orthodox priest John Turkevich as its chaplain, had long been one of these groups, as was a smaller Unitarian-Universalist contingent with its part-time chaplain. Along with the Princeton Evangelical Fellowship and the more Pentecostal Alpha-Omega organization, there was a fellowship led by the minister of the Nassau Christian Center. There was also a volunteer Buddhist chaplain. By maintaining rapport with these chaplains and having them meet from time to time with the UCM chaplains, we found ways to discuss common problems, to try to model a respect for one another, and to engage in some common ministries.

An example of problems we had to face was the proselytizing efforts by some conservative Christians directed specifically at freshmen Jewish students during their first weeks on campus. Likely influenced by biblical stories of first-century Jews finding faith in Christ, these evangelical Christians evidently assumed that offering to freshmen Jewish students an opportunity for such conversion was their twentieth-century duty. Freedom of speech and the right to witness to their faith were cited as protection for this activity. Our conversations and discussions helped to distinguish between forms of positive Christian witness and unwanted harassment. Advertising focused at a particular faith or knocking on dormitory doors in the evening with brochures in hand and invitations to conversation were not acceptable. New Jewish students were not going to feel welcome and comfortable on campus if such were among their first experiences.

Another time, I heard second-hand that a group of conservative Christians were complaining because there was "idol worship" taking place in Murray-Dodge Hall. That did surprise me, and it took a bit of inquiry to realize that their distress was caused by a bust of the Buddha that a Buddhist group had used when meditating in the West Room of Murray-Dodge. I tried to make the matter an occasion for interfaith understanding, in this case perhaps not all that successfully.

Nor did it help my somewhat suspect reputation with some biblically conservative Christians when I began teaching in the Religion Department. My course, Parable and Miracle in the Gospels, was twice used as a substitute for Professor John Gager's introductory New Testament course while he was on sabbatical. Several students had earlier boycotted Gager's course, and campus ministries had set up corrective alternative precepts for his classes. Now John Gager laughingly told me that my course was being labeled a "faith buster" too. I started to protest that it was just a matter of my using historical-critical methods as well as other approaches to the material before I realized he was trying to pay me a compliment and that my protestations would not have much effect on those who had labeled me as well.

The dean of the chapel had responsibilities as a kind of primus inter pares to be of service to these other chaplains. A university officer, on the inside of university administration and councils, the dean was responsible to see that all other groups and chaplains followed those guidelines for recognized campus religious groups. The dean was also responsible for the chapel expenditures and the use of chapel monies to assist some of these other religious groups and common activities. The dean supervised the use of the chapel and of the Dodge building of Murray-Dodge Hall.[24] Murray-Dodge was prime campus space, headquarters for Hillel and home for most of its services, also providing office space for other of the chaplains and meeting and worship room for other campus faith groups.

Beyond providing some supervision, coordination of resources, and accountability, the major ministry of the dean of the chapel was to see that all groups and chaplains now felt accepted and affirmed in their place on campus. Numbers, of course, counted for something. There were, for instance, far more Catholic students than Orthodox, while yet no one would otherwise receive preferential treatment in the eyes of the dean and so the university. A focus for ministry was to provide pastoral support and encouragement to other chaplains; contact with their boards; and doing one's best to see that they had the space, financial support, and university privilege and access for their work.

Insider status of the dean of the chapel and the assistant dean meant that there would always be some differences in emphases and responsibilities. Not being officers of the university meant that other chaplains

---

[24] Murray-Dodge became the common name for what are in fact two buildings joined by a cloister—Murray Hall (built in 1879 and once used for weekly chapel services, having become since the 1920s a student theater) and Dodge Hall (built in 1900 along with a twenty-thousand-dollar endowment) were both given for the work of the Philadelphian Society.

could be freer in their critiques and to direct their work to their own groups. But when things went well, as they often enough did, we were able to do common programming and sometimes to speak with one voice to the campus.

INTERFAITH PROGRAMS AND ACTIVITIES

We had no blueprint for interfaith programs and activities. I knew, however, that I wanted to bring together a group of students on an interfaith basis, while I was unsure how to accomplish this or what we would do or talk about once we were gathered. I also was aware that Princeton was a very busy campus where students often feel pressured and the most valuable commodity is time. I asked the several chaplains to help me get the names of students active in their groups. I contacted some of them personally, dropped a note to others, and invited them to our campus home where I made them dinner. I sensed that I had two things going for me: students on occasion liked to come to a real home while at college, and they liked to eat. I made lots of spaghetti and told them that the multi-ingredient sauce could be called "comprehensive sauce."

Several of the students already knew one another, and they found that they liked talking about their religious interests and backgrounds. They especially liked hearing one another's stories about their faith or sometimes their concerns and questions. They recruited other friends. A couple of graduate students joined in, and they all returned for a second meeting. I cooked spaghetti again—this time (as part of my learning curve) with a "*vegetarian* comprehensive sauce." That was when they told me that several of them knew how to cook, too. Could they use the kitchen next time?

We decided to call ourselves the Interfaith Council, and soon we were eating meals from the different traditions: Greek Orthodox, Middle Eastern, Indian, Italian Catholic (more than spaghetti!), Ghanaian, Jewish, Chinese. Orthodox Jewish students brought their own food or ate before or after meetings. Food was a main subject of conversation as we talked about what people could and could not eat, of kosher and halal, and the significance of food and food preparation in their cultures and religions.

This experience led us to realize that we could take on other topics: music, scripture, time, money, clothing, prayer, spiritual practices, family, sexuality, evil and suffering, success and failure. We could talk about these topics in the context of our several faith traditions. Some of these same students would become involved in informal discussions held over or after lunch in Murray-Dodge Hall. There we might ask how it is that we human beings not only think but also think about ourselves thinking and are aware of ourselves and the world about us? Is this kind of awareness alone in the universe? Or is it in some way related to a fundamental capacity that undergirds existence? What is the universe made of? How does it run itself? Could there be an Awareness or Spirit of life that cares for humanity? How might we experience this?

Why is there so much suffering in the world? Can our lives be said to have significance? What is a good life? Why am I often restless and unsatisfied? How can we best live together? The students laughed and called our discussions "Big Questions." We were laughing at our audacity and then asked what could be the biggest question of all: whether there was any point in asking the questions. Certainly sometimes the students wanted to be less "universal" and focus the discussion on what they might do in their lives, their work and vocations—often an intense interest among such bright, dedicated young adults.[25] Perhaps it was as much my doing as theirs, but the subject of forgiveness would resurface: Does God forgive sins? Should we forgive one another? What is the role of forgiveness and mercy in our religions? Can we be forgiven unless we are forgiving, as "Forgive us our sins as we forgive those who sin against us" in the Lord's Prayer seems to require? Should all acts of evil and wrong be forgiven? What would that forgiveness entail? What of the atrocities in battles between peoples that perpetuate ongoing strife and wars? In Israel and Palestine? In South Africa? In Uganda? In Vietnam? Can there be reconciliation without forgiveness?

As a kind of "show and tell" I would sometimes walk students over to George Segal's sculpture, *Abraham and Isaac,* outside the northeast corner of the chapel. The university placed the sculpture there in 1979 after Kent State found it too controversial to accept as a memorial for the four students killed by the National Guard at the time of the demonstrations protesting the bombings in Cambodia during the Vietnam War. The sculpture catches a key moment in the story of Abraham preparing to offer his son as a sacrifice—Isaac kneeling before him, with his hands bound and his eyes puzzled and pleading. Some interpreters see it as

---

[25] Something of the story of the Interfaith Council and the exploring of these questions is told in my *The Spirit Searches Everything: Keeping Life's Questions* (Cambridge, MA: Cowley Publications, 2005).

symbolic of a highly emotive struggle between the generations—asking about duty and obedience and how older people should behave toward their children. The emotional intensity is heightened when observers stand to a side and catch sight of the phallic jut of the knife blade. Violence and nonviolence, obedience and love hang in suspense. As Segal himself described the moment, "as Abraham moves to do violence with his right hand, his compassion and love for his son are expressed in the gesture made by his left," whose fingers dig deeply into his thigh in self-torture.[26]

Should one forgive the guardsmen who shot the students? The politicians and fathers and mothers in America who helped them think the students were unpatriotic? What of the Vietcong? Ho Chi Minh? Lyndon Johnson, Robert McNamara and others of "the best and the brightest" who for a time believed it was necessary to send fifty thousand young Americans to Vietnam who would not return?

There were not squads of busy Princeton students at these gatherings, fifteen to twenty-five of us at a time, though a good deal of interfaith learning and sharing did take place, and I am sure that I learned more from them than they did from me. One of the most active members was Mehrdad Baghai, a Bahá'í student majoring in electrical engineering and computer science with a joint degree in public policy through the Woodrow Wilson School of International Affairs. Mehrdad came to Princeton from Toronto and a secondary school that he described as remarkably homogenous and where he was just about the only person of a different culture and religion. Gregarious and curious, Mehrdad made friends from many backgrounds and found the Interfaith Council "a formative experience for me in which I learned how people can bridge differences." It was, he told me recently, "the kind of dialogue that planted seeds and helped me to distinguish between the truth about people and their beliefs and labels—labels that often get in the way of ideas and understanding."[27]

After obtaining joint degrees in law and public policy at Harvard, where he found himself particularly interested in values of self-interest and/versus collective interest and the "micromotives and macrobehavior" studies of Thomas Schelling, Mehrdad went on to work as an educator and then business consultant with a stint at the World Bank. He now lives with his Australian wife in Sydney, where he has coauthored several best-

[26] George Segal in "PAW Prints," *PAW*, June 25, 1979, 4.

[27] Quotations from conversation with Mehrdad Baghai in early 2010, when the conversations with Whitney (White) Kazemipour and Cathy (Slemp) Branam also took place.

selling business books and heads up his own firm investing in worldwide technology companies while also devoting time (with his wife) to High Resolves, an educational program they began that is used by fifty Australian schools to help train young people "to work across borders" with those of different backgrounds and cultures. A feature of High Resolves is major service activities that enable students "to put spiritual principles from a variety of faiths into practice."

During Mehrdad's junior year one of his roommates dropped dead of a heart attack while in training for cross country. We held John's service in the chapel where another roommate, who was Catholic, did a remarkable job of speaking of their friend and of enduring care and courage for living. Many other friends, including members of the Interfaith Council, came to the service and an opportunity for conversation and a discussion afterwards in Murray-Dodge Hall. In was a time, Mehrdad remembers, "when we seemed all of one faith in sympathy and care for one another."

One of those friends was Whitney White (now Kazemipour) who came to Princeton from what she described as an atheistic household in southern California. Princeton provided her a place to begin exploring religion. She reminded me of a number of students, and even some faculty, who could begin a conversation with, "I am not religious, but . . ." She wanted to study the Bible and then became an active member of Campus Crusade, but found she had too many questions. She was, for instance, surprised to be told that as a woman she could not become an ordained minister. Whitney joined the Interfaith Council, "drawn by the possibility first of ecumenical and then interfaith harmony and the idea that people of differing faiths could work together on projects." It was contacts off campus as well as on that led her to become a Bahá'í, which then brought about strong reactions from former Campus Crusade colleagues. Now married to a Bahá'í and with three daughters, Whitney is busy completing her thesis for a doctorate in anthropology—researching and writing about parenting issues of Iranian American mothers. The possibilities of interfaith harmony keep her, she tells me, active in her faith and always ready to talk with others about better understanding and cooperation.

Cathy Slemp (now also Branam), on the other hand, came to Princeton as an Episcopalian and stayed one—although passing through a period with the Princeton Evangelical Fellowship and attending Sabbath services with Jewish roommates who sometimes came with her to Episcopal worship. Her time on the Interfaith Council helped her "learn about differences in cultures, values, and perceptions" and "to develop respect and trust, not only with people of different faith, but among Christians." Before medical school, residency, marriage, and children, she worked for a year in a medical and family services clinic directed by a priest of the Church of North India and his spouse. Cathy is now a state health officer and director of the Center for Emergency Services in West Virginia, where she finds her understanding of peoples' differences in religious and spiritual practices and values helps her in her work and in helping others to work together.

One member of the Interfaith Council that a number of us will not forget is Sam. Samiran Mitra had an infectious smile that lit up his face and drew other students to him. One afternoon during his senior year he borrowed a van to pick up some films for a club to which he belonged. Not that familiar with the traffic patterns on and off New Jersey highways, Sam somehow turned the van into the path of a semitrailer truck.

Sam's parents and sister came from New Delhi and, though Hindus, asked me to conduct the memorial service. All the members of the Interfaith Council were present for that liturgy. Our devastated council found that it had another profound question with which to deal.

Another program the Interfaith Council cosponsored was called "What Matters to Me and Why?" The conversations took place in the late evening in the basement of Murray-Dodge—an alternative social space called Café that was sponsored by the chapel office and UCM. Here on many evenings student-led discussions and music were offered. But now the music was quieted, and faculty members and others spoke of what they were passionate about and why they believed this was so for them. Understandably, presenters tended to focus on *what* mattered to them, but the students would sometimes then press them on *why*. Often as not the remarks and the questions and responses that ensued were quite personal. Dean of the Faculty Aaron Lemonick was the first in the series and spoke of his love of physics and education. My former teacher and professor of religion, Malcolm Diamond, told of his disillusion with much of religion and his turn to psychology to discover meaning and purpose for his life. Biologist John Bonner made the study of slime molds sound beautiful and told us why he cared so much for the study of them as part of the circle of life. Others also spoke of family and friendships along with vocation. Near Eastern studies Professor Norman Itzkowitz and Albert Raboteau (scholar of slave religion in America, at the time Catholic and who came to Princeton from Berkeley the year after I did) were among the cadre of faculty solicited into volunteering by the students. Professors John Fleming (English), Robert Connor (classics), Stanley Katz (professor of American law and liberty), Walter Murphy, Nancy Weiss (history, later Nancy Malkiel and dean of the college), Steve Slaby (mechanical engineering), and Joel Weisberg (physics) took their turns. Several alumni, one of them William Ruckelshaus, first head of the Environmental Protection Agency (also remembered for his role in the "Saturday Night Massacre" when he refused an order from Richard Nixon to fire the Watergate special prosecutor, Archibald Cox, and at that time again interim director of the EPA), spoke of the ideal of service in his life. He and others (Admiral William Crowe, a 1965 alumnus of the Graduate School and John Gregory Dunne of the class of 1954) talked of the significance of faith in their lives—of doubts and questions and renewed commitments.

The chapel and a variety of student groups cosponsored other campus events. Each year the Office of Dean of the Chapel and the UCM initiated campuswide activities addressing themes of peace and justice and service. Princeton being Princeton, we often received a positive response from well-known figures willing to come and talk with students: Elie Wiesel, Robert Coles, Coretta Scott King, Joseph Lowery, James Forbes, Annie Dillard, Allan Boesak, Frederick Buechner, Robert Bellah, and Robert Drinan spoke. Bellah and Drinan gave what were in effect sermons in our Interfaith Service for Peace. Bellah's was one of the most challenging sermons I heard over the years in the chapel. Drinan, to my embarrassment, however, somehow did not get the message that it was an interfaith service. Senator Jack Danforth, whom I knew from undergraduate days and who is also an Episcopal priest (and whose daughter was a student in one of my classes), came to preach in the chapel several times and to talk with students about foreign policy and other issues of the day.

Another year the series offered "Alternative Futures: New Perspectives on Vital Human Issues." Representatives from the Fellowship for Reconciliation, Heifer International, a kibbutz in Israel, and Habitat for Humanity talked with students. The following year, "A Different Adventure: A Year of Service" was the theme when we brought back to campus recent graduates who had given a year or more of service in the Peace Corps, the International Rescue Committee, the Jesuit Volunteer Corps, Interns for Peace, Legal Aid, and the Rural Coalition. Vocation and what students would do in their lives (in business, medicine, law, engineering, teaching) was, in these and other programs, often a focus of students' questions and conversations.

Concerts and organ recitals in the chapel were other ways to invite the mind and heart to pause, to reflect, sometimes to yearn. It is music, George Steiner also mused, that "puts our being as men and women in touch with that which transcends the sayable, which outstrips the analyzable."[28] Music, plays, and related events in the chapel were means to make people aware of the invitation of the building itself, although on a few occasions we could receive complaints if the offerings were thought to be too "edgy" (mild by later standards). Peace activist, feminist, and at that time lesbian Holly Near came to sing; and the Paul Winter Consort made the building sonorous with the jazz of his "great symphony of the earth."

Faculty Forums and Conversation

Creating opportunities for faculty to talk together about issues that mattered to them and about their values seemed like it would be a tougher proposition. Nor was it an assignment in the Faculty or Trustees' Reports, although the Faculty Committee did reference "ministering . . . to a lesser degree, to members of the faculty and staff."[29] It was my experience, however, that a good deal of chaplaincy ministry in an institution is to those who do the paid work—the "regulars," as it were: those who are there year after year: the nurses, staff, and doctors in a hospital; the guards and wardens in a penitentiary; staff and faculty in the academy. With a few exceptions, however, Princeton faculty who had a faith practice or leanings attended church, synagogue, temple, or mosque near where they lived rather than on campus. Their religion tended to be a private matter. In a secular environment they may even have had professional reasons for reticence with regard to their faith aspirations and commitments. From time to time I found myself introducing faculty colleagues to one another as Christians. Members of the same department might not know that their colleague was, say, a Lutheran or Catholic or even of the same denomination as theirs.

This reticence about matters religious or spiritual was, I imagine, one of the reasons why a number of faculty members seemed as surprised as

---

[28] Steiner, *Real Presences*, 218.
[29] Faculty Report, 7.

I was to see how many colleagues began to come to a series of Faculty Forums that we offered over lunch in Murray-Dodge Hall. It was common then, as still is true today, to complain that while a university hopes to be a community of shared interests, there is often too little "uni" in university—that even in a relatively compact university like Princeton, learning, scholarship, and the work of teaching are so time-demanding, often competitive, and divided up into departments, guilds, and subspecialties that faculty have few opportunities to talk together about common or community interests and may not even have a common vocabulary to do so. Whatever the causes of that sense of too little community of common interests and opportunities to talk across disciplines, the Faculty Forums seemed for some a welcome antidote.

Lunch at a modest price and the convenient location of Murray-Dodge were part of the attraction. A sense that the space and the sponsorship at Murray-Dodge were neutral with regard to any specific religious or ideological commitments, and yet could allow discussion of significant and perhaps even spiritual matters, was also helpful. We had a session on the topic "Religion: Society's Prop or Foil?" There was some conversation about the reasons for the growing "faith/knowledge divide" in much academic life and criticism of the limits that "scientific" and reductionist forms of rationalism could put upon human ways of knowing. But we soon realized that addressing religious questions directly—especially issues of a theological nature—was not our forte. Once, when he had come to speak at the Princeton Theological Seminary and in our Peace and Justice program, I invited the gifted Christian theologian and ethicist Stanley Hauerwas to talk to a Faculty Forum on the subject of community. It did not go that well. I think he may have been tired from other engagements and expecting that more participants would share some of his biblical and theological understandings about community. He seemed surprised in that multifaith and yet informal secular setting by the sharpness of their questions, and I should have done a better job of preparing him and our group for the character of the gathering.[30] We had better luck when Hans Küng was in town. I think, however, that had more to do with his notoriety and storied struggles with Vatican authority than our discussion of interfaith dialogue with him. One of our most interesting

---

[30] I now wonder how that Faculty Forum group would have responded had it been asked to deal with the theological critique of the modern university and the role for theology set out in several of Stanley Hauerwas's essays in *The State of the University: Academic Knowledges and the Knowledge of God* (Oxford: Blackwell Publishing, 2007).

sessions was with John Polkinghorne, formerly professor of mathematical physics at Cambridge and an Anglican priest. I remember how Richard Toner, professor of chemical engineering, ordained as a deacon in the Episcopal Church, contributed to that discussion, and since I lived across the street from Peyton Hall and was always intrigued by what emanated from that building, I was pleased when faculty from the Astrophysics Department entered in to the conversation.

What we did discover is that the faculty group had a collective desire to talk more indirectly about matters that might be described as spiritual, especially across disciplines, not least scientists and engineers with faculty in the arts and humanities. More specifically they seemed pleased to mosey around value issues as a way of talking about ethics, including values in the university itself pertaining to education and the work and art of teaching.

The fact that Dean Lemonick came and contributed to some of the forums, as did Dean of the College Joan Girgus, Dean of Students Gene Lowe, along with well-respected faculty members such as Marvin Bressler (professor of sociology and formerly chair of the university's Commission on the Future of the College), no doubt encouraged others to attend. Stanley Katz and Michael Mahoney (professor of the history of science) were other thoughtful participants from time to time. Younger faculty, among them Ellen Chances (professor of Russian literature) and Valerie Smith (professor of English with a special interest in African American literature), also brought colleagues with them. President Bowen once initiated our conversation. Professor of mechanical engineering David Billington illustrated his topic, "The Cathedral and the Bridge." Physics Professor David Wilkinson and Freeman Dyson from the Institute for Advanced Studies told us why they had refused to work on President Reagan's newly proposed "Star Wars" defense system. We had a session on the nuclear arms race. William Ruckelshaus (some of our speakers did double duty) talked about care for the environment. There was a discussion on the work and ethics of journalism with Don Oberdorfer (Princeton class of 1952), then with the *Washington Post*.[31]

There were several lively discussions about teaching and learning—the role of grades, competitiveness, how academic violations were dealt with, and admissions policies at Princeton. I brought the insights of Parker Palmer to the attention of the group, particularly from his book *To Know*

---

[31] Oberdorfer would later provide the text for the semiofficial, pictorial study *Princeton: The First 250 Years* (Princeton, NJ: Princeton University Press, 1996).

as We Are Known: A Spirituality of Education.[32] Those who were present
for that forum seemed more interested in the issues raised than Palmer's
ways of raising them, and I realized I should have invited Palmer to the
meeting to be part of the conversation. We had an even better discussion
with Ernest Boyer, president of the Carnegie Foundation for the Advancement of Teaching, whose offices at that time were just down the street
from my campus home.

Perhaps as much for myself as for others I suggested that we try to give
some shape and content to the word *spirituality*. For some people, I attempted, it might be understood as a form of sacramental insight into
life—a "way of seeing all life lived before and in relation to God, or to
that which gives highest value to life."[33] Someone referenced Paul Tillich's
view of religion as "ultimate concern" and suggested that it was what
"religion in the broadest sense has always been about," and I recalled
how the Faculty Report on the chapel had described a liberal arts university as, "by its very nature, based, 'however implicitly,' as one observer
has put it, on the assumption of a transcending—even ultimate—unity of
meaning and value, however elusive or ineffable that unity may be."[34]
Spirituality might then be a sense of relationship with "that which let's
be" and makes possible a world of language and reasoning. A major theologian of that language of Being also held that "spirituality is . . . the
process of becoming a person in the fullest sense," arguing for more comprehensive ways of knowing and against understandings that would see
the spiritual as only the "interior life" or that would divide the spiritual
from the material world.[35] Or, more broadly still, spirituality was "meaning, ideas, and the deepest of human values." "It is about the 'big questions' of life" another tried. Several faculty suggested that "what is beautiful" must be part of the definition. "Spirituality," someone then added,
a bit cynically but not entirely unsympathetically, "is the quintessential
American way of being religious without being religious—without any
burdens of particular beliefs, practices, and community."

After a pause, "Not entirely," came one response. "Compassion and
some kind of service to others need to be part of the equation." Marvin

---

[32] Parker Palmer, *To Know as We Are Known: A Spirituality of Education* (New York:
HarperCollins, 1983).

[33] See my efforts at description in *Coming Together in the Spirit* (Cincinnati: Forward
Movement Publications, 1980), 10–12.

[34] Faculty Report, 2.

[35] John Macquarrie, *Paths in Spirituality* (New York: Harper and Row, 1972), 47.

Bressler, wry and ever willing to point out some of life's and religion's absurdities to me, set out his belief that education is akin to religion and spirituality as directly as anyone could: "I think of education as a secular church, the university as a worldly church, and the faculty as lay priests pursuing a calling." "A sense of our common humanity and of community with all others and with the natural world," was added. Someone chuckled and said that the trouble with words like *spirituality* is that "they are as big as all-out-doors" and then went on to share his love of the world of nature in almost mystical terms. I floated the theological notion of panentheism, and we realized it might be better to speak of "spiritualities."

Values, too, seemed difficult to define yet important to talk about. Value issues had come up in broader discussions about what higher education is and should be about, the advantages as well as problems that derive from the dividing up of knowledge into departments with their separate disciplines, the emphases on "old knowledge" versus "new knowledge" (primarily of the sciences but in other fields as well), and related and perennial issues of curriculum and "what an educated person should know." Someone suggested that the word *values* had become a diluted way of talking about bases for morality and ethics—even matters of right and wrong, and we recognized that as academics from different fields, we were exploring these questions in a university in which rationalism had become a kind of new hegemony—still leaving the need to try to articulate its core values and virtues. Some of these might be called *intellectual* or *academic* virtues, important to the life of the university: seeking to be truthful, to be fair to the ideas of others, striving to be objective, doing one's own work, avoiding false beliefs, intellectual humility—qualities that many people, religious or nonreligious, would affirm.

One year we did a Faculty Forum series begun by Professor of Religion Jeffrey Stout who was at that time working on his soon-to-be influential book about different ethical voices, philosophies, and moral relativism in America: *Ethics after Babel: The Language of Morals and Their Discontents*.[36] Some of us remembered that Stout's Princeton mentor had written widely about Christian ethics, and now Stout was critically exploring the diversity of ethical languages and criteria and the ways in

[36] Jeffery Stout, *Ethics after Babel: The Language of Morals and Their Discontents* (Boston: Beacon Press, 1988). New edition: (Princeton, NJ: Princeton University Press, 2001).

which individuals and groups might talk helpfully together about ethics in a world where no ethical language or religious or philosophical context could have sure preference or authority.

In a second session I shared an essay I had written, later published in the *Chronicle of Higher Education* as "It's Often Difficult Helping Students to Learn More about Values and Ethics."[37] The essay sought to raise questions about the overt or subtler claims of higher education to teach only "the logic of the facts" and to do so in a value-free atmosphere. ("Beware," I was taught early on, "of any teacher who claims only to be teaching the facts.")[38] In reality, the forms (or sometimes deliberate formlessness) of curricula and the institutional life of the academy are, I argued, replete with value-laden understandings that were often influential to students if rarely brought to critical examination by the teaching institution.

During these discussions questions about "caught rather than taught" would resurface. Several faculty members noted that a student's values and virtues largely came from their family and culture or culture and religion and were fairly well formed by the time they came to Princeton. It was at best difficult to teach about them in ways that would make significant difference. One anthropologist suggested that students in our society might even be thinking and acting more out or honor/shame codes than we realized, which led a colleague to ask if faculty were somehow exempt. Others wondered if the sources of morals and ethical values were not too deeply buried in evolutionary biological and psychological layers to bear fully rational examination and noted that most individuals, groups, and organizations are motivated by a mixed set of values, not always complementary. All the more reason, was the reply, that in a university education those values should be "put under a microscope." If one wished, echoes could be heard of those debates between President McCosh and President Eliot of Harvard a century earlier, and I pointed out how Harvard was now beginning to require students to choose from a

---

[37] In the *Chronicle of Higher Education*, September 5, 1984, and later published in *Points of View on American Higher Education: A Selection of Essays from the Chronicle of Higher Education*, ed. Stephen H. Barnes, vol. 2, *Institutions and Issues* (Lewiston, NY: Edwin Mellen Press, 1990), 158–63.

[38] The phrase from the 1960s *Handbook for Faculty Members of the University of California* is quoted in my Chronicle of Higher Education essay. On facts as "value-laden," see the helpful discussion in his chapter "Trouble Maintaining the Fact/Value Dichotomy" in C. John Sommerville, *The Decline of the Secular University* (New York: Oxford University Press, 2008), 39–46.

cluster of courses in moral reasoning and social analysis.[39] At a later forum, Robert Bellah helped us think about this and related issues, not without some heat in the discussion. We were forced to recognize that it is easier to talk about values and virtues and decision-making than it is to explicate the motivations and inspiration that would lead people to live by them. One of the issues we kept returning to was the place of the "common good" or more communal values (a major interest of most religions) in relation to emphases on individual rights and more individualistic values. Complex questions about "justice" as deserving and/or fairness—just process and/or distributive justice—continually recurred. These were addressed in the third forum in our series initiated by Michael Walzer, then at the Institute for Advanced Studies.

The fourth of the forums was led by Professor Amy Gutmann, who was teaching a course with Dennis Thompson on challenging ethical issues of the time. There was some discussion of the proposition that all ethics might be seen as variations on the golden rule, which some interpreted as calling for a measure of genuine altruism and others as the best form of enlightened self-interest.

I like to think that our discussions made some contribution to the founding (through Amy Gutmann's leadership) in 1990 of the university's Center for Human Values, established "to foster ongoing inquiry into important ethical issues in private and public life." While some were concerned that the study of values was now being "departmentalized" and professionalized so as no longer to be a responsibility of other faculty and the university as a whole, the center was intended to support "teaching, ethics, and human values throughout the curriculum and across the disciplines of Princeton University." Much of the funding came from Laurance S. Rockefeller (class of 1932), who as an undergraduate, in addition to being president of the Student Christian Association and a director of the Princeton Summer Camp, was clearly involved in a search for values that would bring intellectual heft to his Baptist upbringing. Becoming a philosophy major, he titled his senior thesis "The Concept of Value and Its Relationship to Ethics," concluding that the validity of value "intu-

---

[39] On the ongoing debate and discussion as to whether and how ethics and morality were, should, or can be taught in colleges and universities, see Elizabeth Kiss and J. Peter Euben, eds., *Debating Moral Education: Rethinking the Role of the Modern University* (Durham, NC: Duke University Press, 2009). At the time I referenced an article by Derek Bok on the challenges and opportunities of teaching ethics. See Derek C. Bok, "Can Ethics Be Taught?" *Change*, October 1976, 26–30.

itions must rest on metaphysical grounds and so are a matter of faith. It is at this dropping off place of values and facts that the basic religious experience is found."[40] I could not help reflecting that a generation or so earlier, Rockefeller money might have seen to it that religion was still at the heart of any search for human values. Now, however, in a university caught between the Enlightenment's modernism and forms of postmodernism (once described to me as a celebration of what modernism mourns) religious teaching would have no privileged position in ethical discussions. In a world of competing religious ethics and secular views and philosophies, some nontheists would in a few more years make their point with slogans that might also be heard as questions: "Goodness without God" or the catchy and pointed "Be Good for Goodness Sake."

There were also matters of applied ethics and action to consider in the life of the university. I recall what I believe was a mutually helpful exchange with a faculty member who had maintained that biblical and other religious teachings about human domination over the natural world, its imminent end, and a spiritual-material dualism contributed to a lack of environmental care and concern in society. I tried to explain why many Christians and others viewed stewardship of the environment as among their primary responsibilities. Human beings have a need both "to till and to keep," as I put it, quoting from a creation story in the Book of Genesis.[41] Frank von Hippel, on the other hand, who was then chairman of the Federation of American Scientists, readily saw faith groups on campus as collaborators in teaching about the dangers of the proliferation of nuclear weapons and was a participant in several campus programs dealing with peace and justice issues.

Another matter of importance to several groups on campus was the problem with the unevenness and quality of public education in America. Princeton, like other elite universities, because it has its pick from many of the brightest secondary school graduates in the country (whatever the quality of their school), and due to the unlikelihood that many of its graduates would enter, much less stay in, the generally poorly remuner-

[40] Quoted in Robin W. Winks, *Laurance S. Rockefeller: Catalyst for Conservation* (Washington, DC: Island Press, 1997), 31–33. See also Axtell, *Making of Princeton University*, 343.

[41] Genesis 2:15. See also my later essays, "Our Fragile Island Home" and "Environmental Economy," in *Outrage and Hope*, 33–38

ated field of public education or send their own children to anything but the best private or public schools, seemed rather inured from the problems. Princeton was also without a professional school of education. The university's annual honoring of several secondary school teachers, the Program in Teacher Preparation directed by the dedicated Henry Drewry, Student Volunteer Council tutoring programs, and then Wendy Kopp's (class of 1989) *Teach for America* were helpful steps.[42] Yet while it remained evident that more needed to be done, it was also held that Princeton made its best contributions to society when it adhered closely to its core mission and purposes of undergraduate and graduate education, scholarship, and the creation of new knowledge.

Dean Morrow; chaplains John Walsh, Timothy Cogan, and Frank Strasburger; other chaplains; and I felt we had a role to play in bringing up other ethical issues in sermons and other venues. I found that I had a wider audience with occasional short pieces in campus publications—the *Nassau Weekly* and, more often, the student newspaper, the *Daily Princetonian.* Concerns such as racism, how to strive for full inclusion and acceptance of all students, faculty diversity, the downsides of wealth influencing Princeton (through too much of the interlocking interests between the university, and some faculty, of the world of finance and government funding), sexuality and pornography (mainly its sexism and economics) were among the topics. I joined with Professors Katz, Slaby, and others in asking the university to consider replacing the federal loans that had been lost by students who refused on conscientious grounds to register for the draft. I found that it took some courage to speak to such an educated and often opinionated audience. I was linked with a student group, Princeton Alliance to Reverse the Arms Race, and when I wrote an editorial piece for the *Daily Princetonian* urging students to become more informed

---

[42] President Shirley Tilghman (who herself once taught in a high school in West Africa), noted in her president's page in the *PAW* (November 4, 2009, 5) that almost nine hundred Princeton students have gone forward over the years through the "Teacher Prep" program to be certified teachers—60 percent staying in the field for five or more years after graduation. Commendable as this is, many of them have become teachers in private schools and the total represents less that 2 percent of Princeton undergraduates (presumably few graduate students) during this period. Yet more positively, see Tom Krattenmaker, "The Highest Art: For Alumni Who Teach in Public Schools, the Pay Is Low but the Rewards Are Real," *PAW*, March 10, 1999, 10–16, and "Schoolhouses Rock," *PAW*, March 2, 2011, 29–33, which tells of Princeton graduates playing lead roles in new inititaives in public education. Notable also in recent years is the Princeton University Preparatory Program (PUPP) through which Princeton students and faculty encourage and assist low-income, high-achieving Mercer County high school students to attend selective colleges.

about nuclear weapons proliferation and active about their concerns, it was countered by a professor of politics who maintained that I "knew next to nothing, to say the very least" about the real issues.[43] My twin sons, who in that relatively small community were in high school with the professor's son, laughed at the "to say the very least" emphasis and sought to console me: "Oh, dad, you know at least something about it." I thought that I did, too, having recently listened to alumnus George Kennan express his concern as to how "almost involuntarily, like the victims of some sort of hypnotism ... we have gone on piling weapon upon weapon, missile upon missile, new levels of destruction upon old ones." My resolve was strengthened when professors such as Richard Falk (who on other occasions shared with me his interest in religion and politics) wrote in support, and several of us were later able to put together a faculty committee to advocate for a freeze on nuclear weapons and related peace and justice matters. With further leadership from physicist Joel Weisberg, two results of our efforts were a "Statement and Recommendation regarding Nuclear Weapons," published in the May 13, 1983 *Daily Princetonian* and signed by more than one hundred faculty, and a conference, "The Nuclear Arms Debate," sponsored by the Center for International Affairs.

On a number of such issues one also met with the general criticism coming from some alumni, media pundits, and a few faculty that these concerns were just part of the "knee-jerk" bias of most faculty in another liberal university. Then it was my turn to smile somewhat ruefully for when it came to several of the radical biblical injunctions that affected peace and structural economic justice issues (e.g., that the United States, in part for economic reasons, was the largest purveyor of military weaponry in the world; severe wealth inequalities from which universities often benefited versus Roosevelt's dictum about progress meaning first providing for those with too little), I found most university administrators and faculty to be caring and often concerned (and, yes, with a few radicals and mostly socially liberal and voting Democratic) but generally moderate in their views. Moreover, while the institution's policy of being "the home of the critic and not the critic itself," and not speaking out or taking sides on issues not directly affecting higher education, was often commendable,[44] silence and neutrality could, as in any era, be misinterpreted and seem to place the *weight* of the university on the side of moderation and accepting

---

[43] My editorial was called "Let's Not Just Sit There," in *DP* of October 5, 1981, 4.
[44] See William Bowen, *Lessons Learned: Reflections of a University President* (Princeton, NJ: Princeton University Press, 2010), 35–41.

economic structures and excesses as they are. While our hope (and, I suppose a form of faith, whether with religious underpinnings or not) was that the ongoing creation of new knowledge—better knowledge—and deeper understanding would have salutary effects on the society's and the world's problems, some of us would on occasion reflect on how surreal it could seem to work and live in Princeton, there to preach, to teach, and write about the difficulties of other societies and peoples, when so much of the rest of the world, and too many in our own country, lived in degrading poverty, and with war or strife and lack of opportunity that had relatively little effect on our lives or those of our students.

University-Wide Service

During that period the dean of the chapel, reporting directly to the president of the university, was also a member of the President's Cabinet. This group that included the provost, other deans, and several vice presidents met weekly and was a good context in which to build friendships and to provide the opportunity to contribute to planning and decision-making in the university. Through the cabinet, the President's Council and other meetings I was able to enter into conversation with Princeton faculty members, such as the brilliant population biologist Robert May, then professor of zoology and chair of the University Research Board, and Theodore Ziolkowski, professor of German and comparative literature and dean of the Graduate School. Bob May had no personal use for religion, especially of an authoritarian or fundamentalist kind, but recognized how some religious folk could be enlisted to cooperate in defense of the environment, not least its biodiversity. Ted Ziolkowski had an abiding interest in Christ figures and stories about the loss of faith in European literature.

By office Princeton's chapel dean also met and interacted with a number of university service departments and their heads: Health Services, Counseling, the Dean of Students Office with its range of student support and disciplinary issues, and the group of junior and senior students known as resident advisors. Dean Morrow and I met with the masters of the residential colleges and their associates to talk about the spiritual needs and opportunities of the students and pastoral care when it was needed. One came to know the campus proctors, and after time, doctors, nurses, the athletic director and some of the coaches, secretaries, electricians, and food servers. The dean's advice was sought on a number of issues dealing with student welfare, conduct, and discipline.

Given the student age group, the issues frequently had to do with drinking and sex. With my undergraduate memories, I had to chuckle to myself recalling how we then thought the proctors and deans, still acting in some measure in loco parentis, seemed solely concerned with keeping young women out of our dorm rooms and seeing to it that we did not drink too publicly or to excess. A quarter of a century later as dean of the chapel—and after the "sexual revolutions" in America—I did not want to rehearse those roles with religion and morality seen primarily as a means of controlling undergraduate sexuality and other potential vices and myself as "Dean No Fun." I took it as a compliment when two sophomore pranksters ordered a subscription to *Playboy* magazine for me.

At the same time a university chaplain wants to be helpful in matters that involve physical and emotional as well as moral health. We held discussions about the best ways to offer sex education and how Health Services could wisely provide means for contraception. From a religious and more general ethical and health perspective, I tried to share with undergraduates willing to enter into conversation my understanding that what was most important in any relationship that involved genital sexuality was trust—a trust of mutual care, trust of protection from unwanted pregnancy, disease, and emotional harm—and that this trust called for relationships of significant caring for the other and hence a genuine form of fidelity. Still more serious were issues of the sexual harassment and rape that happen on every college campus. A young woman working in my office was assaulted on the edge of campus on her way home from work. In "date rape" cases alcohol is often involved. Students will sometimes first come to talk to chaplains like Dean Morrow because they are not sure they want to make their complaint public. They are afraid of the consequences or that nothing will be done. Often, that is the first hurdle to get over, often followed by considerable further counseling while open discussion, education about the issues, and campus security need to be continually emphasized.

What later came to be called *binge drinking* was a major concern. As our campus house was located close behind the eating clubs, my wife and I more than once experienced the issue directly, with inebriated students (the age of our sons) mistakenly coming through a window of our home, evidently thinking it was one of the clubs. One night I was sent downstairs at 3 a.m. with a baseball bat in my hands to find that the source of the noise we had heard was a student now passed out on the floor of my study. Another morning after breakfast we discovered a sobering and chagrined young man arising from behind the living room sofa in only his undershorts.

Because I knew too many classmates who had suffered from alcoholism (which in some cases could have begun at Princeton), I was deeply concerned. Other university administrators tended to find the best responses to the problem mostly in terms of education with counseling for the more severe cases. That could be helpful, but I also saw roots of the problem in the pressures and anxieties that students were dealing with and their attempts (Thursday and Saturday evening seemed to be the worst) to blot them out.

One afternoon several alumni talked with me about their concern for fellow alumni with alcoholic histories who were reluctant to come to reunions where liquor flowed freely, to a setting where they had once drunk with classmates. We were able to set up and advertise a "Friends of Bill" outpost in Murray-Dodge that then became a regular Alcoholics Anonymous oasis as a feature of reunions. Murray-Dodge also became host to a local branch of Alcoholics Anonymous.

This group was mostly composed of university staff, a few alumni living in the area, and an occasional student or two or three. Faculty members were understandably reluctant to attend, but, when some did, it encouraged a few others. A problem developed when those of us who worked in Murray-Dodge realized that people who had struggled with one addiction often had another. Cigarette smoke wafted through the building and embedded itself in the East Room. I was afraid that AA might feel evicted when I told the group they could no longer smoke there. To my surprise they smiled and, at least at their Murray-Dodge meetings, quit cold turkey.

Other issues surfaced from time to time. The university was not well prepared during the early 1980s to talk openly or officially about students (even less so faculty) who were homosexual. Yet there were gay and lesbian graduate and undergraduate students, and some pastoral relationship with them seemed part of the ministry of a chaplain, if they wished it. Had I, or the majority of my 1950s classmates at Princeton, been asked whether any of our peers were homosexual, we would have answered in the negative. Except for rumors about a W. H. Auden, E. M. Forster, and a few other literary figures, and, of course, reading snippets of or hearing about *The Kinsey Reports*, the subject was not on our radar screens. Yet as the years went on, we began to discover (as some of them had) that several friends and distinguished classmates were gay. Also, as the head of a theological seminary in Berkeley, California, in the 1970s, I knew both men and women students who were trying to understand and accept their same-sex orientation while believing that they were called to an ordained ministry. In 1978 Bishop Paul Moore of New York (whom I later invited to preach in the chapel) had ordained the first openly lesbian deacon in the Episcopal Church and promptly sent her out to be a graduate student in my seminary in Berkeley.

Then in early 1984 an Episcopal priest, several years younger than myself who had followed me on the path to ordination from the same Chicago-area parish, came to tell me that he was gay and was dying of AIDS. Even then one needed to recognize that AIDS was an issue of sexualities and blood exchange and not just homosexually, but it was becoming a major concern in the gay community. Somewhat gingerly, I tried to address the issues around homosexuality and, still more directly AIDS, from the pulpit. I discussed the "moral neutrality" with regard to homosexual orientation with the head of Counseling Services. There was a "Gay Disco" advertised on campus, gay and lesbian issues drew the attention of the *Daily Princetonian*, and a small group of students had formed the Gay Alliance of Princeton (GAP) and held some of their meetings in Café in the basement area of Murray-Dodge. I met with them, but I do not think that successfully. They were understandably somewhat suspicious about talking with a university dean of religion, and one spoke up quite pointedly and told me that he did not want anything to do with religious moralism. Nor did I find much interest then (in that age group) in the life partnerships or the institution of marriage for gays, though several gay students did want to talk about trust and fidelity issues.

Dean Morrow met with more success in getting to know these students, both undergraduate and graduate, and this led her to the lesbian group that met in the Women's Center in Aaron Burr Hall. After a time, the two groups joined to become the Gay and Lesbian Alliance at Princeton (GALAP), meeting weekly in Murray-Dodge Hall with Dean Morrow as their advisor. Subsequently the Chapel Office provided a part-time seminarian to work with the group and created a Pride Sunday and other programs. Later in 1990 the Chapel Office raised funds for a half-time administrator, leading by the mid-1990s to a small library and a full-time assistant dean in what is now an LGBT Center in the Office of the Dean for Undergraduate Students that yet has a connection to the Office of Religious Life through its monthly, if not more often, Chattin' with the Chaplain.

Still more matters that could be contentious among and between religious groups as well as in the university at large came up. A number of us cared deeply about trying to bring better fairness and peace to Palestine and Israel. For others abortion and prolife and prochoice positions were a major issue. Helping to overcome apartheid in South Africa was an ongoing interest among a group of faculty members and students. Speakers were invited to campus, often sponsored or cosponsored by religious groups, to address the several sides of these issues. Sometimes the Office of the Chapel was asked to join in cosponsorship and provide funding assistance. Most often we did so, finding that promotion of dialogue and conversation about important ethical issues was what we should be engaged in, while sometimes indicating that neither the Chapel Office nor the university was thereby endorsing particular views. On occasion there were angry people in my office. Letters were written, and there were a few demonstrations of protest, but, for the most part, the other chaplains and I agreed that this is how religiously and ethically minded people should listen, converse, and behave in a university setting.

The question about whether the university should support and join in divestment from companies doing business with and in South Africa provided an interesting test case for the role of the dean of the chapel. The president and trustees had taken the stance that for the university as an educational institution, the proper response was to educate about the issue, not least the wrongs of apartheid, and to offer assistance (largely faculty and administrative exchanges and some funding) for progressive educational institutions in South Africa, but not to support policies of divestment that might well, it was argued, do more harm than good to victims of apartheid.[45] In part because of my friendship and respect for Desmond Tutu,[46] I wished to support his call for divestment as a way of

[45] On Bowen's views on this matter, see ibid., 41, 44–46.

[46] The friendship was tested a tad in 1984 when I had Desmond Tutu signed up to come preach and talk with students at Princeton before it was announced that he had won the Nobel Prize. Desmond then pleaded that he had just too many new obligations to make the Princeton engagement. I had to understand, but would have loved to have had Princeton students hear from him.

putting international moral and economic pressure on the white South African establishment and government. When the faculty wanted to offer their views to this effect, I (having already written an editorial for the *Daily Princetonian* on the subject) voted for a recommendation that the university should join in selective divestment. Afterward several of my colleague deans (some of whom may have wanted to vote the same way) wondered if it was proper for a dean of the university to vote against the policy of the administration and trustees. President Bowen replied to them that, at least in my case, and because I was not in an administrative position that could affect faculty promotion and tenure decisions for faculty who might disagree, he found it not inappropriate. Not long after that, during a student protest at Nassau Hall, several chaplains went to join them—to help explain the support some of us had for their cause and also the nature of nonviolent and peaceful protest that would not lead to prosecution for blocking exits and entrances.

The Chapel Office had funds from several small endowments that could be used for emergency pastoral needs and to cosponsor lectures, conferences, and events with other campus groups as well as funding for student research projects and summer study programs, and this brought, needless to say, a steady stream of students to Murray-Dodge. These grants were usually made without controversy, and we were glad to work together with campus organizations such as the Women's Center and the Third World Center. We also had funds to provide assistance to two seminarians from the Princeton Theological Seminary. These students assisted in various ways in the educational, pastoral, and sometimes liturgical and homiletical ministries of the chapel, as did several graduate students in the Religion Department, among them Daniel Nelson and Randall Balmer—Balmer, coming from a conservative, evangelical background and going on to become a significant interpreter of religion in America[47] and later also an Episcopal priest.

Other forms of service the Office of Dean of the Chapel offered were through its support of the Student Volunteers Council (SVC) and the off-campus Princeton-Blairstown Center that provided programs for inter-city youth and a summer camp for underserved youngsters. Since as an undergraduate I had been a counselor and then director of the summer camp, it was a particular pleasure to serve on the board of directors of the center. The SVC was the de facto successor organization of the former

---

[47] Among his works is *Mine Eyes Have Seen the Glory: A Journey into The Evangelical Subculture of America* (New York: Oxford University Press, 1989).

Student Christian Association—now open to all regardless of any religious affiliation or interests. Headquartered in Murray-Dodge Hall, the SVC had a small student board that directed students to several agencies in the greater Princeton and Trenton area where they might tutor, visit the elderly, or spend part of an afternoon with the mentally disabled. I asked Dean Morrow to be the SVC's advisor, and she found challenges, small and large, from the beginning. On her first day of work she discovered a dead car battery from one of the SVC cars awaiting her on her desk with a note requesting a new battery. More difficult were the hours of help she gave the student board as they were deciding whether to maintain their relationship with Planned Parenthood when a group of prolife students petitioned the Campus Fund Drive (which had its headquarters in the same Murray-Dodge offices) to withhold funding from the SVC if they continued to work with Planned Parenthood.

The SVC also began to grow and change. The student leadership came to see the SVC's role as that of a lead and umbrella organization involving the university in the surrounding community and a wider variety of social service projects while also holding its volunteers accountable to a higher standard of reliability and service. With the chapel and the UCM, the SVC cosponsored weeklong programs on hunger and homelessness, social advocacy and justice, and vocations of service. Community Service Break Trips began, where students would go off to build a house with Habitat for Humanity, sometimes to team up with other schools like Morehouse College in Atlanta. The SVC took on responsibility for the Special Olympics of central New Jersey and began a clothing drive each May that collected thousands of pounds of clothing for the Rescue Mission. Several of the athletic teams were matched with kids from Trenton for an annual "Communiversity," and some of these one-time programs grew into weekly projects for the students as well.

Elizabeth "Liz" Duffy (class of 1988 and now the headmaster of Lawrenceville School), student administrator during her senior year, then became the SVC's first full-time administrator. The brainchild of Lisa Jann (also 1988), the Urban Action orientation program (now Community Action) was begun, enabling entering freshmen and upper-class leaders to participate in community service projects in Mercer County. Much of this growth and activity, Dean Morrow loved to point out, took place in an era when students were dubbed the "X generation" who were only interested in themselves. On into 1990s, and with connections with the Princeton Project 55 (sponsored by members of the class of 1955) and the launching of the Community Based Learning Initiative and the hiring of a second administrator with funds raised through the Chapel Office, more than two-thirds of the Princeton student body would engage in SVC projects by the time of their graduation.

For a number of these years the thriving International Students Association also found a home in Murray-Dodge, with an office and shared meeting and event space. It could become crowded. Working with its entrepreneurial director Paula Chow, we had to learn to schedule carefully, but their presence provided the Murray-Dodge chaplains with contact with students from other countries who were sometimes Muslims, Hindus, and Buddhists or of other faiths. Because a number of these students were graduate students, it also gave us additional reason occasionally to meet with both Christian and interfaith groups of graduate students either in Murray-Dodge or at the Graduate School.

My teaching in the Religion Department and becoming part the Program in the History, Archeology and Religions in the Ancient World offered further opportunities for contact with students and other faculty. I also was asked from time to time to teach in other departments—a class on the gospels in an English literature course that caused me to reflect on all those much earlier years when the Bible was central to the college's curriculum. With the students of civil engineering Professor Steve Slaby, an innovative and interdisciplinary teacher if there ever was one, I discussed values and ethics in the work of engineering and technology. Steve Slaby was passionate in his hope that future engineers would think about *why* and *what for* along with *how to*. Such relationships gave me a sense of being more of a colleague with other faculty and Princeton figures. Marvin Bressler, Lou Pyle, the head of Health Services, and on occasion basketball coach Pete Carril (often with the stub of a cigar in his mouth) never let up on me on the tennis court. Professor of engineering Enoch Durbin ended every match with an explanation of why his specially designed and well-advertised racquet would save me, and others, from tennis elbow, as well, of course, as improving my game. I remember coming out of a faculty meeting late one afternoon, where I had become visible for offering a prayer. Walking beside me was a young assistant professor who wanted to talk for a few minutes, sort of whining about how many papers he was going to have to grade and how busy and demanding the university seemed to be, making it difficult to get his scholarship done. I felt honored that he believed I would understand.

OTHER PASTORAL, LITURGICAL, AND INTERFAITH ROLES

All these relationships provided more opportunities for pastoral ministry to people of various religions or little or maybe none—perhaps the most important service any chaplain can render. On rare occasions there can be a local or even national emergency or tragedy that seems to call for a campuswide response in which a university chaplain can play a major role. Or, though not affecting everyone, some severe accidents, illnesses, or death may have a profound effect on campus, and the chapel becomes a place to offer sympathy, to pray—perhaps to give thanks for a life and wonder at the mysteries of life and death. The wife of President Dodds dies. A student stabs himself to death. Another student dies of a sudden infection. Mehrdad's roommate drops dead while running cross country. The son of a faculty colleague is killed in a car accident. The spouse of a faculty member commits suicide. A well-known alumnus and former trustee dies young. The head football coach succumbs to cancer. The son of a Nobel Prize–winning physicist dies in the prime of life. Samiran Mitra is run over by a semitrailer.

During those years several of my former teachers died: Carlos Baker and Paul Ramsey. Many of us prayed, and all of us wondered again about life's meaning. I remember standing on the north porch of the chapel on a gray winter afternoon with one of Princeton's most distinguished professors. We had just finished the memorial service for a colleague. We exchanged a few words of consolation. He was of a different faith background than mine. We were silent until he gestured across the plaza to Firestone Library and said, "That is my temple." I understood.

The chaplains of the United Campus Ministries shared in making daily rounds of the infirmary. Fortunately, most illnesses of the young are brief, but some cause more anxiety about missed classes and assignments and can be troubling to parents at home. I recall telephoning my mother just to double check to be sure that I had had chicken pox before visiting half a dozen students who were in isolation due to an outbreak of the disease.

There were happier occasions: many weddings in the chapel—a few who wanted a garden or other nonchapel nuptials. Some of those marriages we blessed were of graduate students. I particularly recall the wedding of Alice Gast and Brad Askins, both of whom were part of the chapel congregation. Alice Gast is now the president of Lehigh University, and she invited me there for blessings at the time of her inauguration. There were also recent graduates to marry and some older alumni, occasionally a faculty member and partner. Some of the weddings were decidedly multifaith and challenging to perform. One Saturday I presided at the wedding of, as I recall, a Hindu and Baptist in the late morning and a Christian Scientist and a Mormon in the afternoon. The meetings of families and their different customs at the rehearsals and parties afterward would have made for good movies. Dean Morrow proved more creative at these affairs than I was, and unless I knew the couple well, I often tried to get her or another chaplain or clergyperson to preside.

At other times students were troubled; they had faith questions, vocational or ethical concerns. There was counseling before weddings to do and at the time of memorial services and afterward. All of these can and should take a significant amount of a chaplain's time. There was the space of a couple of years when several students came to me with versions of their same concern. They were African Americans (as I recall, sophomores) who had been admitted to Princeton from a lower socioeconomic background—one of them from the south side of Chicago where I had lived my early years. They found themselves vaguely depressed, uncertain as to how well they were doing and fitting in at what seemed to them a wealthy, elite college and environs—uncertain, too, about their future path. They wanted to think of their futures in terms of vocation—of calling and service. Yes, they realized they had already "made it." Back at home people kept congratulating them on their admission to Princeton. They confessed to a fear of failure or of not doing as well as seemed expected of them. Princeton can be a challenging place for those who have regularly been at the top of their class in high school and then find themselves mixed in with everyone else who had been at the top too. But their problem was more complex. The message they were hearing from Princeton about success and accomplishment was translating to them as getting ahead and excelling as individuals. The message from their community at home, however, and from their religion, had a more communal orientation. It sounded to them something like, "Who do you think you are apart from us? We all put on our pants one leg at a time—you included. Yes, we are proud of you and, please, go ahead and do well at Princeton. Even get rich, if you want to, if that will help you to help others. But don't forget to whom you belong. Your main job is not to get all excellent and famous, but to come back and help your sisters and brothers and to serve your community."

Obviously one could counsel them that they could excel as individuals and see that as a way of contributing to the common life of the society and being in service to families and communities. They could, as that values mantra went, "Do good by doing well." They could return as doctors, teachers, business entrepreneurs, or whatever they wanted to do vocationally, but the dissonance these students were hearing between cultures and values was not easily silenced. Their concerns—often hard for them to articulate—made me again aware of how communal in experience and values much of religion needs to be in order to thrive, and the challenges that a number of students (and faculty and others for that matter) experience in a society and at colleges and universities that so honor individual achievement, autonomy, and success. Of course, many of the benefits and other aspects of American individualism have been imbibed from forms of Protestantism (also having become a challenge to Protestantism's coherence and growth), and the issues and tensions between the communal and individual are forever present in any society. But here I found myself talking with young people directly experiencing the strains.

Some of these students did find community around their faith—at times in local churches with other black students, particularly in the Witherspoon Street Presbyterian Church, which is one of the oldest African American congregations in America.[48] Music, once again, helped. A gospel ensemble was formed, and for a couple of years we had a black seminarian who could give eight hours of ministry on campus. But Dean Morrow and I also began agitating for a third chaplain on the university staff—an African American who could conduct services on campus, counsel, and mix it up with the rest of us. At first we could only afford the services of that part-time seminarian, but, after some further endowment was secured, the administration agreed to the need and opportunity, and the Reverend Floyd Thompkins, ordained in the National Baptist Church, became the first black person to serve as an assistant dean of the chapel.

Now, however, we had three "protestant" Christian deans in the Chapel Office, and one could understand how this might raise a few eyebrows and questions as to how well we were fulfilling that earlier mandate to be supportive of all religious groups on campus while giving preference to none. It remained a complicated challenge with no easy responses. We appeared to be in a process of evolution rather than revolu-

[48] Founded in 1837. Later attempts to bring the two Presbyterian congregations (there was also Second Presbyterian Church) together failed, in more recent years because the Witherspoon Street congregation wanted to retain their historic church and character.

tion. We had also begun a "Latino Hour" service, and I could imagine that at some point in the future there would be other or additional university chaplains of other backgrounds and faiths. In the meantime, however, the Catholic and Hillel chaplains seemed to be satisfied with the new arrangements and the support and encouragement they were receiving. Moreover, they were not at all sure they wanted to have a university-funded and supervised Catholic or Jewish chaplain who might complicate present arrangements and their sense of independence for their faith activities and witness. The other chaplains seemed busy with their own programs and the opportunities there were to work together. Several of us were in touch with small groups of Muslim, Hindu, and Buddhist students about their pastoral and liturgical needs and aspirations. Some of these groups of students seemed more comfortable with off-campus arrangements, but also had leaders who began to hold meetings on campus. The Muslim students organized to use a room in the lower level of the chapel for Friday prayers.

On invitation I went to Jewish, Catholic, Episcopalian, and other services or gatherings. I felt comfortable and accepted at their liturgies, perhaps particularly at Jewish services. "How good and pleasant it is," I said to myself remembering words from Psalm 133, when brothers and sisters can live together and share in what I regarded as the heart of the Jewish covenant: "to do justice, to love kindness, and to walk humbly with your God."[49] In personal terms and as a Christian, participating in the Mass, where I might be asked to give a homily, I felt more awkward. As an Anglican Christian I was at home in Catholic liturgies held in the chapel until it came time to share the communion meal and I realized I was not fully welcome. I understand the theological reasons as to why I could not eat the bread and drink the wine of the body and blood of Christ with them, but I have long regarded these more as rationales for ecclesial and governance issues, and, if I may put it this way, "turf" reasons for Roman Catholics to distinguish themselves from other Christians. I longed for a better, more cooperative and shared Christian witness by us all—Catholics, Protestants, evangelicals.

I do not mean to sound naive. Long histories are involved, and Catholics have known their own discriminations in this country. Yet I still sometimes ask myself why Catholics need to be so insistent on being "Catholics" and not Christians by name—not least in a university setting

---

[49] From Psalm 133:1 and Micah 6:8.

where practicing Christians are now in the minority and might make a better witness by banding more often together as followers of Jesus. I had experienced more integrated ecumenicity with Catholics in the Graduate Theological Union schools in Berkeley than we were able to manage in Princeton, while I do understand that a university—not least one like Princeton—is a very public place for Catholics to conduct a chaplaincy. Probably with all the young and impressionable Catholic students there, it seems more important than ever to retain a strong sense of identity and boundaries. After the Halton controversy of the 1950s, Catholic chaplains at Princeton would be diocesan clergy, and I sometimes felt that the Bishop of Trenton was looking over Aquinas Institute Chaplain Charles Weiser's shoulder. Matters became more challenging for him when a chapter of the conservative Opus Dei came to Princeton. Abortion and "prolife" issues were perhaps not quite as divisive as they were to become in the next decades, but a prolife antiabortion stance already seemed to be turning into the signature doctrine by which Catholics would distinguish themselves. The Opus Dei priest, John McCloskey, was said to often raise the issue of contraception with students and sometimes, too, to object to the content of religion courses at the university.

That being said, Charles Weiser and I had a good professional relationship and became friends. Along with his associates, we shared many a laugh, and they joined in a good deal of our common programming and discussions. With his steady twenty-year ministry at Princeton, he was a good source of history and perspective. We talked of the place of religion in the lives of young people and the challenges of ministry. "Most of them wear their church lightly," was one of his observations. Among the good things we did together was to join with other Christian chaplains and faculty in weekday ecumenical services during Lent and in a Good Friday liturgy in the chapel, one of the most moving services in which I have ever participated. On that day, confronted by the broken body of Jesus, while singing, praying, and confessing together, our differences seemed of little account.

It was also not long before I became aware of how diverse the Catholic community of faculty and students could be in their backgrounds and in their views. One of Weiser's associates evidently caused him other problems when some found this older Jesuit to be much too liberal. Thinking back, it is not surprising to realize that of the six Catholics now on the Supreme Court (evidently they are thought "safer" as far as the law is concerned and find it relatively easier to gain Senate approval), two of the

Princeton justices are as different as Samuel Alito and Sonia Sotomayor. Now, of course, they are joined by Elena Kagan, of Jewish background and culture, who graduated from Princeton (for a time having been my son's resident advisor) in 1981.

Sunday Mornings and the Chapel

Amid all these activities and conversations, the matter of the role of the dean of the chapel in the Sunday morning chapel service (discussed at some length in both the Faculty and the Trustees' Reports) seemed to resolve itself rather easily. As long as the dean was committed to fulfilling other aspects of the policy to support all religions on campus, and as long as the chapel congregation knew it was otherwise receiving no special support from university funds, even many religious folk who were not Protestants seemed to accept or even like the idea that the dean would be a member and leader in a particular congregation. At the cost of a little over an hour a week in public time, the dean's presence at that service gave, amid all the changes, a sense of continuity as well as a place where the dean could speak to important issues of faith and ethical concerns. I had also to recognize, however, that this entailed a more visible role than many other things the dean would do. Part of my response was to share the eleven o'clock pulpit with Dean Morrow, with outside preachers, and on occasion, with UCM clergy. We invited prominent Catholics to preach. It also did not take a large amount of our time for Dean Morrow and me to continue to work with the students who wanted to join in the chapel fellowship programs and for us to meet with the relatively small group of chapel deacons. Some of that ministry could be shared with the graduate student and seminarians working through the Chapel Office. Dean Morrow proved especially adept to gathering small groups of women students together—sometimes at breakfast. On one occasion the young men and I received a special invitation to join the women for a breakfast meeting that was purportedly going to include steak and eggs. When we arrived, the central menu item, perhaps predictably, turned out to be quiche.

There was even more support for the dean's role as custodian and keeper of the chapel and its fair use by others. As Gerson Cohen (who shared with me his concern that a university's efforts in acceptance of all religious traditions could come to mean support for none) had understood, this great structure had now become a kind of buckler and shield, sign and symbol for the place of all religion at Princeton. It also served as a valued link to the wider community with townsfolk and alumni among the Sunday worshippers and attending concerts and other special events. On Easter the building was full to overflowing; it was also the site of an annual community Thanksgiving service with then Mayor Barbara Sigmund reading the president's Thanksgiving Proclamation. These cathedral-like roles for the chapel gave good reason for the dean to come to know and participate in regular meetings with Princeton borough and township clergy. I was grateful when a large new endowment for the maintenance and upkeep of the chapel, as well as for further chapel ministries, was secured.

As with any cathedral-like building the chapel also had its entertaining nooks and crannies. One of them in which I took particular delight was the outdoor pulpit attached to the south side of the building and facing into the courtyard further framed by the classrooms and faculty offices of Dickinson and McCosh Halls. This Bright Pulpit (named for the British parliamentarian, Quaker, and champion of the common man and democracy, John Bright) made one think of centuries past when a preacher might actually address crowds assembled outside a cathedral. I had a fantasy of waiting for a sunny spring afternoon when the young men and women bring their blankets to lie out in the courtyard showing a good deal of skin and drinking beer. Although I had not worked out exactly what I would say, suddenly I would pop up in the outdoor pulpit. A colleague suggested the text, "When Jesus saw the crowds, he had compassion for them,"[50] that he thought had to be the quintessential proof of Jesus's superhuman love. I considered offering the curious students, whose attention I imagined I now had, a short discourse on how the pelican atop the courtyard's Mather Sundial pecking its breast to feed its young with its blood was symbolic of Christ's sacrifice and the Eucharist. That ought, I reasoned, to give them pause for a few moments.

One actual use we did find for the outside pulpit came on Palm Sundays. I had decided that the ecumenical but rather "low church" Sunday morning congregation could use a few liturgical enhancements—one of these being an outdoors Palm Sunday procession that would pass through the courtyard and then back into the church and up the center aisle. The service would begin with my reading from the Bright Pulpit the opening

---

[50] Matthew 9:36. I believe it was William Willimon, toward the beginning of his remarkable and prolific twenty-year tenure as dean of chapel at Duke University, who suggested the text to me.

prayer and Gospel passage of Jesus's entrance into Jerusalem. The first Palm Sunday we did this (having had the pulpit cleaned of the attentions of birds and other elements), I climbed the steps from the chapel interior to the pulpit, gave myself a little smile of triumph, and closed the door behind me. When I finished the prayer and reading, and as the congregation and choir took off that chilly morning bravely singing "All Glory, Laud and Honor," I turned to open a door that I discovered to have locked itself. Since there was now no one in the church to answer to my pounding on the heavy panels, I turned about to shout at the receding procession. Finally it was Dean Morrow who either heard me or wondered where I was who came back inside and up the steps to unlock the door. With whatever scraps of dignity we had left, we then ran in flapping vestments to catch up with those honoring Jesus's riding on his donkey into Jerusalem.

Far more challenging was the news that we needed a rebuilt organ. There were three problems: the failing condition of the original Aeolian-Skinner, the need to raise money for its rebuilding, and the acoustics of the chapel. The original organ, which for many years the renowned Carl Weinrich had lovingly kept functioning after gerrymandering it in order to play his Bach, had come to need repair on almost a weekly basis. It was generally agreed, moreover, that it had never been the right organ for a building of that size.

I put together a committee to make recommendations: the music director of the Chapel Choir and Glee Club, Walter Nollner; Professor Eugene Rohn from the nearby Westminster Choir College; Nathan Randall, the university organist; and David Weadon, director of music at the Princeton Theological Seminary. They came to me after their first meeting and announced that they could do nothing about the organ until something was done about the acoustics in the chapel. The Guastavino tile that had been attached to the ceiling and upper walls of much of the chapel was an invention that helped secure the acoustics for speech. Indeed, a strong voice could be heard from the pulpit throughout the chapel without amplification. But the tiles were not conducive for music. As one of the committee members grew fond of repeating to me, "The most important stop on the organ is the building."

I told the committee that the expense of dealing with such major acoustical issues was beyond my pay grade and, I suspected, the interest of the university administration. They were to go back to their assignment of planning for a rebuild of the organ.

Several weeks later they were back in my office, insisting that they could not do anything until the matter of acoustics was dealt with. Otherwise, whatever new organ was built would never be satisfactory. Nor, I was assured, need I fear because modern acoustical engineers would be able to fix things so that we would have a "room" that would be fine both for music and for sermons and addresses.

Consultants were brought in from the School of Sacred Music at Yale Divinity School and elsewhere. Money was raised from a generous alumnus and lover of music in Los Angeles, and a firm that, among other things, painted the decks of aircraft carriers erected scaffolding through much of the chapel, and began applying coats of sealant to the Guastavino tile.[51] An acoustical expert from New York went to work on a sound system for the chapel. Plans for the organ rebuilding kept expanding. Usable pipes from the old organ were shipped by boat to England. Several years later, finished and installed under my successor Dean Joe Williamson, a rebuilt and virtually new Mander organ was inaugurated at its first concert in the chapel. The music was splendid. The sound for the spoken word, however, has never been the same. After repeated efforts and, I am sure, several hundreds of thousand dollars in further work, the acoustics for the spoken word in the chapel are improved and tolerable. A number of people have advised me since that one cannot, no matter what one is told, have both great musical acoustics and those for speech in the same measure in a building of that size. But the sound of music, for all the university community, is glorious.

THE CENTER FOR JEWISH LIFE

I noted earlier that the Hillel rabbi, Eddie Feld, was satisfied with the way things were going. That was largely true, but Chaplain Feld also had a dream. He had his own challenges in trying to minister to the eight to nine hundred Jewish students on campus—estimating to me that (except for many more on high holy days) perhaps a third of them participated in some way in the many activities and programs that were offered. He came up with the idea that just as Christians had their dedicated building

---

[51] A similar treatment was soon to be given to Rockefeller Chapel in Chicago.

on campus, so now could Jewish students. Their space in Murray-Dodge might be barely adequate (and, as I reminded him, was central campus and in a place where Hillel could best interact with other religious groups), but, he told me, he and other Jewish leaders now saw the advantages of having a place they could call their own. There, they imagined, they could have room for worship and for study—a little library. They could have meals together, so important for Jewish life, especially during holy days—a kosher kitchen. It could be their "home," where they could invite interfaith conversation and dialogue. Rabbi Feld knew that my support would be crucial and was so willing to stay in conversation with me on the subject (sometimes with student leaders like Yoram Hazony, a 1986 graduate who went on to found the Shalem Center in Jerusalem) that he made it seem almost like my idea.

I sensed, however, that there might be differences of view within the Jewish community. Although the location had not proved all that popular, and new underclass colleges were changing freshmen and sophomore living and eating arrangements, some of the Jewish students were attached to the kosher kitchen and their facilities in Stevenson Hall, down Prospect Street past the other eating clubs. There were a few other students and faculty, and, even more so, some of the older Jewish alumni, who were not sure that it was best for Jewish students on campus to set themselves apart in a new Jewish center. They could be Princetonians and Jews without having their own separate building. Eddie Feld told me he understood. Not everyone would agree. That was the way with Judaism. But times had changed. Many would rejoice, and such a building would be a splendid further sign of the full inclusion, acceptance, and participation of Jewish students and faculty and their religion and culture at Princeton. I then asked whether it would not be better if Hillel and other Jewish donors were to build their own independently owned facility on or near the campus. But my rabbi friend convinced me that the university's commitment to the facility would demonstrate Princeton's willingness to support a place for Judaism as well as Christianity in the university.

A first idea was that Hillel might have its own chapel and meeting area in East Pyne—a gracious older building near to the chapel and Murray-Dodge Hall that the university was preparing for renovation. But the administration had other priorities, in particular the need for graduate student space on center campus. Prospects for some form of new facility stayed alive, however, in conversations with Rabbi Feld, Dean of Students

Gene Lowe, and President Bowen and in discussions about the future of Jewish life at Princeton in the President's Cabinet. The possibility of a use of the former Prospect Club, now owned by the university, began to emerge, and I found myself one afternoon in the fall of 1985 walking over to Nassau Hall with a small group of excited students (the Hillel Committee on Jewish Life at Princeton that was chaired by junior student Mara Fox and sophomore Janine Schloss) to meet with President Bowen. Dror Futter, who would graduate in 1986, was another member of the group. (Rabbi Feld did not come with us, for, after all, this was supposed to be primarily the students' idea with the dean of the chapel.) I was less surprised than the students to be met with Bill Bowen's enthusiastic agreement. He heard their ideas for three areas for worship, a kosher kitchen and dining hall, a library, study rooms, offices, and a small auditorium. "It is a great idea," he responded. Study and planning would need to be done. He wanted a poll to be taken to be sure the plan had the strong backing of Jewish students. Funds would have to be raised, and Provost Rudenstine was among those insisting that such a center campus building must remain in university ownership with its overall administration through the Office of the Dean of the Chapel. "But, with your help, we'll all get to work on it," Bowen concluded the meeting.

Not to say that fund-raising at Princeton is not work, but finding the initial major gift for the new Jewish Center started off to be some of the easier fund-raising work I have ever done—and then it became more interesting. The university has many ideas, causes, programs, scholarships, centers, and projects to build and develop that are attractive and of value. And they have a number of foundations, government resources, and a wide range of individuals and families from whom they can ask. With few caveats Princeton is glad to accept funding from anyone because the purposes are seen as so worthwhile to the university's mission and programs. And it can be fun, if also a bit of an adventure. I once found myself in the private dining room of the headquarters of Forbes Magazine, with the sometimes zany Malcolm Forbes, trying to raise money from a wealthy gentleman who had been expelled from Princeton in the 1920s. Dick Riordan and classmates Carl Icahn and Dick Fisher were among the wealthy alumni I solicited for programs I was interested in without much success, although they would later be generous with projects that interested them. On a still happier occasion, my wife, Barbara, and I were able to stop in Hong Kong to meet with Gordon and Ivy Wu on our way to an international Anglican Church meeting in Singapore. Gordon was in the class just behind me at Princeton and had become highly successful as a developer and builder of infrastructure, much of it in communist China. He had named his firm Hopewell Industries after the town of Hopewell near Princeton because he liked the sound of the name. Gordon was in the process of giving over one hundred million dollars to Princeton for new buildings and also had taken a keen interest in helping international students, a number of whom would come from different faith backgrounds. Barbara and I were there primarily to say thank you, and we found ourselves invited to a dinner with a group of Japanese financiers and executives who were celebrating with Gordon a recently completed project. Somewhere I probably still have a collection of thirty or so Japanese business cards from bowing gentlemen, none of whom spoke more than a word or two of English, which, since this was also the sum total of my Japanese vocabulary, made for an evening of considerable pantomime.

When it came to the new Center for Jewish Life at Princeton, we hoped the founding gift (for the center and another project) would come from Ivan Boesky. Boesky had a son attending Princeton at the time and had evidently expressed interest in giving to the university. He was known for his generosity with an impressive list of trusteeships or associations with other institutions, among them the Columbia and New York University Schools of Business, the Metropolitan Museum of Art, the Jewish Theological Seminary, the Albert Einstein School of Medicine, the Harvard School of Public Health, and Yeshiva University. Earlier in 1985, Bill Bowen, Neil Rudenstine, and I had met with Ivan and Seema Boesky to discuss their interests. Then in the fall there was a meeting with Boesky, President Bowen, Rabbi Feld, and Michael Walzer, and myself. There was another meeting or two (one with Princeton students in New York in Boesky's Fifth Avenue offices) to work out details. Some months later Bill Bowen and Neil Rudenstine suggested that I might go visit with Boesky again. Everything was fine, they opined, but we had not heard from him for a while. It is always good to stay in touch and show appreciation. I took the train to New York on a warm day in late July and was ushered past the large Chinese vases into Boesky's rather ornate office. Ivan Boesky was formally gracious, recalled our previous conversations, and told me that he always wanted to be good on his word. But he seemed to me almost overly formal and at the same time agitated. I reported to Bill Bowen that he appeared unable to sit still. "That's the way he is. Full of energy," Bowen responded.

Several months later the news was front page. Ivan Boesky was being indicted for insider trading and had been at times wearing a "wire" to record conversations as part of a forthcoming plea bargain deal with prosecutors. I was kidded about prosecutors even now going over my July conversation with Boesky. It was typical of Bill Bowen that his first concern was for Boesky's family. Others in the university wondered if Boesky was really alone in this activity and how he had been so blatant or unsophisticated as to be singled out.[52]

The Monday after the Boesky news broke I was in the president's office when next steps were being discussed with Director of Development Van Williams and one or two others. It was then that a fax came through from Boesky's lawyer. Because of changed circumstances Mr. Boesky would have to rescind his pledge to the Center for Jewish Life and the other project. "Thank God" someone muttered as brows were wiped. I thought to myself that I would never again be sitting inside an institution where such heartfelt thanks would be given over the loss of a nearly two-million-dollar gift.[53]

Within two weeks I had been sent with Van Williams to meet with another potential giver who readily agreed to become the new lead donor for the Center for Jewish Life, though, as an alumnus of Princeton and then a friend, Michael Scharf chided us for having first asked Boesky. I soon found myself on a committee with Associate Provost Conrad Snowden and several students and faculty to begin planning for the center in earnest. Rabbi Eddie Feld provided more ideas and public vision for this new Jewish "home," and Professors Tom Spiro, Norman Itzkowitz (then also master of the underclass Wilson College), Julian Wolpert, and Thomas Stix (who at one point would also serve as the center's interim director) were, in the years ahead, among faculty members who were especially generous in time and commitment to the project. President Bowen, picking up on the idea of a "home" asked who was the best "home architect" in the country. Hearing tell of Robert Stern, he personally persuaded Stern (who at first said he had too many other projects) to

---

[52] And, of course, there were others—infamously spelled out in James D. Stuart's *Den of Thieves* (New York: Simon and Schuster, 1992).

[53] Several years later I saw Ivan Boesky on Nassau Street in Princeton. To my shame, I crossed over to the other side of the street to avoid him. But then, something got hold of me, and I recrossed the street and went into the store I had seen him enter. We chatted for a few minutes. He had served his time in prison and volunteered that he regretted serious mistakes he had made and now had other priorities for his life.

take on the assignment, to which Stern then devoted himself in many meeting with students. Before long some of the center's activities were begun, and then in 1993 (although there was, I came later to understand, considerable disappointment on Michael Scharf's part due to Princeton's agreement that national Hillel alone would best provide the leadership for the facility and for its breadth of inclusivity, followed by subsequent gifts from the Posner family and others), Princeton's Center for Jewish Life moved into its, by then, four and a half million dollar new building.[54] Some of us longer associated with the university were aware of the irony that it was the footprint of the former Prospect Club, at one time regarded as the "seventeenth" eating club during the bicker process, that had been transformed into the new center. So had the Jewish presence and multifaith life and ministry at Princeton taken this major step forward. It was, it was said, now "cool to be Jewish at Princeton. It's something people identity as positive."[55]

[54] The official dedication was put off until September of 2002 with major donors Henry Posner Jr. (Princeton 1941) and Henry Posner III (Princeton 1977) both speaking of their appreciation of the leadership of just-retired President Harold Shapiro.

[55] So the center's assistant director, Martha Kohl, "A Community to Turn To," by Van Wallach, *PAW*, April 19, 1993, 12–16, on 13.

FOUR

Religion and Religions at Other Universities

W hen Fred Fox conducted his informal survey regarding the role of religion in institutions of higher education in 1979, he may have known that in 1928 Princeton had hosted a major conference to discuss the "problem." Fifty-eight presidents, thirty deans, sixty-eight professors, and thirty-two headmasters attended the meeting. Because they represented denominational and public as well as private schools, no consensus was reached on the issue of required chapel, but, while indicating concern regarding student interest in religion, many of these educational leaders expressed enthusiastic support for voluntary religious organizations, for university chaplains, and for religion courses that would have "an academic dignity equal" to other courses.[1] Such support was believed to be vital for the building of student character and a spirit of service and hence for the benefit of society. Although several of the representatives spoke of their care for those of other denominations and religions, the support focused on the role of Protestant Christianity in the academy.

However, when "the day of pluralism and secularism [had] definitely arrived," a number of educators saw the "problem" as various forms of Protestantism's still lingering official role in the university. Certainly the constituencies of students, community leaders, major donors, and faculty at many of these institutions were no longer predominantly Protestant, and already in 1965 the "secular theologian" Harvey Cox, while developing his understanding of God immanent in the secular world as opposed to a transcendent God of traditional religion, had contended that it was better for the common life of the university, as well as the country and for religion, that Protestantism no longer play the role of "established church."[2]

[1] See P. C. Kemeny, *Princeton in the Nation's Service: Religious Ideals and Educational Practice, 1868–1928* (New York: Oxford University Press, 1998), 215.
[2] Harvey Cox, The Secular City: Secularization and Urbanization in Theological Perspective (New York: Macmillan, 1965), 20–21, 234–35.

In this chapter I wish to continue the overview begun in chapter one reflecting on how a number of universities responded to their changing times and constituencies with respect to religion and religions. There we observed the general movement of a number of the older schools from their earlier sense of mission to serve God and church and community, to service to the larger society and nation. Along with Princeton many a college and university also experienced a significant but in the end shallow swell in campus interest and support for forms of Protestant Christianity in the two decades following World War II that has been described as the "last, major attempt by mainline Protestantism to have a significant influence on American higher education."[3] This was followed by the turbulence of the late 1960s, a lessening of theological confidence and engagement, and a precipitous drop in both interest and support by Protestant institutions—perhaps nowhere better indicated than by the withdrawal of the Danforth Foundation's involvement with higher education ministries and the Society for Religion in Higher Education renaming itself the Society for Values in Higher Education.[4] Meanwhile, student demographics had also been changing dramatically, as from 1950 to 1970 the number of students attending institutions of higher education in America tripled while students were becoming less campus residential, more vocationally oriented, and more diverse ethnically, socioeconomically, and in terms of religion. I can note again that as institutions in some competition with one another for students, faculty, funding, and their roles in "service to the nation," major universities were and continued to be learning from what was taking place at other schools. The McCosh-Eliot debates of the 1880s were but one indicator, while the 1928 conference at Princeton and Fox's survey were others, and I have subsequently been in a position to share in that mutual education. In particular, in this chapter I want to focus the learning by offering closer attention to seven universities with which I and Princeton's policies and programs have had some opportunity to interact. While each of them, influenced by similar but changing social and cultural circumstances, has moved along a trajec-

---

[3] Douglas Sloan, *Faith and Knowledge: Mainline Protestantism and American Higher Education* (Louisville: Westminster John Knox Press, 1994), vii. Notable is his discussion of the influence in America of Sir Walter Moberly's *The Crisis of the University* (London, SCM Press, 1949), along with other literature of the period, as a critique of universities, their curricula, and culture without a significant unifying role for Christianity and theology. See *Faith and Knowledge*, particularly 39–50. Significant also in this regard was Julian N. Hartt's *Theology and the Church in the University* (Philadelphia: Westminster Press, 1968).

[4] See Sloan, *Faith and Knowledge*, 172, 189–91.

tory from a predominantly Protestant influence to a more pluralistic stance with respect to support of religion, we shall again recognize how differing histories, constituencies, finances, urban or non-urban settings, buildings, and personalities have affected the support they have given to religions on campus. In doing so we are able to provide some larger context for the Princeton story while also delineating interesting and significant stories in their own right.

A valuable resource for learning about challenges and opportunities for the role and place of religion and religions in campus ministry has been meetings with other college and university chaplains and visits to their schools. The Ivy League chaplains gathered annually for discussion and for conversation with the university presidents and others on the respective campuses. Several of us also went to consult and sometimes to preach at those universities that continued to hold Sunday services. One by-product of the meetings and conversations was *A New Hymnal For Colleges and Schools*, which included words and music from a variety of cultures and traditions.[5] While predominantly Christian, it included Jewish hymns and music and hymns suitable for multifaith use and for academic occasions. Yale's university chaplain, John Vannorsdall, spearheaded the effort, several of us became members of the editorial board, and I had the pleasure of getting John Updike to contribute a hymn, the words of which I think, however, leave most if not all singers puzzled.[6]

In the spring of 2010 I managed to get an invitation to the Ivy League chaplains' meeting, held that year (as had been our first meeting in 1982) at Dartmouth. We all became aware again of similar issues and concerns as well as differences in the respective ministries: Dartmouth with its Tucker Foundation, the mission of which "is to educate Dartmouth students to think and act as ethical leaders and responsible citizens in the global community through service, character development and spiritual exploration"; Cornell, begun as a public university with a long tradition of Christian association activity and service, but a determinedly nonsectarian and non-establishment-of-religion stance; and Brown with its founding in a spirit of freedom for religion and now broad multifaith encouragement and support. We reflected on the major difference that the

[5] Jeffery Rowthorn and Russell Schulz-Widmar, eds., *A New Hymnal for Colleges and Schools* (New Haven, CT: Yale University Press, 1992).

[6] Hymn 525: "We Pattern Our Heaven."

presence of a large church structure and a strong tradition of worship made on campuses, and we noted how in the Ivy League, as well as at other universities, there had developed a propensity for appointing university chaplains who had experience in multifaith ministries in institutions of higher education. I listened as Peter Gomes, nearing the end of more than forty years at Harvard, and Sharon Kugler, formerly the chaplain at Johns Hopkins and relatively new university chaplain at Yale, described their distinctive emphases in ways of viewing and doing chaplaincy ministry—emphasizing advocacy for religion and presenting a theological vision, on the one hand, or more one of hospitality, programming, and support for religious and spiritual diversity. Several chaplains spoke of decisions that had been made to end any official connection between chaplaincy offices and volunteer service organizations at their schools, while Dartmouth's new president had decided that a relationship between service opportunities and the Tucker Foundation would continue to be beneficial to all.[7]

During my years at Princeton, visits to universities in other parts of the country were also helpful for gaining perspective and learning about similarities and differences in the policies, programs, and activities of the schools. There were, as well, meetings of the National Association of College and University Chaplains (NACUC) and the Association of College and Religious Affairs (ACURA) where one could meet and talk with chaplains from a wider variety of schools. From my own contacts and informal survey of private educational institutions it would not be unfair to say that a number of them have been drifting in their attitudes toward support of religion on campus. Allowing such a significant but potentially controversial matter as religion a measure of drift toward a more Jeffersonian model of providing for religion can seem a wise institutional response. Or still more secular models may prevail as religious language comes to be seen as far more a part of the school's heritage than present practice. At some schools prayers at ceremonies may be the last features of what were once more explicitly religious-toned celebrations. In a few cases the prayers would be further minimized or dropped altogether. Religious symbols might be removed from buildings or not replaced when rebuilding. Chapels that were suitable for other purposes could be used as lecture halls or for school assemblies. At some schools this drift may

[7] The meetings of the Ivy League chaplains take place in a spirit of confidentiality so that the participants can speak openly with one another. These general observations are matters of public knowledge and are made with permission.

have come to be guided by a more determined secularism in the guise of a form of philosophical neutrality having become itself an ideology.[8] Still these institutions wished to attract students who were Catholic, Jewish, at times Episcopalian or from other Protestant groups, sometimes including small numbers of Muslims, along with those of other religions. These were important constituencies. Yet the easiest and perhaps safest response to the challenges of religious diversity and way to appear respectful of the religion of all seemed to be a form of neutrality that gave no support to any faith group while affirming the right of all to have chaplaincies and/ or houses of worship near campus. Since some denominations were finding it harder to support the full-time chaplains whose ministries had proliferated in numbers in the 1950s and '60s, there could yet be the availability of nearby churches, synagogues, or other religious institutions. The opportunities for faith practice and the pastoral needs of students could be met by these part-time or other ministries rather than by the university or college itself. The religious aspirations and needs of faculty, largely now regarded as privatized, could also find support in this manner. Moreover, endowments or funding that had formerly been spent for religious personnel, buildings, or programming could be better used for the benefit of all, including nontheists. This might be done through the support of programs or lecture series dealing with ethical and values issues, development of an office to support diversity and antidiscrimination, and service opportunities. Since education itself was seen as service to society, such funds might reasonably be regarded as fungible in a school's expenditures. Support of a religion department or a small multifaith religious studies program could be seen as a particularly appropriate use.

The attractions and benefits or responses along these lines were and are apparent. It is the ultimate, so to speak, in nonsectarianism—officially avoiding any specifically religious issues or sense of preference. This approach could be seen as fairest to all while allowing the academy better to concentrate its resources on its primary mission of education, even if this could mean excluding exploration of questions of ultimate purpose

---

[8] Indeed, this is the stance of universities in general in the United States and a reason for their considerable loss of influence, argues C. John Sommerville in *The Decline of the Secular Universities*, though he does not detail differences among institutions. On a critique of seventeen formerly denominational institutions of higher education, most of whom, he argues in great detail, have drifted far from the light of their church influences, see James Tunstead Burtchaell, *The Dying of the Light: The Disengagement of Colleges and Universities from Their Christian Churches* (Grand Rapids, MI: Eerdmans, 1998).

or meaning. In emulating a kind of church-state separation, the schools can be seen as following the American way, as it were, and—as semipublic institutions (often, in fact, receiving considerable government funding in the sciences and for other forms of research)—becoming more like public colleges and universities in America. Benign in their attitude toward the role of religion in student lives, they can be seen as neutrally supportive of none.

However, it must be noted again that while there are common trajectories in this regard, each college and university has its own history and constituencies, along with its distinctive permutations in its responses to modernism, postmodernism, and religious diversity. Princeton was one among a number of private institutions that sought ways to continue to use university resources to support religious activities and offer forms of pastoral care and concern on its campus. Other colleges and universities would respond in similar ways, if only because they recognized religion to be an important interest among the extracurricular activities of students they wished to attract. Even among public, state-supported institutions of higher education (many of which at one time had or still have very active YMCAs, YWCAs, Student Christian Associations, or now successor groups, as well as privately supported denominational chaplaincies, religious studies offerings, and administrations supportive of a place for religion on campus) there can be ongoing and expanded space for religious ministries.[9] The Pasquerilla Spiritual Center at Pennsylvania State University, with its Center for Ethics and Religious Affairs, and offices, meeting rooms, and worship space for over forty religious and spiritual groups, claims to be the largest multifaith facility in the country. That efforts to make some form of accommodation for religions while responding to pluralism can also bring about controversy at public universities was recently evidenced at America's second-oldest college, William and Mary, where a wrenching public debate took place (that in some part cost the president his job) over the placement of a cross in its historic Wren Chapel.[10] It was a symbolic struggle echoing Princeton's tiff over the place of the cross in university assemblies in 1980–81.

[9] On something of the history of these associations and programs, references to previous literature about them, and several efforts in denominational and interreligious cooperation, see Seymour A. Smith, *Religious Cooperation in State Universities: An Historical Sketch* (Ann Arbor: University of Michigan, 1957).

[10] I first heard of this controversy in conversations with William Bowen and with Taylor Reveley, once a colleague on Princeton's Board of Trustees and its Advisory Council for the Center for the Study of Religion and now the president of William and Mary College. For

Another sign of interest in keeping some place for religion in universities in recent decades has been a resurgence in support for baccalaureate services at a number of schools. This traditional service, which in America goes back to a time when colleges were educating many students for ministerial vocations, had in more than a few institutions eroded to become a poorly attended addendum to closing exercises and commencement for graduates. Following renewed interest in Christian services of baccalaureate,[11] there has now also come impetus for the ceremony to take on multifaith characteristics and be welcoming to all who wish to attend—sometimes even at public universities. Indiana University, for example, in 2002 restructured its traditional baccalaureate service into a multifaith ceremony attractive to a diversity of students, family, and friends.

Roman Catholic, specifically Jewish colleges and universities, historic black colleges, and smaller Christian colleges still affiliated with their denominations, also have stories to tell with regard to growing pluralism.[12] It is of particular interest to observe how Catholic schools, now

---

an argument in favor of retaining the place of the cross, see "Save the Wren Chapel: An Astounding Bit of Blabber from the President of William and Mary," by Vince Haley, *National Review Online*, November 17, 2006. On the ramifications of the establishment clause and the place of religion in public universities more generally ("The controversy over the presence and placement of the cross in the Wren Chapel . . . represents a spectacularly teachable moment," 994), see Ira C. Lupu and Robert W. Tuttle, "The Cross at College: Accommodation and Acknowledgment of Religion at Public Universities," *William & Mary Bill of Rights Journal*, 16, no. 4 (2008): 939–97.

[11] See Donald Shockley, "Back to Baccalaureate," *Christian Century* (June 2, 1982): 666.

[12] On the struggles of Catholic institutions (with a focus on The Catholic University of America), see Philip Gleason, *Contending with Modernity: Catholic Higher Education in the Twentieth Century* (New York: Oxford University Press, 1995) and Burtchaell, *Dying*, 557–742. For a relatively positive assessment of smaller colleges and universities from seven Christian faith traditions, see Richard Hughes and William Adrian, *Models for Christian Education: Strategies for Success in the Twenty-First Century* (Grand Rapids, MI: Eerdmans, 1997). For a study of considerable religious activity and the teaching of religion on four anonymous campuses (large state, Lutheran, Roman Catholic, and a private college with Presbyterian roots and a traditional commitment to African American students) that finds pluralism a better description than secularism, see Conrad Cherry, Betty A. DeBerg, and Amanda Porterfield, *Religion on Campus* (Chapel Hill: University of North Carolina Press, 2001). Among other books dealing with religion in these institutions are Robert Benne, *Quality with Soul: How Six Premier Colleges and Universities Keep Faith with their Religious Traditions* (Grand Rapids, MI: Eerdmans, 2001); Paul J. Dovre, ed., *The Future of Religious Colleges: The Proceeding of the Harvard Conference on the Future of Religious Colleges, October 6-7, 2000* (Grand Rapids, MI: Eerdmans, 2002); and Merrimon Cuninggim, *Uneasy Partners: the Colleges and the Churches* (Nashville, TN: Abindon Press, 1994).

with their more diverse student bodies and faculties, labor to retain "Catholic identity." Although in retrospect but a minor incident, the 2009 flap over whether President Obama, because of his advocacy for abortion rights and stem cell research, should be allowed to speak at Notre Dame's commencement and receive an honorary degree, occasioned considerable commentary and reflection on what it means to be a Catholic university in America today. In the meantime one notes that Jesuit Georgetown University, the nation's oldest Roman Catholic university, hosts an interfaith baccalaureate service, and that Brandeis, "the only nonsectarian Jewish-sponsored college or university in the country," also now holds an interfaith service as part of its commencement activities.[13]

Here in overviews made up of snapshots and vignettes are the stories of seven universities with which I have had the opportunity to interact, sometimes as a consultant or serving on a study committee dealing with religion and spirituality in these institutions. It is also the case that several Princeton chaplains have gone forth to these other universities taking their experience of interfaith ministry at Princeton with them. The influence has come the other way with Deans Alison Boden and Deborah Blanks bringing their learning and insights from their previous chaplaincies to Princeton. In each case I am grateful for friends and colleagues in ministry who are or have been at these universities for conversation and research and responses to my questions and curiosity.

COLUMBIA UNIVERSITY

I first met James Pike and heard him preach when he was dean of the Cathedral of St. John the Divine that borders the Columbia campus. The colorful, chain-smoking, hard-drinking, one-time lawyer, former Roman Catholic, former agnostic, Pike was the first chaplain of Columbia University (1949–52) and already something of a media figure and proponent of contemporary theological language that would speak to the postwar generation. It was a heady time for Protestant Christianity and neoorthodoxy and other forms of modern theology. In his opening ser-

---

[13] I am indebted to William Gipson for his research on end of academic year interfaith services in his unpublished paper, "Baccalaureate Services and Pluralism."

mon as chaplain in St. Paul's Chapel ("The Place of Religion in a University"), Pike spoke out against the secularism in academia that had been turned into a compulsory option that was no friend of academic freedom. To the contrary, Pike enlisted the names of Reinhold Niebuhr, then Columbia's president Dwight Eisenhower, and others in a ringing endorsement of his trust "that Columbia aims to promote among students and faculty, and in the nation, an understanding of and a devotion to the great religious heritage which underlies the best values of our free society—the free society which makes possible the very existence of a nation like this." Noting also his role as chair of the "Counselors" of other religious groups (Catholics, Jews, Lutherans, and Episcopalians were named), Pike looked forward to their working together for the same causes and spoke enthusiastically of recent meetings in Earl Hall, one of which "swamped us; they were coming in the windows as well as the doors, the stairs were packed as was every inch of room in our lounges."[14]

Pike was succeeded (1952–65) by Episcopalian John Krumm, who also later became an Episcopal bishop and then a friend with whom I sometimes discussed college chaplaincy and ministry. Three decades later my twin sons were graduate students (one also a teaching assistant) at Columbia and gave me some insight into life on campus.

Columbia had its beginnings by royal charter in 1754 as King's College in lower Manhattan with a spirit of religious liberty guaranteed at its founding. In early years the school was strongly influenced by several Christian denominations with Anglican predominant. But during the War of Independence the college was virtually closed as a number of these Anglicans either had or were suspected of having divided loyalties. When reopened by the state legislature in 1784, it was mandated that no preference be given to any religious group, but after the failure of an unwieldy arrangement with a composite board of regents and opportunities for several religious groups to endow professorships, the school was returned to local control. By 1800 Columbia again had an Episcopal clergyman as president, while members of other denominations, particularly Dutch Reformed and Presbyterian, could also be found on its board and among its faculty.

This relatively benign religious influence continued through much of the nineteenth century. A note of controversy arose when in 1853 a distinguished candidate for the faculty, Oliver Walcott Gibbs, was turned

---

[14] "The Place of Religion in a University. Opening Sermon of the Reverend James A. Pike J.S.D., Preached at St. Paul's Chapel on Sunday, October 2, 1949," no pagination.

down by a close vote of the trustees because he was a Unitarian. In 1857 the college moved to midtown and affiliated with the new women's college, Barnard, in 1879. Officially becoming a university in the same year, 1896, as did Princeton, Columbia then moved to Morningside Heights. Already present in the neighborhood were the Union Theological Seminary (begun by Presbyterians but an ecumenical Protestant school) and the Jewish Theological Seminary. Both would become affiliated with Columbia, and through the next century there would be considerable cross-influence of ideas and some sharing in teaching and library resources.

In 1902, just west of Low Library at the center of campus, the stately Earl Hall was built as a YMCA-like center for religious gatherings and service and other activities. Over the years it would be used for additional purposes with the health services in the basement and, for a time, the offices of the Department of Religion. Engraved over the entrance in large capital letters are these welcoming and encouraging words: ERECTED FOR THE STUDENTS THAT RELIGION AND LEARNING MAY GROW HAND IN HAND AND CHARACTER GROW WITH KNOWLEDGE.

Five years later, in 1907, just to the east of Low Library, St. Paul's Chapel was dedicated, "forever to be and remain a house set apart and dedicated to the service of Almighty God," and became the main center for worship at the university and the site of its baccalaureate service. In succeeding decades the building of the neighboring Cathedral of St. John the Divine and the Protestant ecumenical cathedral-like Riverside Church provided further opportunity for worship and service for both faculty and students. The progressive spirit of Riverside Church and the Union Theological Seminary—with their leading preachers and theologians, among them Harry Emerson Fosdick, then Reinhold Niebuhr and Paul Tillich, along with the National Council of Churches headquarters—made Morningside Heights the voice of liberal Protestant Christianity in America. The development of Columbia's Western civilization curriculum in 1919 provided rationale for the study and discussion of the religious texts of Christians and Jews.

Through much of the twentieth century Jewish students were the most rapidly growing religious and cultural group on this increasingly urbanized campus, for the most part using Earl Hall for meetings and services until the opening of the Kraft Center for Columbia/Bernard Hillel in 2000. Through these years the university had also become a leading institution for Jewish studies. A program for these purposes was begun in 1950, endowed in 1980 as the Center for Israel and Jewish Studies, and further strengthened to become the Institute for Israel and Jewish Studies in 2005.

In 1967 the political scientist and then president, Grayson Kirk, asked that a study be done on Earl Hall and St. Paul's Chapel, which resulted in a report by a faculty committee headed by Edward Leonard, professor of chemical engineering. The committee included the anthropologist and active Episcopalian Professor Margaret Mead. The report, likely delayed and clearly much influenced by the sit-ins, altercations, and disruptions of the life of the academy by the student protests of the late 1960s, was completed in 1971. Eschewing any idea of indoctrination of specific religious and moral values in academic programs, the report, oddly prolix and abstract in its language, yet contended for a place for religion as a value system within the university community. But it did not find reason to continue the office and ministry of chaplain to the university. Instead, the administration of Earl Hall and St. Paul's Chapel were to be "co-joined," and "cocurricular"; opportunities to aid in the study as well as practice of spiritual, religious, and philanthropic (defined as the love of mankind) values were to be directed by a student governing board. Among other things, this board would decide which groups were to use Earl Hall. There would also, however, be an administrative director of the center, appointed by the trustees, who would work with the students in their study and practice of religious values and who would superintend the use of the chapel. There was to be an advisory board as well, to assist if problems arose that were too difficult for the governing board to handle and to provide advice as necessary.

It is hard not to gain the impression that the report was striving to find a useful place within the university for a role in governance for students and perhaps at the same time no longer to have any distinctive university religious officer who might become a focus for or become involved in future student protest activities. With the end of the Vietnam War, however, students' interest in protest and their appetite for governance waned, and religious, spiritual, and ethical values issues fell more into the hands of the director and the Earl Hall denominational chaplains, with the chapel being used for weddings and memorials and for worship, primarily by Catholics and Episcopalians. The upkeep of both aging buildings was also a challenge to the lay Catholic J. Paul Martin (the director from 1974 to 1986), who had a strong interest and expertise in human rights issues, and Rabbi Michael Paley (director, 1987–95), who helped give further new life to student-led neighborhood community services, such as the Community Impact organization headquartered in Earl Hall.

Through these years Columbia also continued to experience controversy over Middle Eastern issues involving politics, cultures, and religions, along with questions about academic freedom and the use of the classroom for partisan purposes. Heated debate, accusations of faculty bias, and objections to outside speakers reoccurred. Security and support for Israel and justice for Palestinians were often the focus of concern, and my Princeton classmate Edward Said, Columbia professor of English and comparative literature, was a sometimes cause and subject of controversy. More recently, the invitation to President Mahmoud Ahmadinejad of Iran to speak on campus (partly organized by my son's doctoral thesis advisor, Professor Richard Bulliet), and President Lee Bollinger's introduction to Ahmadinejad's speech, which, among other things, again denied the Holocaust, was a cause célèbre in controversy.

All the more reason, it was argued, for interreligious meeting and dialogue. After the 9/11 deaths and the destruction of the World Trade Towers—so near to the first site of the college, the Institute for Religion, Culture, and Public Life was established to offer instruction and programs dealing with issues in which politics, culture, and religion mix. Also begun were the Interfaith Fellows Program and the funding for the Kraft Family Intercultural and Interfaith Awareness Fund to be administered through the Office of the University Chaplain.

The office and ministry of the university chaplain was reestablished in 1996 by President George Rupp, who had previously been the dean of the Harvard Divinity School and president of Rice University and who had considerable insight into religious and multifaith issues. The Reverend Jewelnel Davis, a National Baptist by ordination, who had been chaplain at Carleton College, also became associate provost (reporting to the provost) and director of Earl Hall—having oversight of the United Campus Ministries also now known as the Religious Life Advisors. Her Office of Religious Life has oversight as well of the Kraft Center and Community Impact and is charged with ministering "to the individual faiths of Columbia University's diverse community of scholars, students, and staff from many different traditions while promoting interfaith and intercultural understanding" along with providing programs in justice and spirituality.[15] Together with the president's office, the Office of Religious Life bears responsibility for the baccalaureate service that continues to over-

[15] From the website of the Office of the University Chaplain, Columbia University, 2010.

flow the 650 seats of St. Paul's Chapel and where the speaker is a religious or moral leader from the Columbia faculty or community or the city of New York.

On this urban and busy campus much of the religious worship and activity takes place within the many religious groups in the undergraduate college and graduate schools. Columbia/Barnard Hillel and other Jewish groups meet at the Kraft Center and the Catholics worship in St. Paul's Chapel and the Church of Notre Dame (along with study groups and other activities including the Thomas Merton Lecture named for their best-known Columbia graduate). Today, while some students attend Riverside Church, the Cathedral of St. John the Divine, or other local churches, the Protestant groups are significantly smaller. Several, including the Intervarsity Christian Fellowship, use St. Paul's for their worship. The Hindu Campus Ministry holds worship in the chapel's underground space. Other groups, including the Muslim Campus Ministry, use the auditorium or other rooms in Earl Hall for worship and meditation, and a number of them share office space there. Even when they are attending to their own faith opportunities, they cannot be unaware, however, that they are doing so on a multifaith campus and world. Just past the entrance rotunda of Earl Hall one finds a display case with versions of the Golden Rule from seventeen religions.

UNIVERSITY OF PENNSYLVANIA

While Princeton's relatively near neighbor, with several similar constituencies as a mid-Atlantic Ivy League university, the University of Pennsylvania (Penn) and Princeton are different in a number of significant ways—not least in the roles religion has played in their institutional lives. I first began to learn about religion and religions at Penn from my colleague there, Stanley Johnson, an Episcopalian who was Penn's university chaplain for thirty-five years. When he retired in 1996, William Gipson, who had been Princeton's associate dean of religious life, became Penn's university chaplain and special advisor to the president, serving in that position until 2008. Over the years there have been a number of other comings and goings between Princeton and Penn. During my time at Princeton I came to know Penn's president (1981–93), Sheldon Hackney, who had been Princeton's provost (1972–75). Then in 2004 Amy Gutmann, Princeton professor and later provost, became president of the University of Pennsylvania. The current university chaplain, Charles "Chaz" Howard, recently received his PhD from the Lutheran Theological Seminary at Philadelphia, where I have taught and lived for seven years while several times visiting the Penn campus.

The University of Pennsylvania traces its origins to a time in 1740 when a group of Philadelphians that included Benjamin Franklin launched an effort to raise funds for construction of a chapel for George White-field's preaching and a charity school for "the instruction of poor children." Franklin's 1751 acquisition of the property for his "Publick Academy of Philadelphia" and a charity school in accordance with the intentions of the original donors (minus Whitefield's chapel, though the revivalist does have his statue on campus) presaged Penn's distinctively nonsectarian and nonecclesiastical character. Unlike other early American colleges that first focused on a classical education for the clergy, Penn would prepare students for practical lives in applied science, business, and public service. Franklin stressed the discovery and application of knowledge to improve human welfare. Tellingly, less than two centuries after his famous stormy kite flight in 1752 to prove that lightning is a stream of electrified air, his university would invent the first electronic computer.

Raised in Boston, Franklin retained a commitment to Puritan virtues of education, industry, thrift, honesty, temperance, charity, and community spirit. As a young man he rejected Christian dogma in favor of Enlightenment Deism, the belief that God's truths can be found entirely through nature and reason. He later returned to a support of organized religion and a respect for all churches on the pragmatic grounds that without them individuals would be prey to immorality. The Quakers (to this day the nickname of Penn's athletic teams) of Franklin's adopted city emphasized individual morality, too, out of their belief that individuals can have a direct experience of God without mediation by the church and its clergy, preaching, and sacraments, but therefore must be responsible for their own conduct. As all were agreed that individual freedom required morality, since 1756 Penn's motto, borrowed from the Latin poet Horace, has been *Leges Sine Moribus Vanae*, "Laws without morals [are] useless."

While the first head of the college, Franklin's hand-picked provost, the Reverend William Smith, was an Anglican, as were three-fourths of Penn's original trustees and five of the clergy who headed the university for all but fifteen years between 1802 and 1868, it was Franklin's pragmatic outlook along with Quaker-influenced views of religion and morality that generally prevailed within the institution. Smith led Anglican services at the college, but welcomed students of all denominations to the services. He encouraged discussions of religion outside of the classroom but did not include courses on religion in the curriculum. Students, he held, learn true religion from exposure to truthful teaching. He had designed a curriculum to teach not only the classics but also, as Franklin wished, the pragmatic sciences—eventuating in the college founding the first medical school in the colonies in 1765 and presaging Penn's predominance today in biomedical research.

In 1779, Smith, unfairly suspected as an Anglican of loyalist sympathies, left Philadelphia for Maryland, and the revolutionary Pennsylvania state government seized the college, which it regarded as a Tory bastion, and transformed it into the University of the State of Pennsylvania under the Reverend John Ewing, a Presbyterian. The new university was more egalitarian than any before in the colonies, with members of the board of trustees from several denominations and the only nonsectarian faculty in the new nation. Then in 1789 the College of Philadelphia and its administration under Smith were reinstated, coexisting alongside the University of the State of Pennsylvania until two years later when the state legislature merged the schools into the University of Pennsylvania under Ewing. Although privatized, it retained its resemblance to an American state university in terms of religion's place on its campus.

Strongly influenced by the German model of higher education, Penn transformed itself through the nineteenth century into a research institution and pioneered professional education by founding its Law School in 1850 and the School of Engineering and Applied Science in 1852. With the campus relocated to west of Philadelphia's Schuylkill River in 1872, Franklin's spirit of discovery and invention flourished as blocks of labs sprung up and additional professional schools, including the Wharton School of Finance and Commerce, were established. During the latter part of this same period, Penn began to take account of the nation's increasing diversity as it admitted its first students of color in 1879. Women were admitted to the graduate school from its inception in 1882, and in the undergraduate programs after the establishment of the School of Education in 1914. Today at Penn, which was the first Ivy League university to have a woman as president, over 50 percent of the 10,000 undergraduates are women and almost 40 percent are Asian, Hispanic, African, or Native American.

Penn's first president, Thomas S. Gates, appointed the school's first university chaplain in 1932, using $600,000 of his own funds to do so. While every chaplain since that time has been a Protestant, they have been expected to provide a pastoral ministry for a whole campus that has long understood itself to be open to people of different religious beliefs.

When William Gipson came to Penn from his ministry at Princeton, he brought with him plans for interfaith ceremonies, an interfaith council (that students soon solicited university funds for and renamed Programs in Religion, Interfaith Spirituality Matters [PRISM]) and other programs like "What Matters to Me and Why?" Gipson was asked by President Judith Rodin to work with the Netter Center for Community Partnerships in developing initiatives begun by President Sheldon Hackney to engage the university with churches and other faith communities in largely black west Philadelphia. The Interfaith Programs in Universities, Communities of Faith and Neighborhood Organization, now knows as CHORDS, provides opportunities for university students, faculty, and staff to become involved in a variety of projects including mentoring, health care initiatives, and academically based community service courses.

While the Office of the Chaplain sponsors no regular worship of its own, it encourages the many opportunities for worship and fellowship offered by nearby churches and religious groups on campus, varying from Episcopalians, Lutherans, Quakers, the Harvest Christian Fellowship, and Penn Students for Christ to the Muslim Student Association, the Hindu Student Council, the Penn Sikh Organization, and some thirty other groups. A number of these organizations use the basement area called The RAC (Religious Activities Commons) for their meetings; interfaith activities also take place there. The space is under heavy demand while the three largest faith organizations—Jewish, Catholic, and the Christian Association all have their own centers.

Historically, Quaker Philadelphia's spirit of religious toleration made the city one of America's more welcoming places for Jews, and Jewish students, attracted, too, by the urban setting, have long been an important constituency of the university—at times making up as much as 35 percent of the student body. Today, in addition to a Lubavitch House (Chabad) presence on campus, Penn Hillel provides one of the more vibrant centers of Jewish campus ministry in the world. Since 2003 it has been housed on the Penn campus in the 35,000-square-foot Steinhardt Hall, with its comfortable lounges and meeting rooms, Internet access, a Judaic library, Beit Midrash, and university-run kosher dining where 250 to 350 students eat lunch or dinner every day. Steinhardt is home to Reform, Sephardic, and Conservative services on Shabbat, celebrations on all the Jewish holidays, and daily Orthodox services.

In 1893 the first Newman Club in the country was founded at Penn, and Catholics are now the largest faith group on campus, with students attending a variety of classes, discussions, and weekday masses at the

Newman Center and Sunday masses at the adjacent St. Agatha–St. James Church. The still older religious organization at Penn is the Christian Association begun in 1891. Having recently sold its large campus head-quarters building, it is still today the inheritor of many years of ecumeni-cal Christian service, missionary activity, and social justice advocacy, "promoting open minds and working faith at the University of Pennsyl-vania." The Reverend Beverly Dale, sometimes known as "Rev. Bev., the conscience of the University," is a Disciples of Christ minister and was an outspoken presence from 1989 to 2010, leading a staff of seven and several seminarian and student interns in advocating for workers rights, gender equity, good race relations, and the civil rights of sexual minority communities. Because of the growing support for multifaith religious activity and engagement with its neighborhood, the university added the position of associate chaplain in 2005, primarily to convene and help direct CHORDS. Charles Howard, who had been active in religious life at Penn as an undergraduate, was the first to serve in that position, and when William Gipson became associate vice provost for equity and ac-cess, "Chaz" Howard succeeded him as the university chaplain. Recently I have been in conversation with them as for a few minutes we wondered rather pointlessly about what happened to Gates's $600,000 and what it might be worth now if held and reinvested in a restricted account. More to the point, they described to me the scope of religious and inter-faith activity at Penn and in the west Philadelphia area. They believe that as many as half the students at one time or another participate actively in one or more of the religious programs on campus. While a number of the students identify with their own faith group, there are many others who do not affiliate denominationally and see themselves as "spiritual" rather than formally religious—sometimes as seekers, searchers, and ex-plorers. The university chaplain is viewed as a key player in this diver-sity, reporting directly to the provost while encouraging and supporting much of the faith and spiritual activity. The chaplain has chief responsi-bility for the interfaith baccalaureate service that now is offered twice to accommodate all the students and family who wish to attend. The uni-versity chaplain is also called upon to offer prayers at the university's opening-of-the-year convocation, at trustee meetings, and to offer an invocation and benediction at commencement. In addition, the univer-sity sponsors what is now an interfaith chaplaincy to its hospitals and medical school.

I learned of the recent appointment of a part-time campus minister to the Muslim community and of how the Muslim Student Association had sufficiently grown in numbers that there had been some requests for a Shia as well as a Sunni service. We spoke of the course offerings and the generally good relationships with the six-member Department of Religious Studies and of the Graduate Group in Religious Studies comprising some additional thirty scholars. Gipson noted the significance on campus of the energy and ideas of John Dilulio, professor of politics, religion, and civil society, director of the Program for Research on Religion and Urban Civil Society, and first, if brief, director of the White House Office of Faith-Based Community Initiatives.[16] There is perhaps no clearer example of Penn's inclusiveness and pragmatism with regard to religions on its campus than the three-point Policy on Secular and Religious Holidays it adopted in 1996. First, while Penn does not formally recognize any secular or religious holidays, in setting the academic calendar it tries to avoid conflicts with holidays like July 4, Thanksgiving, Labor Day, Christmas, and New Year's, which involve most of its members. Second, no examinations may be given or required work assigned on days like Martin Luther King Jr. Day, Rosh Hashanah, Yom Kippur, the first two days of Passover, and Good Friday, which affect large numbers of its members. Third, students who wish to observe holidays like Memorial Day, Sukkot, the last two days of Passover, Shavuot, Shemini Atzerat, and Simchat Torah, as well as the Muslim New Year, Ra's al-sana, and the Islamic holidays Eid Al-Fitr and Eid Al-Adha must inform their instructors within the first two weeks of each semester of their intent to observe the holiday so that alternative arrangements can be made for completing the assignments. I concluded that Benjamin Franklin would be pleased with the sense of inclusiveness and the pragmatism.

Harvard University

As a young seminary professor, I once was interviewed for the better part of an hour by Nathan Pusey regarding the future of Episcopal seminaries. Many of us were impressed that the president of Harvard was an active Episcopalian taking an interest in theological education. Nearly twenty years later I had two interesting dinner conversations with President

---

[16] On his views of the role of religion at Penn and several other universities, see John J. Dilulio Jr., "A Level Playing Field for Religion in Higher Education," in *The American University in a Postsecular Age*, ed. Douglas Jacobsen and Rhonda Hustedt Jacobsen (New York: Oxford University Press, 2008), 45–62.

Derek Bok, who shared memories with me about the teenage years he had spent at the Harvard School in Los Angeles when it was still an Episcopal military academy. At that time I was a candidate for a position at the Divinity School, which caused me to learn something of its history, character, challenges, and opportunities. Bok, wisely I think, chose someone else for that post.

My fifteen minutes of fame at Harvard began on an icy Saturday night in January when my World Airways DC-10 jet from Newark was unable to stop on the runway at Boston's Logan Airport and went lunging into the harbor where the front part of the plane broke off. Although two people lost their lives, the rest of us (the plane was full of college students returning from the holiday break) were able to make our way to shore— wet, cold, but uninjured. Realizing that I was going to live and then would still need to preach at Harvard's Memorial Church the next morning, I managed—before exiting the plane via the escape chute we had swung over to the wing—to stuff my sermon notes into my pants. The essayist, storyteller, and Princeton graduate Frederick Buechner found this to be the quintessential preacher's tale: Just escaping death, the preacher yet remembers his sermon notes.

Later that night I was able to find the Pusey Minister in the Memorial Church Peter Gomes having a beer with students and seeming, I thought, rather unfazed by news of my ordeal. The next morning I blew one of the more remarkable opportunities a preacher will ever have. Donning the inflated life jacket I had worn off the plane, I spoke for several minutes about the crash, but then reverted to my prepared sermon notes. As I did, I could see the congregants' eyes begin to wander. I performed a little better at Milton Academy that evening and eventually was able to reflect on what happened in "Where Was God When the Plane Crashed?"[17]

Harvard College, I had learned, was founded in 1636 with the motto *Veritas* soon joined by *In Christo Gloriam*—meaning that all Truth was to be found in Christ and the college was to prepare the leadership for the ecclesiastical and civil order that was theocratic Massachusetts. Each student was to "well consider that the main end of his life and studies is to know God and Jesus Christ which is eternal life." He was to attend religious exercises, pray privately, and read Scripture twice daily. Saturday was for Bible study, and Sunday primarily for hearing two long sermons. Late in the eighteenth century the words on Harvard's heraldic seal be-

[17] In the *Christian Century* (March 13, 1985): 262–64.

came *Christo et Ecclesiae*—still stressing this sense of the school's fundamental mission.

Yet Harvard, although charged with helping to fashion a theocracy, was never an enclosed theological circle. Based on the Calvinist doctrine of common grace, Puritans could also embrace the secular realm and study the natural order, believing that the creation could be known through reason. Harvard taught mathematics, astronomy, English composition, philosophy, natural philosophy, as well as theology. While slightly over half of its seventeenth-century graduates became clergy, many entered other fields. Coming from Cambridge and Oxford Universities where individual colleges laid greater claim on their loyalties than the universities themselves, a number of the Harvard faculty felt some affinity for what we today call "pluralism."

Pluralism brings conflict, and by 1701 ten Harvard alumni, perceiving a decline of orthodoxy at their alma mater, were founding Yale, even attracting to their camp Harvard's president. With the establishment in 1721 of the Hollis Chair of Divinity, theology was clearly one, but no longer the only, subject taught. When the liberal theologian Henry Ware occupied that chair in 1805, the Trinitarians departed, leaving Harvard largely to the Unitarians, under whom moral philosophy became the essence of a Harvard education. From 1810 to 1933, every Harvard president was a Unitarian committed to a liberality in religious teaching, a pursuit of truth and intellectual freedom that were part and parcel of their faith. The nondenominational but Unitarian-influenced Divinity School was established within the college in 1816 for the education of a learned clergy and to ensure that "every encouragement be given to the serious, impartial, and unbiased investigation of Christian truth."[18]

When in 1833 Massachusetts disestablished religion, the theocratic ideal died and the educational goal of creative human development began to displace Calvinist views of human nature that emphasized obedience to God. With a commitment to science, the individual's intellectual quest, students' freedom to regulate their own lives, the cultivation of character through humanistic education, and professional rather than theological criteria in faculty hiring, Harvard appeared to be more and more secular. But as Professor Hedge of the Divinity School explained in 1866, "the secularization of the College is no violation of its motto, '*Christo et Ecclesiae*,' for I interpret those sacred ideas, the cause of Christ and the

[18] From the website of the Harvard Divinity School, 2010, at http://www.hds.harvard.edu/history.html.

Church, as advanced by whatever liberalizes and enriches and enlarges the mind."[19] When in 1884 *Veritas* was restored to a central place in the school's seal and shield, it was yet encompassed by *Christo et Ecclesiae*, signifying some ongoing belief in the unity of faith and knowledge.

In other words, whatever Harvard did was Christian. Liberal education *was* the driving force and content of that religion, and its canon was to be not only the Bible, but the world's great literature published in the fifty-one-volume *Harvard Classics*. The anthology's editor was Charles Eliot, Harvard's president from 1869 to 1909, who once debated Princeton's James McCosh on the benefits for religion of no longer requiring specific religious studies or chapel attendance (an idea said to have been recommended in order to encourage deeper religious commitments by the famed and beloved then rector of Trinity Church, Copley Square, Phillips Brooks). Eliot hired professors regardless of their religious affiliation. He championed a religion of the future that would be based in the love of an "immanent and loving God" and of neighbor and in service that would promote all human welfare. Without dogma or the supernatural, this "simple," alternative to traditional Christianity would be based in the best knowledge of the human race that was "in essential agreement with the direct personal teachings of Jesus."[20] By 1945 Harvard could contend that the great books "can be looked at as a secular continuation of the spirit of Protestantism," while "rejecting the unique authority of the Scriptures."[21] By the time of the school's three hundredth anniversary in 1936, *Veritas* had come regularly to stand alone on the university's shield.[22]

Upon becoming Harvard's president in 1953, Nathan Pusey declared his "sincere hope, that theological studies can here be given a fresh impetus and a new life within this University."[23] He brought Paul Tillich to

[19] Quoted by George W. Marsden, *The Soul of The American University: From Protestant Establishment to Established Non-Belief* (New York: Oxford University Press, 1994), 186.

[20] Eliot's "The Religion of the Future—Present Tendencies and a Forecast," was first delivered to Harvard's 1909 Summer School of Theology and printed in full in the *New York Times* of Sunday, September 19, 1909, part six, 6–7. Widely admired, it was also criticized by, among others, the pope.

[21] *General Education in a Free Society: Report of the Harvard Committee* (Cambridge, MA: Harvard University Press, 1945), 43.

[22] For a summary story of Harvard's shield motto, see Julia A. Reuben, *The Making of the Modern University: Intellectual Transformation and the Marginalization of Morality* (Chicago: University of Chicago Press, 1996), 1–2, 15.

[23] Quoted by Marsden, *Soul*, 411 (which see for a fuller discussion as Pusey was con-

Harvard to be one of its five university professors. Opponents quickly pushed back at his efforts to strengthen the place of religion and, in their view, particularly Christianity at Harvard. Then undergraduate Stanley Katz remembers seeing nearly one hundred Harvard faculty members lined up outside Pusey's office to present a petition for a change in the policy that people had to be Christian to have services, weddings, and burials in Memorial Church (the nondenominational house of worship built in 1932 on the site of the 1858 Appleton Chapel that stands opposite Widener Library in Harvard Yard to frame the outdoor Tercentenary Theater where students graduate and that is the symbolic center of Harvard's spiritual life). Pusey soon agreed that the chapel should be open to private services of all faiths.

When in 1972 Episcopalian Charles Price, later my sometimes colleague who had often demonstrated his ecumenical and interfaith interests during his Harvard ministry, resigned his post as preacher to the university and Plummer Professor of Moral Theology (first established in 1855), President Derek Bok appointed a committee chaired by the highly respected dean of the Divinity School, Krister Stendahl, to address the question, "How can Harvard provide appropriate recognition to the diverse religious needs of its community while still maintaining the vitality of the traditions and programs associated with Memorial Church?" This was also a time of ascending secularism at Harvard and in academia generally, and there were some who questioned whether religion should have any established role. The Divinity School's Professor Harvey Cox had (as noted earlier), in his book *The Secular City*, promoted the demise of establishment religion and encouraged Christians to advance secularism as a way of helping to break down barriers of divisiveness. Frustrated after eighteen months by what it called "the sharp divisions of opinion that exist throughout the Harvard community concerning the question under review," the committee disbanded. With their "difficult assignment" and being unable "to achieve a clear consensus," the committee had, however, in what Bok diplomatically referred to as "a preliminary report," come as far as proposing the possibility of hiring three ministers—a Protestant, a Roman Catholic, and a Jew. But for reasons of administrative efficiency and "financial considerations," Bok kept Memorial Church under one

---

trasting his understanding of religion with that of President Eliot's emphasis on religion as service only), from Pusey's "A Faith for These Times," in *The Age of the Scholar: Observations on Education in a Troubled Decade* (Cambridge, MA: Harvard University Press, 1963), 7–8.

individual, and, to honor Harvard's heritage and the terms of the Plummer bequest, a Protestant. To accommodate Harvard's diversity, he changed the position's title to Minister in Memorial Church, renamed the Board of Preachers the Board of Ministry, created a faculty committee for Memorial Church, and built offices for recognized religious groups on campus in the basement of the church.[24] In 1974 the Reverend Peter Gomes, an American Baptist, became the first African American to be the chief preacher and pastor in Memorial Church.

It is hard to know all that was in Bok's mind in the appointment of Gomes. As Harvard was seeking racial diversity in its faculty and senior administrative positions, the choice of an African American, who was already on the staff at Memorial Church, would have been well received by many. Peter Gomes was also just thirty-two years old and styled himself as Republican in his politics and rather conservative in his theology. After the campus and alumni problems that Chaplain Bill Coffin's antiwar and other views had recently caused at Yale, Gomes may have seemed like a safe choice as well. Bok had noted that if he had to choose whether to emphasize abilities as a scholar, speaker, or pastor in the post, he would choose Harvard's need for a chaplain's pastoral skills.[25] My reading of Bok is that he also wanted a committed Christian and a talented and thoughtful preacher in that position.[26] If so, Bok has earned his credits as a talent scout for great preachers, for Gomes went on to an extraordinary career as a preacher capable of drawing many students and others to Memorial Church, as well as becoming widely known for his preaching and teaching well beyond Harvard. Through his sermons, books, and student teas at his campus residence, Gomes became as iconic of Harvard as anyone then living—his stature enhanced by the vibrancy of Sunday morning worship and music at "Mem Church," its Christian Morning Prayer services Monday through Saturday, a monthly service of Compline, adult educational forums, fellowship groups, off-campus overnight retreats, vocation dinners, and more. Indeed, although not bearing the title of "Preacher to the University" (a designation whose loss he attributed more to Stendahl than Bok), Gomes told me that he still saw himself as having that role, along with being a "custodian of the virtues and values of the University." Among those virtues, he came to insist (after an-

---

[24] See Bok's "Report on Memorial Church," in *Harvard Gazette*, May 31, 1974, 1–4.
[25] Ibid., 3.
[26] Derek Bok reflected again on his choice at Gomes's April 6, 2011, memorial service. The text of his address was made available through memorialchurcharvard.edu.

nouncing in 1991 that he was a Christian who happened to be gay while celibate by choice), were full acceptance of gay men and lesbians in the university, society and church.[27]

One further sign of the visibility that Gomes retained for Memorial Church is the "Service for Seniors" that takes place at eight in the morning on Commencement Day, a service that he recognized may be somewhat of an anachronism but "a very pleasant one." The church, which can officially accommodate 900, is filled to overflowing with an estimated 1,600 seniors, a number of whom, one can imagine, had to struggle to get out of bed and dress themselves properly for the occasion. Gomes would give them a final sermon in the midst of a brief service that could be described as a kind of Judeo-Christian civil liturgy, complete with the singing of "My Country, 'Tis of Thee" . . . "Protect us by thy might, Great God, our King."

The traditional baccalaureate service, held in Memorial Church on the Tuesday afternoon of Commencement Week, at which the president is regularly the speaker, is also overcrowded by the graduates in academic dress. Their family members and friends are invited to hear the service in the Tercentenary Theater. Over the years the readings, prayers, and participants have become multifaith and multicultural. Indeed, during Gomes's long tenure Harvard has become increasingly diverse with regard to the religions of its students. As Gomes put it, referring to the growing number of international students as well as other non-Christians, these are "people who don't leave their religion at home."[28] All the major religious traditions of the world, and many smaller ones, are well represented on campus, most of them ministered to by one or more of the forty chaplains that are members of the Harvard Chaplains, an umbrella group that also includes a very active Humanist/Agnostic/Atheist chaplaincy. Gomes, who described himself as "the secretary of state for religion at Harvard," was interested in their ministries and responsible for their licensing and for hospitality to other denominations and faiths on campus but focused on his primary ministries in and through his position at Memorial Church with two associate clergy and seminarians from the Divinity School to assist him in meeting the pastoral needs of a campus with some 6,700 undergraduates and over 12,000 graduate and professional students.

[27] The story is told more fully in his *New York Times* obituary, March 2, 2011, A21.

[28] Gomes is quoted by Alan Finder, "Matters of Faith Find a New Prominence on Campus," *New York Times*, May 2, 2007, A16

Catholics and Jews form the largest of the religious groups in the student body. Harvard has long had a significant Jewish population, not always with the best of relationships due to both covert and overt efforts to keep some kind of a lid on their admissions.[29] With Jews now, however, making up an estimated one-quarter of students and one-third of the faculty, Harvard Hillel (there is also a Chabad group) embraces a pluralism that respects the dignity and lifestyle of every Jew and the development of Jewish leaders. In May of 1994, Rosovsky Hall, the home of the Rieseman Center, was dedicated; it has a student lounge, dining hall, library, offices, and a place for worship by four distinct congregations. From this center Hillel can offer initiatives for interfaith programming as was done with the 2008 "Day of Faith," held to address such questions as "How can we deepen and nurture our own roots in classical faith traditions and yet open our hearts and minds to others?" and "How can groups of people whose history, traditions, and worldviews radically differ communicate effectively?"

Even before the time of Gomes's appointment, Harvard was beginning to see itself as an international university reflecting global diversity that included the world's religions. The Center for the Study of World Religions had been established in 1960 and the Women's Studies in Religion Program in 1973. When in 1991 the Harvard Pluralism Project began its study of the changing religious landscape in America, it drew a distinction between mere diversity and a pluralism defined as engagement with diversity and the knowledge such engagement brings. In the Divinity School, while understanding its mission as "rigorous historical and comparative studies of Christian traditions in the context of other world religions and value systems," courses are taught by faculty members who are personally knowledgeable about these other traditions. Harvard also has an Islam Awareness Week, an introductory course called Islam 101, and offers another twenty-five courses through the Prince Alwaleed Bin Talal Islamic Studies Program.

The importance of the study of religions' roles in the world recently led to the recommendation that undergraduates be required to study religion in a category first called "reason and faith," which was then changed to "culture and belief." "As academics in a university, we don't

---

[29] See Jerome Karabel, *The Chosen: The Hidden History of Admission and Exclusion at Harvard, Yale, and Princeton* (Boston: Houghton Mifflin, 2005), 77–109, 139–99.

have to confront religion if we are not religious," noted philosophy professor Alison Simmons, "but in the world they will have to."[30] "Religion has historically been, and continues to be a force shaping identity and behavior throughout the world," reasoned a task group's report on general education. "Harvard is a secular institution, but religion is an important part of or students' lives. When they get to college, students often struggle to sort out the relationship between their own beliefs and practices and those of fellow students, and the relationship of religious belief to the resolutely secular world of the academy."[31] The recommendation (supported by a group led by Professor Louis Menand) was vigorously opposed by Professor Steven Pinker and other faculty—some who rejected it as the study of an irrational subject.

Whatever the future place of religion in the curriculum, interest in faith matters seems to have grown at Harvard in recent decades. For some years the longtime Hollis Professor of Divinity, Harvey Cox, taught a course he called "Jesus and the Moral Life." The last such course at Harvard had been taught by the philosopher George Santayana in 1912, and in the intervening period much of the teaching of religion had been confined to the Divinity School, which by midcentury the chemist and president James Conan Bryant had seriously considered giving away. But if it had come to seem to many that secularism and relativism reigned at Harvard, quite a number of students, Cox observed, were nonetheless "uncomfortable relativists."[32] Seven hundred of them showed up annually for his course.

"There is probably more active religious life now than there has been in 100 years," Gomes maintained.[33] Certainly there has been some resurgence among Christian evangelical groups and, under Gomes, of Trinitarian Christology. "There is a rumor about . . . that this University has long since abandoned its ancient motto and is conformable only to 'Veritas.' That simply is not true," Gomes contended from his pulpit in Memorial Church in 2002. "The seal by which the President and Fellows of Harvard College continue to conduct their business is still the seal that says:

[30] "Harvard Wants Undergraduates to Study Religion," at Buzzle.com, accessed October 6, 2006.

[31] "Report of the Task Force on General Education" (Cambridge, MA: Harvard University, Faculty of Arts and Sciences, 2007), 11–12.

[32] Harvey Cox, *When Jesus Came to Harvard: Making Moral Choices Today* (Boston: Houghton Mifflin, 2004), 8.

[33] Gomes in "Matters of Faith," A16. The article reports on growing interest in religion and spirituality on a number of campuses.

'*Veritas Christo et Ecclesiae*' . . . *Veritas*—that is, true *Veritas*, and not simply correct information—can never be separated from the one in whom it is most perfectly and fully seen: Jesus Christ."[34] One cannot help but observe, however, that it is hard to find the Harvard shield with anything other than the word *Veritas*,[35] while many at Harvard regard the faith of contemporary Christians as the views of but another tolerated minority and would prefer to stress the positive aspects of the university's pluralism of religions, cultures, and diverse forms of secularism. As at other universities, the role of religion and religions at Harvard has its particular history, circumstances, and personalities and continues to change, leading to questions about the future at the time of this writing and after Peter Gomes had announced he would retire in 2012 and then his death in the late winter of 2011.

YALE UNIVERSITY

During the 1980s I visited Yale several times, to preach in Battell Chapel, to talk with students, and to deliver convocation lectures at the Berkeley Divinity School at Yale—coming to know University Chaplains John Vannorsdall (1976–85) and Harry Adams (1986–92). Then in 2002–3 I lived in New Haven for the better part of two years, serving as interim dean of the Berkeley Divinity School and associate dean at Yale Divinity School during transitions in leadership at both schools. I was later asked by President Richard Levin to chair a University Council committee to study religion and spiritual life at Yale. During these periods I had the opportunity to come to know more than a few students, faculty, administrators, and alumni and to value friendship with University Chaplain Frederick J. "Jerry" Streets (1992–2007), and once more with Harry Adams, and to talk with them and others about how Yale had moved on its trajectory from Congregationalist and then more liberal Protestant hegemony to become a far more religiously diverse and largely secular university. Some friends were still discussing Law School Professor Stephen Carter's 1994 *The Culture of Disbelief*, which took to task the cli-

---

[34] Peter J. Gomes, *Strength for the Journey: Biblical Wisdom for Daily Living* (Boston: Houghton Mifflin, 2004), 56, 60.

[35] Sometimes with the word *Harvard* below. The first page of the *Harvard Gazette* of May 31, 1974, says *Christo et Ecclesiae* that it "is strictly speaking a 'seal legend'" that "may be used on a motto ribbon beneath the shield if so desired."

mate of law and politics in America for forcing those with strong religious faith to bend to the viewpoint of what he regarded as a largely faithless "public faith."[36] More recently I have come to know Sharon Kugler, who became university chaplain in 2007 and has been in conversation with me about these changing times and circumstances and her present ministry.

We have reflected on how Yale was born in 1701 out of an energetic concern for Christian orthodoxy—thought to be no longer the governing faith at Harvard. Although the founding Congregational Connecticut clergy—intent on establishing an institution that would prepare young men "for service in church and civil state"—at first sought to avoid the endorsement of specific creeds, the declaration of the school's first resident rector, Timothy Cutler, that he had become an Anglican, forced the trustees to rid Yale of Cutler and any suspicion of Anglican broadmindedness and "Arminian" ideas about free will. For years to come future rectors and tutors would be required to subscribe to the Saybrook Platform version of the Westminster Confession. As the spiritual enthusiasms of the Great Awakening and "New Lights" preaching and teaching moved through the college and local churches in succeeding decades, there would be struggles (with some expulsions) over who was teaching true orthodoxy and avoiding "spiritual laxity." Moreover, while the attendance of some Anglican students and the endowments of Anglicans Bishop George Berkeley and Eli Yale himself were to be appreciated, the strictly orthodox rector (and first to be called President, 1740–66), Thomas Clap, made it clear that the gifts were to be regarded as "donations" that would in no way "buy" the theological and moral teaching of the college.[37] Although Clap's views and those of Yale's first professor of divinity, the Reverend Naphtali Daggett, became somewhat more accommodating to the views of other Congregationalists, the establishment in 1757 of the first college church, followed by the building in 1767 of the Athenaeum— where prayers led by the presidents were held twice daily—were regarded by many as a means to keep the Yale community free from heterodoxy. After personal objections, Anglicans were, however, permitted to attend their own church in town.

With the influences of the Enlightenment and the political excitement and fervor over the War of Independence, more pluralism in religious

[36] Stephen L. Carter, *The Culture of Disbelief: How American Law and Politics Trivialize Religious Devotion* (New York: Anchor Books, 1994).

[37] See Marsden, *Soul,* 56.

thought, some free thinking and what many regarded as laxity in religion entered into the college. By the end of the century it was estimated that less than 10 percent of the student body openly professed their religion. President Timothy Dwight (1795–1817) then, however, strengthened the college in a number of ways, including—with his "Edwardean [*sic*] Divinity" views of the role of human will—its religion.[38] Professors of law, chemistry and mineralogy, and mathematics were added to the faculty, and Dwight conducted personal conversations and prayer meetings with students. The number of students who called themselves Christians, joined the College Church and willingly attended required daily chapel (5:30 a.m. and 6:00 p.m.) and Sunday services grew considerably. A new Second Chapel was built in 1824, and the next decades were years of relative Congregationalist Protestant stability—enlivened by several times of revival. As a sign of fading Puritan attitudes toward worship, a Beethoven Society and a student choir were formed to add beauty to the worship, and in 1851 an organ found a place in the chapel. Earlier, in 1822, the Divinity School had been organized as a separate department of the academy, enabling it to focus on the training of Congregational ministers, and allowing the rest of the college further to broaden the curriculum for a growing number of students with a wider range of vocational ambitions.

Change continued in the college with the challenges of the Civil War and more diversity among the students in Protestant belief and practice. Although compulsory evening services were abolished in 1859, the Victorian Gothic Battell Chapel, large enough for the whole student body, was dedicated in 1876 to members of the college fallen in the Civil War, and a variety of distinguished preachers were invited to its pulpit. What seemed for a time to be less interest in religion was counteracted by the activities and missionary spirit of the new YMCA programs centered in the first Dwight Hall. Well attended lectures and prayer meetings led to rescue missions and boys' clubs in New Haven and Yale-in-China missionaries who went abroad to found schools and hospitals.

The Dwight Hall dedication in 1885 was attended by President Noah Porter, a moral philosopher, abolitionist, and Congregational minister

---

[38] See George P. Fisher, *A Discourse, Commemorative of the History of the Church of Christ in Yale, during the First Century of Its Existence* (New Haven, CT: Thomas H. Pease, 1858), 80–82, and into the modern period, Ralph Henry Gabriel, *Religion and Learning at Yale: The Church of Christ in College and University, 1757–1957* (New Haven, CT: Yale University Press, 1958).

who understood there to be intellectual and moral warfare between
Christianity and secularism. Porter presided over Yale's last public struggle regarding a faculty member's religion when he maneuvered William
Graham Sumner, an Anglican minister become scientific naturalist, into
dropping the course in which he used Herbert Spencer's *The Study of
Sociology*, which classified Christianity with the "superstitions of the
Mohammedans and South Sea Islanders," as a major text. Porter's successor, Timothy Dwight V, the son of the first President Dwight and the last
in the line of Congregational ministers to head the school, managed to
avoid such controversy in the college (which officially became Yale University in 1887) even while the faculty was becoming more departmentalized and "scientific" in its approaches to knowledge and more diverse and
liberal in its religious and philosophical views.

This liberalism and a spirit of secularism would grow in the next decades, especially with the challenges of the deaths and tragedies of the
Great War. Questions regarding human moral progress, which long had
been tied to religious belief, took root among faculty and students. Pluralism also was becoming more evident in the Yale community. The development of graduate professional schools added to the numbers and
complexity of the institution. Yale gained its first Catholic chaplain in
1922, and by mid-decade one out of every ten Yale undergraduates was
Jewish. In 1927, noting that the student body could no longer fit into Battell Chapel, all chapel requirements were abolished, while at the same
time the Fellows of the Corporation announced the appointment of the
first full-time chaplain and entertained plans for a new chapel, which,
however, was never built.[39]

In the face of these changes and less churchgoing by Protestants, Protestant Christianity yet had a significant presence on campus. Through his
ministry in what was now known as the Church of Christ in Yale University, his teaching, conversations, and pastoral work, the Reverend Sidney
"Sid" Lovett (university chaplain for twenty-six years, from 1932 to
1958) touched the lives of many, being remembered for his consistent
pacifism and genial but firmly liberal Protestant views. One could point
to a number of committed Christians on the faculty, several teaching religion courses, and the place of the Divinity School in the overall university. At his 1937 inauguration, President Charles Seymour called on members of the faculty "to recognize the tremendous power of the teachings

[39] Recall that Princeton and Chicago were building grand new ones and Harvard soon
would, but then came the Depression.

of Christ in our life-and-death struggle against the selfish forces of materialism" and called for "the maintenance and up building of the Christian religion as a vital part of university life."[40] Immediately after World War II a Yale committee declared that "a university that fails to promote a vigorous religious life among its students is shirking one of its major responsibilities," for, although the "guns are silenced, . . . the spiritual battle is not yet won."[41]

All this to the sharp eye and rhetoric of the 1950 graduate William Buckley was, however, window dressing for the reality of the paltry role Christianity had come to play at the university. Along with a rather confused opposition of individualism and "collectivism" and his linkage of this individualism with capitalism and Christianity, his *God and Man at Yale: The Superstitions of "Academic Freedom"* zeroed in on "the duel between Christianity and atheism," contending that the Dwight Hall activities of the University Christian Association were no longer particularly Christian in motivation and that the teaching at Yale promoted relativism and the "absolute that there are no absolutes, no intrinsic rights, no ultimate truths."[42] Yale faculty, he contended, were by and large not even neutral to religion. While it was not acceptable (in later parlance "politically correct") to promote religion in the classroom, it was quite permissible to talk it down—even deride it, and he offered up a number of examples to make his point. Critics held that Buckley neither understood the role of academic freedom nor the proper place and strengths of Christianity at Yale. The Reverend Henry Sloane Coffin (Yale 1897, former president of Union Theological Seminary and former Yale trustee) was called upon to chair an alumni commission to inquire as to "the intellectual and spiritual welfare of the university, the students and its faculty." He and McGeorge Bundy (Yale 1940) more than hinted that Buckley's viewpoints and brand of Roman Catholicism (although in the book Buckley never stated that he was Catholic, an omission for which he was also criticized) did not belong at Yale.[43] More remarkably, from the retrospective of the next generations, it may be hard for many to understand

---

[40] In *God and Man at Yale* (3, 43), William Buckley uses quotations from Seymour's inaugural address largely to stress Buckley's understanding of the distance between the rhetoric about the importance of Christianity and the reality. William F. Buckley Jr., *God and Man at Yale: The Superstitions of Academic Freedom* (Chicago: Regnery, 1951).

[41] *Time*, "Religion: Revival at Yale?," August 15, 1945, 90.

[42] Buckley, *God and Man at Yale*, xii, 25.

[43] On the Coffin and Bundy critiques, see Marsden, *Soul*, 10. There were also several critiques of Buckley's social and economic views from Catholic perspectives.

that there could even be controversy over whether Yale should have a strong commitment to any form of religion. Moreover, as time went on it was the Catholics who would grow in their numbers (from about 13 percent of the undergraduates in 1950 to 20 to 25 percent by the turn of the century) and continue to develop their own Saint Thomas More Chapel and Catholic Center at Yale as a hub for worship and activities.

The controversial ministry of Sidney Lovett's successor, and Henry Sloane Coffin's nephew, William Sloane Coffin (Yale 1949, Yale Divinity School 1956, and chaplain 1958–76), may be seen as a hurrah (Bill Coffin would like that description) and last high-water mark for the significance of liberal, prophetic Protestant Christianity at Yale. The picture of President Kingman Brewster, sitting in the president's chair in the crowded Battell Chapel, listening to Coffin's often challenging and moving sermons and then rising to sing the favorite hymn ("Once to every man and nation / Comes the moment to decide / In the strife of truth with falsehood / For the good or evil side") of the chaplain who could cause him no end of trouble is still imprinted in the memory of students of the time.[44] Outspoken both for the civil rights of blacks and in protest against the Vietnam War, Coffin was glad to welcome and work with members of other religions, especially when they shared his vigorous, nonviolent social justice and peacemaking advocacy. On his retirement he suggested that his successor could be a rabbi or a Catholic, but that it should be just one person to speak to the university, and not some troika. I was present at the 2002 commencement when Coffin, not long before his death, was granted an honorary degree. There were smiles of both pleasure and irony as much of Yale and its best-known prophet and pastor seemed to be at peace.

Quieter times called for thoughtful preachers and pastors as university chaplains. John Vannorsdall (1978–85), a Lutheran minister, and Disciples of Christ Harry Adams (1986–92), also continuing as a professor at the Divinity School and serving as master of Trumbull College, supplied both the preaching and pastoring. They carried on a primarily Protestant ministry through Battell Chapel and to the campus, while working in

---

[44] Further on Yale's reactions to Coffin's ministry and his complex relationship with Brewster, see Geoffrey Kabaservice, *The Guardians: Kingman Brewster, His Circle, and the Rise of the Liberal Establishment* (New York: Henry Holt, 2004), 318–23, passim. Kabaservice also frequently notes the important influence of Bishop Paul Moore (Yale class of 1941 and member of the Yale Corporation) on Brewster and religious and social justice issues at Yale. Coffin referenced the opening line of the hymn in the title of his autobiography, William Sloane Coffin Jr., *Once to Every Man: A Memoir* (New York: Atheneum, 1977).

cooperation with the growing Catholic and Jewish ministries and those of other denominations and groups. A 1990 study of religion and spirituality at Yale concentrated on describing the roles and activities of Protestants, Catholics, and Jews. Particularly under Vannorsdall the Office of University Chaplain supported the university's efforts to ameliorate social and economic problems in the school's urban environment and several times attempted to be of some assistance in Yale's often-rocky relationships with parts of its labor force.

Jerry Streets brought to the work of university chaplain (1992–2007) his seventeen years of experience with social involvement as the senior pastor of the Mt. Aery Baptist Church in Bridgeport, Connecticut, which enabled him to be a strong ally of the university's programs in New Haven. Among other undertaking he served on the New Haven Board of Police Commissioners as well as on the State Judicial Selection Committee. Streets developed the cooperative ecumenical and interfaith relations on campus, in particular with Catholic Chaplain Robert Beloin, who has had a twenty-year ministry at Yale, and with Rabbi James Ponet (Yale 1968), who was instrumental in building the Slifka Center (dedicated in 1995) and has been at Yale for nearly thirty years. During Street's fifteen years, and as Yale increasingly came to see itself as a "global university," the numbers of students of other religious backgrounds continued to grow. This was particularly true of Muslim students, both graduate/professional and undergraduate, and a Muslim Student Association was officially begun and a place found for Muslim prayer services. When our committee to study religious and spiritual life at Yale met with Muslim students in early 2004, they, however, told us of the difficulties they had been experiencing in obtaining their evening meals during Ramadan, as the school's food services were unable to provide meals as late as sunset. Committee members noted this to Chaplain Streets and others at the university, and when the committee was at Yale during the next Ramadan, Muslim students proudly invited us to share a university-provided dinner with them.

Streets and other Yale chaplains have taught a course at the Divinity School that for many years has otherwise had but a modest involvement with religion in the rest of the campus. The Divinity School provides occasional preachers for the Sunday services and student interns for campus ministry. Programs of the school's Institute of Sacred Music are also part of the full artistic life at Yale. With pluses and minuses, the near-mile-distance between the Divinity School's Sterling Quadrangle and the main campus fosters a certain independence from undergraduate life and even from the twenty-member-strong Religious Studies Department (with ten fields of study and now a PhD program in Islamic studies) with which, however, there are cooperative relationships and some affiliated appointments. The Divinity School's library is one of the world's finest and is an important asset to the university. Its small Center for Faith and Culture, led by Professor Miroslav Volf, focuses on understanding and peaceful relations between Christians and Muslims.

When, during the 1990s, there were questions about the future of the Divinity School (which included the possibility of its relocation to the main campus), Yale's first Jewish president, Richard Levin, while urging the school to lower its percentage of admissions to applicants to something like the high standards of other Yale schools, made a commitment of $40 million to rebuild and modernize the Sterling Quadrangle. His explicit intention was to ensure the school's future as a graduate professional school with its primary mission as the ecumenical education of Christian ministers and leaders. Much of that rebuilding took place during my years in New Haven, and I saw firsthand the administrative and pastoral leadership the New Testament scholar and teacher, Harold Attridge, provided during that challenging period. It was, many others and I agreed with President Levin, one of those "no-brainers" that he should become—at a formerly largely Protestant divinity school that now also had some eighty Catholic students—its first Catholic dean.

With Jerry Streets's retirement as university chaplain, Yale also made a major change in the office and character of that ministry by selecting a Catholic woman. In 2007 Sharon Kugler arrived with her the experience of having been university chaplain at Johns Hopkins for fourteen years and former president of both the National Association of University Chaplains and the Association of College and University Religious Affairs. Having long thought about the most effective ways to be chaplain in a modern multifaith university (her master's thesis is titled "The Limits and Possibilities of Building a Religiously Pluralistic Community"), she now teaches a course at the Divinity School called Models and Methods of University Chaplaincy.

One of the first changes that resulted from the appointment of Kugler was that the Sunday morning congregation of the University Church would no longer be a focus for the university chaplain's ministry.[45] That

---

[45] Now called the University Church, the Church of Christ in Yale University was from the early 1960s until 2005 officially a United Church of Christ congregation with an ecumenical outreach and ministry.

congregation, which had been struggling for some years, would instead have the leadership of the Reverend Ian Oliver, former university chaplain at Bucknell, whom Kugler asked to be her senior associate chaplain for Protestant life and pastor of the University Church, helping to coordinate all Christian campus ministries. Kugler herself "splits her time," worshiping half her Sundays with this Protestant congregation, where she on occasion preaches, and on other Sundays at Catholic services.

Chaplain Kugler then brought new attention to interfaith work and conversation. Now on her staff, succeeding several part-time advisors, is a full-time coordinator for Muslim life and a part-time coordinator for Hindu life. A multifaith council of self-selecting students, which had been begun several years earlier, now meets weekly with Kugler as (on a biweekly basis and along with other staff chaplains) does a new interreligious leadership council made up of the student leaders of campus religious organizations. Meeting regularly as well is the Yale Religious Ministries composed of the chaplains and directors of the many faith groups granted recognition and status by the chaplain's office. The office publishes a "Multifaith Calendar and So Much More . . ." booklet and has a website featuring the calendar and other information and videos that tell of the services and activities of the various denominations and groups and also offer descriptions and definitions of each group's beliefs and practices. Each year the chaplaincy provides training for freshmen counselors regarding these beliefs and practices to guide them in helping new students to an understanding of the diversity and differences of religions on campus.

As university chaplain, Sharon Kugler is active in many other aspects of campus life, often as a pastor and counselor. She sits on the board of Dwight Hall, encouraging its independent volunteer service activities and use of the Dwight Hall Chapel and meeting room for worship by Episcopalians and for other services and events. Although recent reductions in university finances have meant postponing any expansion beyond the limited space in the basement of Bingham Hall for the university chaplain's offices (among other things leaving too little room for the growing Muslim Friday worship), those plans are still on the drawing boards. Reporting to the president of the university, the chaplain has as her primary liaison the vice president and secretary of the university, Linda Lorimer, who takes considerable interest and offers support to religious life and ministry. The secretary's office also takes major responsibility for planning the annual baccalaureate service, which has long been held in Yale's largest auditorium, Woolsey Hall, with its renowned Newberry

Memorial Organ. For this university assembly, held three times to accommodate the numbers, the president and provost are regularly the speakers, while the chaplain's office helps to provide prayer, hymns, readers from three faith traditions, and a benediction by a rabbi, priest, or imam. The chaplain also offers interfaith prayer at the freshmen assembly at the beginning of the year. At commencement the lay Catholic Kugler presents the opening prayer with the head of the Divinity School, the lay Catholic Dean Attridge offering the benediction. One wonders what the Presidents Dwight would think of that—what Bill Buckley would say.

THE UNIVERSITY OF CHICAGO

Born on Chicago's south side and raised in one of its suburbs, later living and working in Oak Park and Evanston and coming to know a number of the school's graduates, I sometimes wondered what it would have been like to have attended the University of Chicago as an undergraduate or graduate student and perhaps to have remained a midwesterner all my life. My wife lived her earlier years in Hyde Park, and we both came to know of the tensions and challenges the still largely all white university was experiencing in the 1960s and '70s, particularly with blacks and other neighbors in Hyde Park, Kenwood, and Woodlawn, with regard to issues of housing, schools, and other services. We grew up hearing stories of the fame of a university where scientists had opened the atomic age by creating the first controlled nuclear chain reaction under the stands of the then-unused Stagg Stadium, and where the dynamic and iconoclastic President Robert Maynard Hutchins had, with his emphasis on the "great books" of Western civilization and a kind of metaphysics without theology, insisted that the university's work was to bring a moral, intellectual, and spiritual revolution to the world. During my years teaching in Evanston, I was involved in establishing a network of theological seminaries in the Chicago area, and I attended seminars and programs at the Divinity School and affiliated theological schools. Over the years I had several opportunities to preach in Rockefeller Chapel, and I came to know my Episcopal colleague Bernard "Bernie" Brown (dean of the chapel 1979–95) and then Alison Boden (dean 1995–2007), now dean of religious life and the chapel at Princeton. The present dean of Rockefeller Chapel and director of spiritual life, Elizabeth Davenport, was previously senior associate dean of religious life at the University of Southern California and is an Episcopal priest whom I ordained in Los Angeles in 1991.[46]

The University of Chicago arose like a full-fledged phoenix (the emblem of the school) from the ashes of earlier Baptists' attempts to join in America's growing enthusiasm for higher education. Their newly formed American Baptist Education Society provided a founding organization that looked beyond a seminary mode of education and was sufficiently nonsectarian in attitude as to be open to new learning, pedagogical innovation, and a spectrum of students and faculty. Coupled with the extraordinary generosity of John D. Rockefeller and Chicago's bustling entrepreneurial spirit, this openness enabled the university quickly to establish itself as a major institution of higher education—soon to build its gothic quadrangles to provide an almost instant sense of academic tradition. Combining this passion for education and for Christian learning and living with his own pioneering spirit and boundless energy was the Hebrew and biblical scholar and first president, William Rainey Harper. Recruited from Yale, Harper, who had earlier taught at Chicago's Baptist Seminary in Morgan Park, used that institution to help form the Divinity School as the university's first graduate school. At the heart of his educational vision was his belief that the Bible, properly taught in a modern, "scientific" manner, would provide a necessary foundation for a college education and also for the enlightenment of the larger community. The Bible's inspiration, values, and moral principles could uplift and help build the new America. Biblical studies and church services were, therefore, mandatory for all students at the new university, and Harper regularly addressed the students about the importance of contributing to the "higher life" through the cultivation of a strong religious character.[47]

The services were planned so as to be accessible to students of all Protestant denominations. It was, as George Marsden describes it, "low church Protestantism"[48] along with a Chicago pragmatism and optimism that provided much of the school's early inspiration. Harper, several of the trustees, and the faculty he brought to the new institution put considerable hope and energy in a higher religion that educated for and would inspire a life of right living, industry, and service—a Christianity that was fully allied with the ideals of freedom and democracy and was free from unreformed church teaching and ecclesiastical control. It was also possi-

[46] Dean Boden, in particular, and Dean Davenport have contributed to this overview.
[47] See William Rainey Harper, *Religion and the Higher Life* (Chicago: University of Chicago Press, 1904).
[48] Marsden, *Soul*, 239.

ble for talented and dedicated supporters, teachers, and students from different backgrounds to share in the vision for the future of the school and nation. Several of the university's earliest donors were Jewish industrialists from the burgeoning city that was diversifying almost by the day from new waves of immigration. Many bright young men would join the student body from the incoming white-ethnic groups, and women, too, were accepted from the start. Chicago was glad to compare its modernity and openness, as well as the quality of its education, with any elite eastern university.

One of Harper's first recruits from Yale was Amos Alonzo Stagg, who believed that he was called to a Christian ministry that would, through sports and athletics, help form educated men of moral character who would live out the best of their religion in a spirit of service, leadership, and teamwork. Another new colleague on the faculty was John Dewey, whose moral and educational philosophy was developing in a manner that would, however, no longer have much place for particular religion or churchgoing.

The first several decades of the university's existence kept it well within the camp of liberal Protestantism. The second and third presidents were (as was Harper who had died in early 1906 before he was fifty) also Baptist clergymen, while a developing schism between conservatives who called themselves "fundamentalists" and those more inclined to liberal exegesis, theology, and polity, found the university's leadership set at the liberal end of the spectrum. The sharpest criticism of the university's overall values came from social and economic liberals like Thorstein Veblen and Upton Sinclair, who viewed the "university of Standard Oil" as far too indebted to business interests and the role of money.[49]

In 1910, John D. Rockefeller gave to the university his "final gift" (so stated in the letter of deed—don't even think of asking for more!). He designated $1.5 million of the $10 million gift to be used for the building of a chapel that was to be "the central and dominant feature of the University group." The building would be able to accommodate the entire student body at one time. Its physical prominence was to ensure that the "spirit of religion should penetrate and control the University," so that "all its departments are inspired by religious feeling, and all its work is dedicated to the highest end."[50] The influence of Oxford and Cambridge

---

[49] On these criticisms of Veblen, Sinclair, and others, see ibid., 236–37.

[50] From the Inscription at Rockefeller Chapel. On the story of the building of the chapel and its place in the university, see Sarah Margaret Ritchey, with an introduction by Alison

was still strong, and university leaders wanted the church to be an important part of the campus. By the time the actual chapel was built and dedicated the best location that could accommodate so monumental a structure was on the east side of University Avenue, across the street from the quadrangles, yet also on the highest ground in the area.

In keeping with the university's self-understanding as nonsectarian, and also with the continually growing presence of non-Christian (mainly Jewish) students and faculty, the original plans for the gothic-style chapel were made simpler and sparer during lengthy years of planning. While the early plans included religious iconography in the great stained glass windows, the architect's final design favored geometric shapes in pastel colors with the understanding that the light of truth and reason would flow in and from as well as through the structure. Further decoration was to be in the small, glittering mosaics in the chapel's ceiling, intending to draw the worshiper's attention and spirit upward. The building remained cruciform in shape; interior wood and stone carvings depicted the story of the Parable of the Talents and other Christian tales, and the church seemed to contemporaries a gothic-moving-to-deco cathedral. For their day, however, the administrators and builders of the chapel were ahead of their time in adapting their new building to the more multireligious community they were becoming. Carved over the great front doors are figures representing "the march of religion." Jesus is at top center, but among the figures "marching" toward him, along with persons from the Jewish and Christian scriptures, are Plato and Zoroaster. Additional iconography offers tribute to other philosophers, artists, and scientists.

At the dedication of the University Chapel in 1928 the position of dean of the chapel was also instituted—in the same year as at Princeton. Previously, the university had recognized a chaplain from among the faculty ranks to participate in services and provide formal spiritual leadership. The dean was to be within the highest leadership group at the university—those known as the deans and officers. Reporting to the provost, the dean of the chapel was the only member of the senior group not at the head of an academic division or school.

Also at the chapel's dedication, John D. Rockefeller Jr., representing his father, announced a gift of $1 million (named in honor of his mother Laura Spelman Rockefeller) to endow the programs and fabric of the

L. Boden, *Life of the Spirit, Life of the Mind: Rockefeller Memorial Chapel at 75* (Chicago: University of Chicago Library, 2004) .

chapel. This highly restricted gift was meant to ensure that no matter what the university's financial condition, a portion of money must always be spent on religious life at the institution. Ironically, between the laying of the cornerstone in June 1926 and the dedication of the chapel in October 1928, all mandatory chapel attendance was ended, and the sanctuary big enough to fit the entire student body was, for this purpose, no longer necessary.

In fact, the dedication ceremony of the University Chapel in October 1928 must have seemed to some observers a last high point for the University of Chicago's institutional commitment to any sense of established religion. While Hutchins (a clergyman's son) maintained his hopes for the moral and spiritual power of education, succeeding presidents were all laypersons, none of whom were asked or expected to provide religious leadership. While many students, faculty, and staff were practicing their faith, the university continued to diversify. A joke on campus became, "The University of Chicago—where Jewish faculty teach Aquinas to Protestant students"—an exaggeration with some ironic merit. The university's self-understanding as a place of rigorous debate with no ideological (and certainly no religious) place to hide encouraged the radical questioning of received norms. Meanwhile, the Jewish and Catholic communities had grown to such a critical mass by the 1940s that Hillel and the Archdiocese of Chicago each purchased buildings adjacent to campus and continued the administration of ever more thriving chaplaincies. The Hillel office had previously been in the large, unfinished basement of the chapel (renamed Rockefeller Memorial Chapel in 1937). The home (to become Calvert House) bought by the Catholic Campus Ministry became available on December 8, 1941, with the deportation of the Japanese Consul and his family.[51] After the war years a Lutheran campus ministry was established, and Brent House became the center for the Episcopal chaplaincy. Hyde Park Union Church and other houses of worship had significant constituencies from the university community as part of their congregational life.[52]

Although through the next half century the university embarked on no official study or plan to divest Protestantism's role as a privileged or de-

---

[51] During a renovation of the building in 2005 a number of wires and cables were found in the walls that turned out to have been installed, not by the Japanese, but by Americans spying on them.

[52] Early presidents of the University of Chicago had been active in the Hyde Park Union Church, and Charles Gilkey was its pastor for some eighteen years before becoming the first dean of Rockefeller Chapel.

fault religion, a process in that direction may be seen to have happened quietly over decades. The chapel and other denominational ministries remained important, but it was understood that if one wanted to participate in such communities, an individual should join them as a part of one's private life. As they do today, services continued to be held in the chapel. For a number of years sermons were broadcast on WGN Radio. Choral and organ performances, considered among the best in the city, were regularly offered. Then and now the chapel serves as a center for music and the arts in the university and as a kind of south-side cathedral for the city where funerals, a popular multifaith Thanksgiving service, and other civic events can be held. Each year there is a "packed out" Martin Luther King Jr. Day service at which then state senator and Law School lecturer Barack Obama was once the speaker.

Of ongoing significance to theology and religion at the university is the Divinity School, which cooperates with several denominational seminaries located in Hyde Park. The chapel and its deans have been partners with "the Div School" in several ways. The dean has often been a member of the Divinity School faculty, has mentored ministry students as chapel interns, and more recently has shared a staff member with the Divinity School. During the 1960s the divinity faculty voted to place greater emphasis on the training of MA/PhD students and to reduce the Master of Divinity (preordination) program. Today, master of divinity degree students comprise approximately one-sixth of Divinity School students, and the school maintains a reputation on campus and beyond for its production of young scholars of religion and for the contributions of its faculty, not least in years past those of Martin Marty, a leading historian and interpreter of religion in America. The school's Bond Chapel is also used by Catholics for one of their Sunday masses, by Muslims for Friday prayers, Episcopalians for a Thursday midday Eucharist, and the Orthodox for Saturday evening vespers.

A tradition of progressive Christianity and politics has long been a part of the chapel's ministry. The first dean, Baptist Charles Gilkey, presided for twenty years, during the latter part of which time his son, the theologian Langdon Gilkey, was held a prisoner of war in China by the Japanese. His wartime letters to his parents were read publicly by the dean, and the chapel community understood itself to be activist in support of the war effort. During the Depression, Charles Gilkey had organized a fund for those staff members laid off by the university. He also continued a tradition of social service to the poorest of Chicago's residents, including those in settlement houses.

The second dean, Presbyterian John Thompson, was a southerner who came to the university with an earned reputation as an early and vigorous supporter of civil rights. Martin Luther King Jr. preached at the chapel in both 1956 and 1959. Eventually, Thompson supported striking workers at the University of Chicago hospitals, and his tenure was not renewed. The third dean, Baptist E. Spencer Parsons, was vocal in his opposition to the Vietnam War, supported draft resisters, and was a leader in the local Jane Roe Society, working toward abortion rights. In advance of a police search of the society's materials, Parsons famously hid his papers and files inside the wooden altar of the chapel. Coming from Yale and perhaps also reflecting on the ministry of Bill Coffin there, President Hanna Gray is thought by some to have chosen a fourth dean, Bernard Brown, based in part on her belief that as an Episcopalian, he would be a thoughtful preacher and leader but somewhat less of an activist. His tenure, however, was marked by a perhaps somewhat quieter, but strong support for the justice issues of his day.

In 1994–95 a study was done that took into account the diverse religious picture at the university and encouraged a further broadening of the chapel's programming and for the dean to be yet more of a resource to people of any religious background, opening the possibility that a future chief religious officer might be other than a Christian. The first woman dean was then appointed, Alison Boden (United Church of Christ), who sought to continue the chapel's tradition of engaged and relevant discipleship. Remembering the university's role in the invention of the first atomic weapons, on the fiftieth anniversary of the bombing of Hiroshima, the chapel served as home to a regionwide observance; Kurt Vonnegut was the guest speaker and Studs Terkel the emcee. On the day of 9/11 and in the weeks that followed, the chapel was open to thousands of people joining for lament and in interfaith prayers for peace. On March 5, 2003, the chapel hosted a student-planned "Teach-in on the Iraq War." More than one thousand students, staff, and faculty listened to senior professors cite their professional and personal opposition to the looming invasion of Iraq. On the day of the inauguration of George W. Bush for a second term in office, the chapel was the site chosen by faculty and artists to stage a "counter-inauguration." None of these and other events went unnoticed by those who opposed them.

During Dean Boden's tenure the chapel structure underwent a major restoration, and with the strong encouragement of President Don Randel (a Princeton educated musicologist), the full restorations of the Skinner organ and the Laura Spelman Rockefeller carillon were begun.[53] For the sake of tradition and because of its size, the major university ceremonies of opening convocation, "Aims of Education," and the summer, autumn, and winter convocations (commencements) are held in the refurbished chapel, although they have no other religious components. The baccalaureate ceremony, designed by the graduating class, does offer a catena of multifaith readings. Due to numbers, the spring convocation is an outdoor event, now without prayer or "religious utterances," as President Robert Zimmer decided that since "the commencement, or convocation, . . . includes people for whom religion is important and for whom it is not . . . it should be reflective and welcoming for the whole community." Commenting on this after her departure to Princeton, Dean Boden thought Zimmer's exclusion of any religious dimension to be a "dated perspective" on inclusiveness.[54]

In April 2006 a ribbon-cutting ceremony was held at the chapel's entrance formally to open the Interreligious Center. The result of years of planning and effort by the dean and the provost, the center makes use of a remodeled chapel basement. It comprises five rooms, one dedicated to the Muslim community's use, one to the Hindu community, plus several rooms that are available to all. With the opening of the center, Dean Boden convened a committee of students from across the more than thirty religious organizations on campus to work together in sponsoring programming, although efforts to create an ongoing body of students interested in dialogue were not successful. At the time of the beginning of the second intifada in 2000, however, a group of Jewish and Arab students had begun an ongoing dialogue group, and several years later Dean Boden also helped lead a continuing Muslim/Jewish dialogue.

With her experience as mentor for the Interfaith Council at the University of Southern California, Dean Elizabeth Davenport has been able to form a strong student Spiritual Life Council at Chicago, and she has developed other programs supportive of the pluralism of religious groups and spiritual activity. With the title Dean of Rockefeller Chapel and Director of Spiritual Life in the newly created Office for Spiritual Life in the Chapel (and now working closely with other university staff leaders through the Office of Vice President for Campus Life and Dean of Stu-

---

[53] In a 2005 sermon in Rockefeller Chapel the soon-to-be-leaving Randel set out his determination to help raise the funds for the restorations. The Randel State Trumpet pipes were named to honor his dedication.

[54] In Stephen R. Strahler, "Math on the Midway," *Chicago Business*, March 24, 2008.

dents), Davenport sees her ministry reaching out to a diversity of students and others with spiritual interests throughout the university community, with the chapel continuing as a vibrant "hub" for worship, the arts, meditation (e.g., Yoga on Tuesday nights; a Zen Buddhist group on Wednesdays), conversation, and pastoral care.

STANFORD UNIVERSITY

B. Davie Napier, Stanford's dean of the chapel during the turbulent 1960s, was later my colleague for several years in Berkeley as heads of schools in the Graduate Theological Union. We worked on a book together, and he gave me an introduction to the role of religion and of Memorial Church at Stanford. He was succeeded as dean by Robert Hamerton-Kelly (1972–86), who had earlier been a friend of mine in teaching New Testament studies in Chicago-area seminaries and who invited me to preach and visit the campus. Later, President Donald Kennedy asked me to consult with him and others at the university about the future roles of religion and religions at Stanford, and it is probably not too much to say that I helped talk Robert Gregg into agreeing to become the next dean of the chapel and then dean for religious life (1987–2000). He had earlier aided me in bringing Sue Anne Steffey Morrow to Princeton, and, in turn, invited Floyd Thompkins to come from Princeton to the Office of Religious Life at Stanford as associate dean. Then Patricia Karlin-Neumann, who had been a Hillel rabbi at UCLA and for a time at Princeton, came to Stanford in 1996 to be senior associate dean for religious life.[55]

George Marsden used a photograph of Stanford's Memorial Church for the cover of his classic study *The Soul of the American University.* Standing at the center of the campus, *MemChu,* as it has been both affectionately and at times dismissively known, represents something of the schizophrenic attitude toward the sacred that has been with Stanford from its beginnings in 1902. Determined to wrest good from the tragic death of their young son, Jane and Leland Stanford established the school in Leland Junior's memory. Although the founding faculty advocated for a library in the geographic heart of the university, Jane Stanford insisted that the mile-long Palm Drive lead to Memorial Church. While the first president, David Starr Jordan, enjoined that "in its religious life, as in its

---

[55] Patricia Karlin-Newman has been my partner in writing these Stanford observations.

scientific investigations, [Stanford] should be wholly free from outside control,"[56] Jane Stanford professed that she would prefer to see church life stand out in the future life of every student. "While my whole heart is in the university, my soul is in that church."[57]

Although in the hearts of the Stanfords the new university was meant to be remarkably egalitarian for the times, and the Stanford Founding Grant (amended in October of 1902) insisted that "the University must forever be maintained on a strictly non-partisan and non-sectarian basis,"[58] that inclusivity did not easily extend to the religion of anything other than Protestant Christian. While with Jane Stanford's strong influence the windows and mosaics of Memorial Church notably featured women, and the iconography was rather eclectic, the church was fully Christian in its overall design, and worship was generally according to the Episcopal Book of Common Prayer.

One could, however, continue to hear the impetus of a trailblazing, progressive spirit in matters of religion as well as education generally. In his charge to Stanford's Pioneer Class, President Jordan held the new university to be "hallowed by no traditions; it is hampered by none. Its finger posts all forward."[59] At the church's 1903 dedication, the first chaplain, D. Charles Gardner, invited Jacob Voorsanger from San Francisco's Temple Emmanu-El to join twelve clergy from several Protestant denominations in the ceremony and to read Solomon's Prayer from the dedication of the temple in Jerusalem. Perhaps somewhat overcome by the spirit of the moment, Voorsanger spoke admiringly of Mrs. Stanford's open-mindedness: "Mrs. Stanford has sat at the feet of preachers of every possible denomination and no denomination . . . Unitarians, Trinitarians, infidels, Brahmins, Buddhists, Mohammedans, materialist, atheists. All have been heard, all were welcomed, the main condition of their welcome being that they must have something to say."[60]

Those who had something to say in Memorial Church and who spoke officially for religion at Stanford remained, however, almost entirely

[56] See Gunther W. Nagel, *Jane Stanford: Her Life and Letters* (Stanford, CA: Stanford Alumni Association, 1975), 14.

[57] See Gail Stockton, *Stanford Memorial Church: An Appreciative Guide for the Not-So-Casual Visitor* (Stanford, CA: Stanford Memorial Church and Office of Public Affairs, 1980), 2.

[58] See "The Founding Grant with Amendments, Legislation and Court Decrees," 21, at https://wasc.stanford.edu/files/Founding Grant.pdf.

[59] "History of Stanford," at http://www.stanford.edu/about/facts/founding.html.

[60] Quoted in Stockton, *Memorial Church*, 8.

Protestant Christian. Certainly the university chaplains were, and through the ensuing decades of world wars, Depression, and recovery, and despite Stanford's continuing sense of itself as a forward-looking Western university during times of a growing secularism and changes in the student population, Jane Stanford's October 1902 stipulation that services in Memorial Church "must be simple and informal in character, and the theological questions, services and observances upon which the sects differ should not be entered upon, so that members of every church may worship and receive instruction therein" were recognized as a prohibition of worship other than what took place in Memorial Church.[61] When Clare Booth Luce's daughter, a student, was killed in a 1944 auto accident and a Roman Catholic mass could not be held in Memorial Church, Catholics responded by turning part of an off-campus residence into St. Ann's Church.

Meanwhile, the Jewish community met above a tire store in downtown Palo Alto. But when in 1965 Rabbi Charles Familant became Stanford's first full-time Hillel director, he with other campus ministers argued that while the school was perhaps adhering to the letter of the Founding Grant, its spirit had been subverted. If the Stanfords' desire had been to prevent the university from becoming an instrument of any religious denomination, then prohibiting sectarian worship had, in practice, unintentionally yielded the opposite outcome. This argument found resonance in the President's Committee on Religious Activities, chaired by Professor Richard Lyman, later to become provost and then Stanford's seventh president. Lyman advocated "opening up Memorial Church" and encouraged President Wallace Sterling to bring this finding to the board of trustees. On February 16, 1966, the board of trustees approved sectarian worship "on a trial basis," enabling religious communities to schedule regular worship in the church. But for the Jewish community, the freedom to worship in a building suffused with Christian iconography was scarcely a tenable outcome. Rabbi Familant conveyed to President Sterling and Professor Lyman that some Jews would "find the general surroundings and symbols of a Church incompatible with the spirit that ought to be generated in a Jewish worship service." Charged with serving "the religious needs of all the Jewish students on campus," Familant con-

[61] "Address, Jane Lathrop Stanford to the Board of Trustees of the Leland Stanford Junior University," October 3, 1902, in "The Founding Grant with Amendments, Legislation and Court Decrees," 21.

cluded, "I would find it impossible to conduct services in the Memorial Church building."[62]

While administrators were considering how to accommodate Jewish worship, Rabbi Familant received a call from a bereaved medical student wanting to honor his father. The student sought to recite the traditional *kaddish*, a prayer to commemorate the dead that children are instructed to say for eleven months following the death of a parent. Rabbi Familant organized a daily worship service to be held at 5 p.m. Arranging the time was not difficult. Arranging a place was fraught with problems. He reserved space in the Women's Clubhouse, a meeting place for faculty wives' teas and ballroom dancing, and he publicized not only the daily gathering but also Friday night worship services in the same location. Three Sabbath services were held before Rabbi Familant received a letter from the Office of the President insisting that he discontinue Sabbath services in the clubhouse, since they violated the terms of the Founding Grant.

"Rabbi Barred from Services," proclaimed the front-page headline of the *Stanford Daily.* The article quoted the university position: "Rabbi Familant cannot participate in worship services in any other worship facility but Memorial Church because of the explicit limitation in the February Trustees' resolution which specifies denominational worship at Stanford may be conducted only within the Church. . . . While the University was prepared to authorize informal assembly of Jewish students for the purpose of private prayer, we simply cannot authorize Rabbi Familant to conduct Sabbath services outside Memorial Church."[63] Recognizing that requiring Jews to pray amid the iconography and symbolism of Memorial Church was indefensible, Robert McAfee Brown, a widely respected religion professor and member of the Committee on Religious Activities, urged the administration to find a solution. Other campus clergy refused to conduct worship for their own denominations in solidarity with the Jewish community until adequate provision was made for Jewish students to worship.

Change came even as Davie Napier prepared to become dean of the chapel in 1966. He asserted that he would interpret "*Memorial Church* [emphasis mine] as all worship taking place under the auspices of the

---

[62] Rabbi Charles Familant, "How Jewish Worship Got on Campus," unpublished reflections.
[63] *Stanford Daily*, May 6, 1966, 1.

person responsible for Memorial Church."[64] Permission was then granted by the trustees for Jewish worship to proceed in the clubhouse, and soon Napier was opening up religious life at Stanford in other ways. He related scripture to the turbulent political times and provided leadership for student activism against the Vietnam War. In 1971, in an act of nonviolent disobedience, he blocked entry to the San Mateo Draft Board office. He experimented with University Public Worship, encouraging congregational participation and pioneering jazz and folk music being played in the services. A *Time* magazine article praised the vibrancy of religion at Stanford, both as an academic discipline and a lived practice. "Religion has become one of Stanford's most adventurous intellectual disciplines," the article claimed, "and Dean of the Chapel B. Davie Napier has turned the once staid services at the pseudo-Romanesque Memorial Church into a continuing experiment in worship."[65]

This general spirit of comity with other denominations and religions carried forward during the ministry of South African–raised Methodist Robert Hamerton-Kelly who, in his 1979 letter to Fred Fox and the committees studying the chapel and religion at Princeton, noted that while "University Public Worship" at Stanford continued to be Protestant in character, he had a good and supportive relationship with the Catholic and Jewish chaplaincies—the Catholics now using Memorial Church for a Sunday afternoon mass and the university providing the Hillel Foundation with worship space. This relationship extended to other religious groups that were associated through the Stanford United Ministry. To their cooperative work Memorial Church funding was granted to promote conferences and the like. Hamerton-Kelly stressed the importance to his ministry of his faculty position and teaching and his close reporting relationship to the president. He concluded on a note of optimism and mission with: "my perception that there is a revival of interest in participation on the part of our students, at least, in the life and work of the University Church and other religious groups. I feel more acutely than ever the importance of the moral and spiritual teaching of the great religious traditions in times like ours, when people seem to be searching for values and direction in life. Our own founders were perfectly clear in

---

[64] "Flexibility Urged in Worship Sights," *Stanford Daily*, May 9, 1966, 1.

[65] "Theology: Faith & Learning at Stanford," *Time*, November 25, 1966, 100. In the article, Robert McAfee Brown, recently recruited from Union Theological Seminary in New York to be part of a group of four to teach religion in the humanities division, concluded that "truth and learning can exist in partnership; they need not be antithetical."

their conviction that rootless learning was dangerous, and in the service of that conviction, established this church at the center of the campus."[66]

When the Reverend Dr. Robert C. Gregg, an Episcopal priest and scholar of early Christianity, became dean of the chapel in 1987, the opening up of Memorial Church took on greater meaning. He would appoint the first rabbi to Stanford's university chaplaincy as associate dean, then renaming the department from Memorial Church to Religious Life and the Stanford Associated Ministries to the more inclusive Stanford Associated Religions. Several years later, Dean Gregg brought to campus Ebrahim Moosa, a Muslim imam and scholar, who, while teaching in the Religious Studies Department, became a visiting associate dean for religious life.

Challenged by the enormous damage done to Memorial Church by the 1989 Loma Prieta earthquake, Gregg for three years moved worship to Dinkelspiel Auditorium, quickly christened *MemDink*. The baccalaureate service that in recent years was held in Frost Amphitheater was moved outside to the campus's main space within the quadrangle near to Memorial Church and became yet more fully multifaith in character. Then Gregg supervised the enlarging of the Muslim prayer space in the Old Union Clubhouse and had stations constructed so observant Muslims could wash their feet prior to worship. When he left the chaplaincy to teach full time in the Religious Studies Department, Gregg founded and was the first director of Stanford's Abbasi Program in Islamic Studies.

With Memorial Church no longer the single focus of Stanford's religious life, the need for new and more inclusive religious space became increasingly evident. When Scotty McLennan, a Unitarian Universalist minister who had previously been a poverty lawyer before becoming university chaplain at Tufts University, became Stanford's dean for religious life, most religious groups had offices in the Old Union Clubhouse, a storied, centrally located but dilapidated building. Stanford's Catholic community worshiped in the student union as well as Memorial Church and worked in offices on and off campus. While Hillel had more space than other groups, the members made their home in the Clubhouse's cramped and overcrowded basement. Eventually the Jewish community managed to fulfill a long-held dream of creating an on-campus center, converting a large faculty home into Stanford's first Center for Jewish

[66] Letter of January 4, 1979 to Committees of the Faculty and Board of Trustees, c/o Dr. F. Fox, in Fox Files.

Life. In the spring of 2008, a new adjacent building was dedicated, with a sanctuary adorned by contemporary stained glass filled with biblical imagery and Hebrew letters. It was a far cry from that tire store attic.

Still, Stanford lacked a more inclusive worship space that was welcoming to traditions other than Judaism and Christianity. When the university decided to renovate the Old Union, students advocated to set aside the third floor for religious-life purposes. In 2007, the deans for religious life, Scotty McLennan, Episcopalian Joanne Sanders, and Rabbi Patricia Karlin-Neumann, presided over the dedication of the CIRCLE—the Center for Inter-Religious Community, Learning and Experiences. Stanford now had a sanctuary designed for and dedicated to multifaith worship, with silk banners reflecting and respecting the Buddhist, Bahá'í, Christian, Jewish, Muslim, and Hindu traditions. On any given week, the CIRCLE echoes with the Muslim call to prayer, Buddhist prayer bells, Hindu chanting, and Shinto and Native American drumming, along with Hebrew *davening* and Catholic mass. Programs from a weekly Fellowship for Religious Encounter, bringing together students from across the religious spectrum, to a summer fellowship in Spirituality, Service and Social Change, manifest the range of religious life at Stanford today.

The University of Southern California

Early on in my ministry as Episcopal bishop of Los Angeles, Steven Sample, the new president of the University of Southern California, invited me to his inauguration. We became friends and met from time to time in the first decade of his presidency to talk about the place of religion in the university and also about the Episcopal Church, of which he was an active member—not always agreeing with some of its directions. I was, of course, supportive of the Episcopal chaplaincy on campus and several times came to talk with the chaplain and other students there.

One result of President Sample's interest in Christianity and the relationship of the churches in Los Angeles to the university was an invitation to the Catholic, Lutheran, and Episcopal bishops to preside at an Ash Wednesday service at the university. Cardinal Roger Mahony, Bishop Paul Egertson, and I, who were already working together in a covenant relationship in Los Angeles, said prayers, spoke, and made the sign of the cross with ashes on the foreheads of those who came forward to us on that day of penitence. Moved by the ecumenical sharing, I still could not escape the irony of a witness in fellowship in ashes when not all of us could share in the bread and wine of full Christian communion.

Steven Sample had previously served public universities and came to USC from the presidency of the State University of New York at Buffalo. When Alvin Rudisill (at one time Lutheran campus pastor) retired in 1995 after a quarter-century of ministry as university chaplain, Sample set in motion a process that would include the possibility of getting out of the "religion business" and operating more like a public university by allowing and perhaps even encouraging religious chaplaincies and activities on campus, but favoring none nor supporting religion per se by discontinuing the office of university chaplain. His decision, however, was simultaneously to affirm the importance of religion at the university and at the same time to enlarge that support beyond its core Christian founding. Rabbi Susan Laemmle, who had been the Hillel director at USC, became the first other-than-Christian chief religious officer of any formerly Protestant-aligned university with the new title that she helped to choose, dean of religious life.

Susan Laemmle invited me to become part of an early-phase strategic-planning process for religions at USC, and later I returned the favor by asking her to help with the 2004–5 review of religion and spirituality at Yale. She also had for some years been a member of the advisory board for the Office of Religious Life at Princeton. She and I have several times reflected on the parallels but also on some major differences between USC and Princeton and the roles of their deans of religious life—not least due to USC's urban setting and the cultures of southern California versus those of mid-Atlantic New Jersey. Susan Laemmle assisted in the writing of this overview. She notes in particular that USC is a much larger institution with 17,000 undergraduates and 18,000 graduate students; USC also is the largest private employer in the region.

The University of Southern California was incorporated in 1880 by the Methodist Episcopal Conference of Southern California and keeps as part of its institutional memory the knowledge that the land was provided by Orzo W. Childs, a Protestant horticulturist; John G. Downey, an Irish Catholic pharmacist and businessman and former governor of the state; and Isaias W. Hellman, a German Jewish banker and philanthropist. They and the Methodist founders were all passionate believers in the benefits of education for their frontier area, and a major mission was providing teachers for the public schools of Los Angeles. The Reverend Marion McKinley Bovard, the university's first president, saw the fledgling institution as "Christian, yet non-sectarian."

The affiliation with the Methodist Church continued until 1928 when a board of trustees separate from the church was created, although only in 1951 did the requirement cease that 51 percent of the board had to be Methodists. This relationship with the Methodist Church ran its course without the wrenching controversy that occurred at one-time Methodist Vanderbilt University, while a few years later in 1956 the School of Theology withdrew from USC to become the Methodist-related Claremont School of Theology. The School of Religion continued within the university as a department of religious studies, to which I was at one time appointed as an adjunct.

In 1996 the Center for Religion and Civic Culture was established in large part as a response to the civic unrest following the dismissal of charges against the police officers involved in the Rodney King incident. The sociologist, fellow Episcopalian and professor of religion and sociology, Donald Miller, became its executive director, and I became interested in its studies and programs—at first pertaining to urban Los Angeles but since expanding to the study of cultural and religious issues in a number of other countries.

Religious diversity grew during USC's early decades. Initially, the YMCA and YWCA were the major campus religious organizations, and the Student Christian Associations provided the dominant ministries. The numbers of Catholic and Jewish students then increased, however, to some 15 percent of the student body, and by 1930 campus religious life included a Newman Club, a Hillel organization, a Latter-Day Saints ministry, an Episcopal Club, and a Christian Science organization. The dean of the School of Religion had a role in overseeing religious activities, duties that were assumed by the first official university chaplain, Dr. Clinton A. Neyman, appointed in 1948.

In the decades after World War II other campus religious groups were established, and in 1966 the Office of University Chaplain was moved to a new University Religious Center—a joint project of the university and five Protestant denominations. By the 1970s a small Muslim Student Association began to form and a Bahá'í Club added to the campus mix. Parachurch organizations had also begun ministries at USC, and several high-pressure religious groups (then typically referred to as "cults") had become a problematic presence.

As the first other-than-Protestant and then first dean of religious life to be USC's chief religious officer, Susan Laemmle's job description included pastoral, ceremonial, and supervisory functions formerly fulfilled by the university chaplain. Her job description also encompassed a heightened desire for interfaith cooperation and "leadership in fostering the spiritual and moral life of the USC community." She decided that she could better carry out these responsibilities by reporting directly to the provost rather than the president. The fact that she had been a USC undergraduate, had a PhD in English literature from UCLA and taught USC courses from time to time, and had previously served as USC's Hillel director meant that she had a good understanding of the academic and cultural as well as religious life at the university. President Sample had set "the development of human beings and a society through the cultivation and enrichment of the human mind and spirit" as a central mission of the school, and Dean Laemmle saw her work as contributing to that broad mandate.

As the first rabbi to be the institution's chief religious officer, Susan Laemmle's appointment was an honor to the Jewish community and was understood as another signal to other religious communities that they were welcome on campus. Dean Laemmle used "seed money" to encourage the formation of new student groups in a region that (she would remind people) was the birthplace of Pentecostalism and in a university that prided itself for having a strong institutional history of innovation and entrepreneurship. By the beginning of the twenty-first century there were over fifty religious groups on campus. There was a proliferation of new Christian groups (several of them evangelical and geared to USC's many native-born and foreign Asian students); there were Jains and Zoroastrians as well as the Secular Alliance, and an atheist/agnostic, free-thinking group that characterized itself as "the loyal opposition." Their roles and activities on campus are guided by a "Guidelines and Governance" document and specifically by a chapter, "The Ethical Framework for USC Religious Life," to which all must subscribe. By 2003, through the instigation of Associate Dean Elizabeth Davenport, the Office of Religious Life had created a multifaith calendar and directory that had been influenced by one designed by Sharon Kugler at Johns Hopkins and that, in turn, was influential at other institutions.

For Dean Laemmle, not having a traditional campus pulpit meant doing much of the prophetic work and speaking to the campus through programming. In addition to the "Genesis Conversations" and "The Seven

Deadly Sins," geared mainly to students, and "Genesis," "Job," and "Science and Religion," for faculty, she believes the most important program begun was USC's version of Princeton's "What Matters to Me and Why?" which became "an instant and enduring success." Interfaith activity and learning is also furthered by the proximity of the Hebrew Union College–Jewish Institute of Religion and the Muslim Masjid Omar ibn Al-Khattab and, in a sense, culminates each year in the multifaith baccalaureate service. By 1995 that service had become so sparsely attended that the university considered abolishing it. Its new multifaith character, the participation of the Thornton School of Music's Concert Choir, together with the creation of a following baccalaureate dinner, have now helped make the ceremony and dinner treasured parts of the university's commencement calendar.

The current dean of religious life is Varun Soni, a Hindu, lawyer, and teacher who grew up in southern California, studied in South Africa, and who has recently completed a doctorate in religious studies at the University of Cape Town. Like Dean Laemmle he prefers the title Dean to that of Chaplain, which could carry, for some, more traditional understandings of Protestant chaplaincy rather than his broader university responsibilities. Not being clergy himself, Dean Soni has appointed a Christian with campus experience to be associate dean. If students come to the Office of Religious Life for conversation or counseling, either dean might engage them, seeing themselves (as did Dean Laemmle) as "of" rather than "for" their particular religion, and so being able to, in some sense, serve and represent all religious approaches and the larger campus community.

UNIVERSITIES AND RELIGIONS IN PROCESS

Change is regularly taking place in many departments and programs of modern universities. In summary we can see this to be true of the place of religion and the Offices of Religious Life, or its equivalent, at the seven universities for which we have provided overviews. As times and circumstances alter, these offices and the role of religions more generally are all works in process. The place and function of religion are much affected by differences in histories, locales, size and composition of constituencies, and personalities, and by the presence of graduate and professional schools, including the presence or absence of a divinity school as well as a large university church or chapel building. Significant also, however, are similarities—not least in the contemporary secularism of these once overtly Protestant institutions and, at the same time, in their broad support for pluralism of religions on campus.

While each institution can speak to the important roles of its university chaplain or Office of Religious Life or equivalent, the influence of these programs in the life of the schools appears today less significant for the identity of the institutions and also appears to have become more incorporated into the professional ranks of other university services such as health and athletics. In searching for new heads for these religious life programs five of the major universities under review have in recent years selected individuals who have had experience in such roles at other universities or colleges.

These individuals have also had experience advocating for religious pluralism on their previous campuses and seem to have been chosen for this proven capability. While only the University of Southern California has so far chosen a non-Christian for its religious leadership position, other of the schools have continued to state an openness to this possibility, and the Stanford (Unitarian Universalist) and Yale (lay Catholic) appointments have brought different Christian traditions into the post. With the appointment of Rabbi Patricia Karlin-Neumann as senior associate dean, Stanford has also incorporated religious pluralism into its Office of Religious Life. In terms of further diversity, several of the universities have or have had gay or lesbian chaplains, and four of them have or had women in the lead role. Harvard, Columbia, Penn, and Yale have or recently had African Americans as their head religious figure, and USC now has an Asian American.

Change is part of the character of religions as well as universities. Newer forms of religions, spiritualities, and blended religions may grow on these campuses. While precise forms of change are not readily predictable, it would certainly seem that encouragement for religious pluralism lies ahead, as can next be seen to be very much part of religious life and religions at Princeton today.

FIVE

Religions at Princeton Today

W hile the overall policies for the support of religious life at Princeton have remained essentially the same through the past twenty years, there have been a number of significant shifts in circumstances and developments. Were time travelers from those two decades ago to arrive at Princeton today and ask about these changes, I suspect the first thing they would need to learn is something about the events of 9/11 and the responses to them. I was in South Africa on September 11, 2001, but not long afterward I was at a trustees' meeting when I heard how important were the religious and spiritual resources of the university that Tuesday and in the days following.[1] During the frightening and confusing daylight hours many came to the chapel or the Center for Jewish Life to pray or to talk with chaplains and one another, and at dusk students, faculty, staff, and others from the community streamed into the McCosh courtyard in the chapel's shadow for a candlelight vigil. For the dead and their dear ones there were prayers, music, and then profound silence. Now foreman of the electric shop and often member of the Chapel Choir Kenneth "Kenny" Grayson was, as he had been for many chapel services and university ceremonies, an important behind-the-scenes player for the event. The following Sunday afternoon many from the university came together again, this time on Cannon Green, to hear Professors James McPherson, Marta Tienda, and Toni Morrison meditate on the tragedy. The ninety-strong Chapel Choir sang *Dona nobis pacem* and Bobby McFerrin's "The 23rd Psalm." Weeks later the Office of Religious Life helped to create a memorial to the thirteen Princetonians who had died that September 11, and again the Chapel Choir sang at the dedication.

---

[1] Elected by the alumni to a board of trustees that had once been predominantly clerical, and then with a long tradition of clergy trustees through the time of John Coburn, I had to wonder if I might be the last clergy and theologian to serve on the board for at least some time—perhaps the most evident indicator of the decline in the influence of Christianity and religion generally in the governance of Princeton as well as any number of other universities.

There followed a surge of interest in the role of religions in the world, and at the same time searing concerns were raised regarding religious fundamentalism and fanaticism. Many people, both religious and nonreligious, had questions about whether there was something deep down in the spirit of religions—perhaps particularly a need to see one's religion, morality, and culture as highly superior or truer—that could cause a fear and hatred of others, a willingness to persecute and even kill in the name of one's faith. At first, because of the religion of the perpetrators of the 9/11 murders, those questions were directed primarily toward the Muslim faith, but fair-minded people were able to cite chapter and verse from the scriptures and/or histories of other religions. In response representatives of the different religions could contend that a radical call to peace, to nonviolence, and even to loving one's enemies was at the heart of their religious traditions, and that it was cultural politics and fanaticism that could sometimes use religion for divisive and even murderous purposes. Although religions and cultures were and are deeply entwined, religion has also served as a prophetic critic of its culture as well as a carrier of some of its better qualities. Jihad was not meant to be about bombings and killing innocent civilians. Nor need the response to terrorism by nation-states that are perceived to be predominantly Christian or Jewish be more bombing and "collateral" killing in the tens of thousands in the name of self-defense, prevention, or smart geopolitics. Certainly there was abundant evidence throughout history of "us against them," and that people could kill one another and commit atrocities in battles over economic leverage, land, food, oil, national pride, sex, water—with or without the *benefit* of religion.

Here were more "big questions" for people of faith to study, debate, and pray about while seeking for better understanding—first in terms of their own faith and then in dialogue with others. Was religion in some sense the problem or could it be part of the solution? Or, in some more complex interaction, was it a cause of both considerable human strife and a number of peaceful and reconciling endeavors? How might one better understand what is most profoundly humane in one's own religion and carry that into dialogue and practice with those of other faiths?

And what of the natural environment? Population growth? Economic development at the expense of stress on resources? Water and food shortages? The need for education? Rights and opportunities for women? These challenges cannot be understood apart from the world's increasing technological, economic, and cultural globalization—the benefits globalization has brought and the problems, along with the positive and negative reactions. Would religions be a major help or hindrance? One might try to leave religion and religions out of the discussions, but where else will several billion religious people find the hope and resolve to make the efforts and sharing that seem to be necessary?[2] What additional resources for human caring and cooperation could be developed? Or could technology do it on its own? And what of the interplay between the benefits and downsides of technology and religion—between science, especially microbiology and cell research, and religion?

Princeton continued to be a microcosm of religion in America. Once reflective of the Protestant hegemony and then the ethics of a liberal Protestantism, it now was more and more a diverse community of the religious and secular. Within its secular nonsectarianism it now included Christians and Jews of many stripes as well as Muslims, Hindus, Buddhists, people of other and blended faiths and spiritualities, as well as many from these backgrounds with little or no religious interests and allegiances. How should the university sponsor welcome for them all and encouragement not only to tolerate but also to engage one another while promoting the values of learning and scholarship and service to the nation and all nations? Could, as the trustees had hoped in 1979, this welcome and encouragement continue to "affirm the religious spirit which helped to give birth to Princeton" and expand the "opportunities given on the campus to explore and practice religious faith and values in a variety of traditions and communities of religious faith?"[3]

Were Presidents McCosh or Wilson, Hibben or Dodds to return to Princeton today I doubt whether they would be that surprised by the attitudes of the majority of the college-age group toward morning church or a number of other formal religious activities, much less of anything that smacked of in loco parentis rules. They had noted plenty of that kind of reaction in the "boys" of an earlier Princeton. I can almost see them nudging one another (well, perhaps not Wilson) and swapping stories with the current administration. Were they able to comment further, however, the decidedly less religious rhetoric of the university and the number of students who now come to the college without any formal

---

[2] Among efforts to explore these questions and issues from the perspective of theological ethics, see the four-volume series God and Globalization under the general editorship of Max L. Stackhouse and now in 2009 editions. 1. *Religion and the Powers of Common Life*; 2. *The Spirit and the Modern Authorities*; 3. *Christ and the Dominions of Civilizations*; 4. *Globalization and Grace* (New York: Continuum International). The study project was begun at Princeton Theological Seminary's Center for Theological Inquiry in 1999.

[3] Trustees' Report, 2, 1.

religious background would probably cause conversation. At the same time, one can imagine that a number of previous Princeton presidents and other faculty and administrators would be surprised—perhaps even astounded—at the measure of religious activity and interest in spirituality issues and the open discussions of them. Indeed, I know this was true for Bob Goheen who continued to worship in the University Chapel as his physical condition allowed and remained interested in all that was happening on campus, including the growing diversity of the student body that he had encouraged during his presidency. Because of his early years in India and then later ambassador to that country, he took a particular interest in students whose religious beliefs came from that part of the world.

THE UNIVERSITY CHAPEL

Robert Francis Goheen, the sixteenth president of Princeton University, died at age eighty-six in the early spring of 2008. Several years earlier he had asked me to preside at his memorial service. I told him that I would be honored to do so, but that I hoped it would not be too soon. I also suggested that it would be helpful to the family and myself if he would put into writing some thoughts regarding the character of the service. He bit off a smile and told me he would think about that. In the times we met between that suggestion and his final days there was an unspoken joke between us that I had come, like some angel of death, to check up on his memorial planning.

He had, however, written to me that he had begun a file labeled "someday." In addition to prayers and a reading that he wanted for a smaller service for family, he had sketched the memorial service in some detail. There were two hymns and a prayer attributed to St. Francis. To the surprise of some of his friends, there was jazz: Duke Ellington's "It's Freedom" from *Sacred Concerts* and "The Single Petal of a Rose" from the *Queen's Suite*. His provost and successor as president, Bill Bowen, was to offer "Words of Remembrance." It was a university ceremony as well as a service of song and prayer including the Prayer for Princeton. The Chapel Choir led in the singing of the hymns and the student Jazz Vespers ensemble played the Ellington. Toward the end of the service his wife, Margaret, signaled to me and asked why we were not singing "Old Nassau" one last time with him. We agreed that we would, and I am sure I was not the only one who noted that we were using the gender-inclusive revision. There were more prayers, tears, and thanksgiving as we concluded with Benny Carter's "Vine Street Rumble" from *Harlem Renaissance*. On that day, as we honored and offered gratitude for one whom Professor John Fleming had described as a splendid Christian humanist, we, whatever our religion or understanding of life, knew why we had a university chapel and also that the representative of an era had passed into history.

As the most visible center and symbol for ongoing prayer and Princeton's religious tradition, the University Chapel continues to have its role at other memorial services and at the annual Service of Remembrance for alumni, which now includes memorials for recently deceased faculty and administrative and service staff.[4] Major reunion classes hold their memorial services in the chapel as well, and the chapel office assists with these services that are designed to be as inclusive as possible for all attending.

For tradition's sake and, no doubt, because it is the largest assembly hall on campus, opening exercises for the new students as well as the baccalaureate for the graduates and their families continue to be held in the chapel. They are amalgams—colorful ceremonies and pageantry of a university that is no longer specifically religious—while they are also services of spirituality and prayers offered by chaplains and students of several religions, who all, like Princeton's founders, are supportive of the university's major mission of education. Over a dozen chaplains of various faiths process in their different garb with administrators, marshals, and representative faculty in academic dress, preceded by the Chapel Choir in black gowns with bright orange trim. The prayers, readings, and music may be described as multifaith in a manner that enabled Princeton's first Jewish president (Harold Shapiro 1988–2002), along with colleagues and students of differing faiths, to find themselves comfortable in the service and the building—in President Shapiro's case fully participating in the hymns and prayers. Recently I had the opportunity to talk about these ceremonies with Christopher Eisgruber, provost and Rockefeller Professor of Public Affairs in the Woodrow Wilson School and at the Center for Human Values, who during his senior year in 1983 came to me several times to talk about prayer. He shared with me how in recent years he had discovered and returned to an awareness and some observance of his Jewish roots and faith. Coauthor, among his writings, of *Religious Free-*

---

[4] The annual Commemoration was merged into the service Remembrance in 1992 in order to provide one memorial service for all the Princeton community.

dom and the Constitution,[5] he has reflected at length on religions' roles in American institutions and tells me how fitting and welcoming to all he finds the Princeton ceremonies to be.

Those of us, past or present, who have helped to provide the more formally religious dimensions to university ceremonies, may still, however, have lessons to be learned. I may have made a mistake when asked to provide the opening prayer at the inauguration of Shirley Tilghman as Princeton's nineteenth president. Mindful that I was writing a prayer for the university and its first scientist president, and that I would be invoking blessing on behalf of a diverse audience, I addressed God as the Creator Spirit ("in whom we live and move and have our being," words drawn from Paul's Areopagus speech in the Acts of the Apostles[6]) and as Reconciling Spirit. (The inauguration was being held seventeen days after 9/11.) Both as a Trinitarian Christian and one trying to be inclusive of the religions and spirituality of as many present as possible, I thought calling upon God in this way would be helpful; I even made reference at the end of the prayer to the words of Princeton's motto, "in Your name may this University flourish." But clearly this was not helpful for everyone. One alumnus wrote to the *Princeton Alumni Weekly*, angered that the word *God* had not been used in the prayer, and that Princeton's "Judeo-Christian" heritage had thereby been given short shrift.[7] I had to recognize that he probably was not alone, and that while I could try to defend and explain my choice of words in attempting to be inclusive, I had not been as inclusive as I had wanted to be.

At the university's opening exercises the Princeton president speaks to the new students about the values and purposes of learning. The baccalaureate speakers, who now are invited to speak of "human values, broadly considered," exhort the graduating students to use their learning for the benefit of others. Garrison Keillor, Princeton professors Toni Morrison and John Fleming, and General David Petraeus (Princeton PhD, 1987) have been recent speakers. In 2002 trustee Meg Whitman, Princeton class of 1977 and the president of eBay and who had recently donated $30

---

[5] Christopher Eisgruber and Lawrence G. Sager, *Religious Freedom and the Constitution* (Cambridge, MA: Harvard University Press, 2007).

[6] Acts 17:28.

[7] Letter of Edward Tiryakian ('52), *PAW*, December 5, 2001, 5–6. Only several years later did I learn that Tiryakian, who had a long tenure as professor of sociology at Duke, had also once taught at Princeton.

million for the building of the new Whitman undergraduate college, called upon the graduates to take risks in their lives and be willing to act selflessly. Several students had questioned whether the donation was not the primary reason she had been asked to be the baccalaureate speaker, but she held up her end well. "Life is not about you. It's about what you can do for others." "Your school, community, and country are relying on you to make life better for others."[8] In 2010 Amazon.com's president, Jeff Bezos (whom I had somehow failed to get to know before he graduated from Princeton in 1986), was selected to address these underlying human values at baccalaureate. Noting in his talk "We Are What We Choose" the hard choices one had to make in life, he emphasized those that were for kindness.

Ecumenical Christian worship continues in the chapel on Sunday mornings, on occasion with a Catholic preacher or a speaker from another faith tradition. Dean Alison Boden tells those gathered that they are "the continuing congregation" of those who founded the university and supported and prayed for it over the years.

At nine on Sunday evenings seventy or more Episcopalians and friends gather for worship. Annually they sponsor a popular Easter vigil service that begins with the lighting of the paschal fire outside the chapel before sunrise. Even more often Catholics use the chapel for Sunday and weekday masses. In the chapel Catholics also now have their own small Blessed Sacrament Chapel where the Reserved Sacrament is held in reverence. On Good Fridays and occasions like the annual Festival of Lessons and Carols, Christians of many traditions come together to worship and sing. Graduation ceremonies for the Princeton Theological Seminary and the Westminster Choir College take place in the chapel. Hindus, with bells, candles, dance, and song accompanied by the Chapel Choir, now celebrate the festival of Diwali in this "shared, sacred space" where the multifaith program, Performing the Sacred, also takes place—on those days helping to make the building a temple for all peoples.

The chapel's endowment guarantees the continual care of the building. With its relatively new organ of 137 ranks and almost 8,000 pipes, the stained glass windows recently releaded and restored (at a cost of ten million dollars), and the audio system improved, the chapel continues to be

[8] Meg Whitman, Baccalaureate Address, June 2, 2002, 3. Copy in files of Princeton's Office of Vice President and Secretary.

the site for plays and concerts where students, faculty, and often alumni and other Princeton residents may gather. At many of these services and events one may hear (or perhaps hear whispered) the lightly revised version of Dean Aldrich's Prayer for Princeton that clearly holds multifaith sensitivities in mind.

> O Eternal God, the source of light and life for all peoples, we pray that you would bestow upon this University your manifold gifts of grace; Your truth to those who teach; Your joy to those who learn; Your wisdom to those who administer. To all who work here and all who bear the name of Princeton, give your guiding Spirit of steadfast love and service.

AROUND THE CAMPUS

Considerably more faith practice, conversation, and study takes place beyond the chapel. On some late afternoons and often in the evenings the entrance to Murray-Dodge Hall seems almost a revolving door with students coming for meetings, meals, and worship. The group now named Princeton Presbyterians invites students to Sunday worship in the Nassau Presbyterian church that is effectively on the campus and holds a Sunday evening fellowship service in Murray-Dodge. The Wesley Foundation uses the close-by Methodist Church on Sundays and offers a discussion group in Murray-Dodge on Thursday evenings. The Unitarian-Universalist Campus Community follows a similar pattern with Sunday transportation to a local congregation and a gathering on late Tuesday afternoons in Murray-Dodge.

At ten on Tuesday nights, Catholics, Episcopalians, and Lutherans hold an ecumenical vespers in the chapel. Lutherans, with part-time chaplaincies, invite students to local churches for Sunday worship and have occasional social gatherings in Murray-Dodge. In addition to their Sunday night worship and a late afternoon Eucharist in the chapel on Tuesdays, the Episcopalians also continue to have a Wednesday service and meal at the Proctor House adjacent to the campus.

On a busy campus the activities of some of the former "mainline" Protestant groups can be relatively small. They do, however, provide pastoral care and opportunities for fellowship and support for students from those traditions or those who want to explore them. They are also indications of the continuing willingness of a number of church traditions to be represented at an elite university, knowing that many Princeton's graduates go on to be leaders in business, finance, medicine, education, and government service in America and beyond.

The Orthodox Christian Fellowship has a considerable history at Princeton. The retiring chaplain, Dan Skivir (Princeton class of 1966), is the son-in-law of former chemistry professor John Turkevich, who was the chaplain from 1965 until 1989. The fellowship worships in Murray-Dodge on Sunday mornings, leaving the building redolent with incense. The group also meets in Murray-Dodge on Wednesday evenings. In addition to their regular use of the chapel for daily and Sunday worship, Catholics hold study groups and other meetings in Murray-Dodge and masses, fellowship, and meals at their Aquinas Institute building several blocks from campus.

The Princeton Evangelical Fellowship (PEF), a campus presence since 1931, over the years has been the largest evangelical Christian group; it sees itself as carrying on the tradition of evangelical Christianity at Princeton. It, too, uses Murray-Dodge for Friday evening worship and daily prayer and Bible study meetings. PEF sometimes has smaller meetings in the colleges and holds annual conferences for missionaries and for dealing with other topics. In some measure the PEF is in competition with the Intervarsity Christian Fellowship, although their Tuesday evening meetings in Murray-Dodge are largely for graduate students. The group has a particular appeal to international graduate students from evangelical protestant traditions. The Faculty Commons (a division of the older Campus Crusade for Christ) is an interdenominational ministry directed to graduate students, particularly those who will become teachers. The group is described as "for professors and future professors." Princeton Faith and Action, an evangelical group with links to the Christian Union organization that seeks the "advancing of the kingdom of Jesus Christ in the Ivy League," offers courses on the Bible, fellowship, and discussions of theological issues.

The Manna Christian Fellowship, which separated from PEF in 1993, is more Pentecostal in its worship, with its Large Group Fellowship held in Murray-Dodge on Saturday evenings and its daily prayer meetings. Manna, which is particularly attractive to Asian and Asian American students, also publishes a magazine, *Revisions*, that contains articles by students and others on topics dealing with ethics, religion and psychology, prayer, and service. Often yet more exuberant in its prayer and praise is Athletes in Action, which meets some seventy yards to the west of

Murray-Dodge in Whig Hall. As many as sixty men and women athletes gather for meetings they sometimes call Game Time, and that one student described as feeling bigger "because the people are bigger."

With the opening of a sixth undergraduate college in 2007, Princeton has expanded its student body from 4,800 to 5,200. This expansion, together with greater scholarship assistance to students from lower socioeconomic situations and the decision in 2001 to offer full financial support without loans to students who otherwise could not attend Princeton, has helped to bring about yet greater diversity. Although still a rather socioeconomic as well as academically elitist school, 37 percent of the entering class of 2013 are Hispanic, Asian, African, or Native American, or they self-identify as multiracial, and 10 percent are first in their families to attend college. Impact is one of several groups that "focuses on reaching black students on campus with the gospel and deepening their knowledge of the Bible, while fostering unity and fellowship of the entire body of Christ." The Gospel Ensemble seeks "to spread the Gospel of Jesus Christ through song," while the Hour of Power, regularly led by Associate Dean of Religious Life Deborah Blanks and Baptist Chaplain David Buschman, offers a weekly noonday service for faculty, staff, and students in which clergy from local churches and the Princeton Theological Seminary often participate. Sponsored by the Office of Religious Life, this interdenominational Hour of Power is the most diverse gathering of students, faculty, staff, and community members on campus.

Ordained in the African Methodist Episcopal Church, and with degrees from the Interdenominational Theological Center in Atlanta as well as Princeton Theological Seminary, Dean Blanks was previously an assistant university chaplain at Brown and a US Navy chaplain. For the Office of Religious Life she also facilitates Hallelujah, a student-led worship service "in the African American tradition" held on Sundays at 1 p.m. in Murray-Dodge. Begun in 1990 with the help of then Associate Dean William Gipson, it continues to meet some of the aspirations for community and a deepened spirituality that were evident in conversations with black students of a generation ago. These feelings can be heard in comments from alumni at the time of a twentieth-year celebration of Hallelujah: "In a place that could sometimes be so oppressive and ostracizing I always felt listened to, cared for and renewed." "It helped me to build upon the spiritual foundation I gained as a child . . . and to deal with some of the academic pressures." "We were a diverse group of backgrounds, denominations, and Princeton social circles and [Hallelujah was] a place where we could celebrate each other's triumphs and struggle through each other's challenges." "It helped set me on the path of service, scholarship, and even ministry that I pursue to this day." "The Hallelujah service was literally and figuratively my weekly serving of soul food at Princeton."[9]

While other factors may be involved,[10] the increasing diversity of Princeton's student body, along with the fact that there are more students who come from outside the United States, is one reason why the percentage of Jewish students is down from its peak of at least 18 percent in the early 1980s. Julie Roth, the present Hillel director, estimates that in 2010 it is something like 10 or 11 percent. This still means, however, that there are as many as six hundred Jewish students at Princeton, along with a considerable number of Jewish faculty. The Center for Jewish Life is a going concern—its programs enhanced by further endowment received in recent years. With the overall supervision of the dean of religious life, the university provides funding for the building and for the administration of the center, while the Hillel Foundation and its executive director offer ministry and programs for some twelve diverse Jewish student groups. Cultural, educational, and social activities fill the daily schedule. On Friday evenings there are Reform, Conservative, and Orthodox services followed by Shabbat dinner. Additional Conservative and Orthodox services take place on Saturday mornings. An Orthodox minyan happens three times a day. The ongoing student organization known as Yavneh House helps facilitate social and religious activities for observant Jews at the center.

Food is a vital part of Jewish life, and students may contract with the university dining services to have some or all of their meals at the center. Other students may attend on occasion, too, and so the center becomes a place of hospitality for people of other religious and cultural backgrounds. Although one might wish there could be more interaction with all that goes on in Murray-Dodge Hall, there are many occasions for interfaith meetings and dialogue at the center. Remarkable adventures in

---

[9] In 2010 correspondence from Princeton alumni Yara Delgado, Tshaka Cunningham, Patricia Garcia-Monet, Clarence Hardy, and Douglas Marshall Jr., shared with me by William Gipson and Deborah Blanks.

[10] Some cite recent admissions policies or at least a lack of aggressive recruiting, the urban setting of other universities with whom Princeton is in competition for students, or Princeton's latent reputation for not being the most welcoming of places socially for Jewish students.

sharing among faiths take place. In the spring of 2007, for example, the Hillel director and Princeton's new coordinator of Muslim life led a study tour to Spain. They visited some of the well-known sites and learned more about the centuries when Jews and Muslims lived together in Spain and then later experienced forms of Christian ghettoizing, pressure to convert, and expulsion. Several of the students had also benefited from the teaching of Princeton's professor of Jewish civilization in the Near East, Mark Cohen, who has written extensively about Arab, Muslim, and Jewish relationships in that part of the world and the implications for better understanding today.

In recent years a test of Princeton's acceptance of diversity in religion has come with the presence of a Chabad ministry to the campus. Chabad (from an acronym signifying "Wisdom, Understanding, and Knowledge") or Chabad Lubavitch as it is sometimes known (after the town in Russia, Lyabuvachi, to which it traces its origin), is a Hasidic movement in Orthodox Judaism. Messianic in its faith and hope, Chabad stresses outreach to nonobservant Jews through observance and education in its understanding of Judaism. Its teaching and practices can be controversial among some Jews, not least in what are seen as its tendencies toward separatism. Chabad has gained a presence and a form of acceptance at a number of other universities where its strategy has been to place a young rabbi with a wife and children in a house near to the campus. There they intend to remain for life, raising a large family and using the house as a center for hospitality, teaching, and services until such time as an additional building might be added. Princeton's administration was not at first sure Chabad was a good fit on campus. Faith groups cannot, of course, be forbidden to be in the area, but the university was unsure if it wished formally to recognize Chabad through the Office of the Dean of Religious Life and to give the rabbi the privileges of other chaplains. That recognition, upon the recommendation of the dean of religious life, comes only through the concurrence of the president of the university. When I came to be the interim dean of religious life and the chapel in the spring of 2007, President Shirley Tilghman was leaning toward a negative decision, and my friend and one-time student, Thomas Breidenthal (dean of religious life 2002–7), had recommended against the university recognizing Chabad at that time. I concurred in that advice. President Tilghman and I agreed that it might be wise to wait and see how well their presence would be accepted on campus. And we both recognized they certainly were not going to go away.

The concerns were several, coming primarily from within the Jewish community. Uncertainty was expressed as to whether Chabad's views of the role and value of liberal higher education for its students were fully commensurate with those of the university. There was also a measure of perturbation regarding Chabad's teachings and emphases, particularly its literalistic readings of the scriptural promises regarding all Israel as a Jewish homeland. Perhaps more important was a concern with a relationship to the Center for Jewish Life. The center had been established with the plan that it would be the cooperative hub for facilitating all the diverse Jewish life at Princeton while Hillel had been granted the overall direction and supervision of all chaplaincy at the center. The Chabad rabbi, Eitan Webb, while offering a spirit of cooperation and willingness to make some use the center, evidently did not believe that he could or should put all Chabad's activities under Hillel's supervision.

It was interesting to me that the chaplain who most questioned the decision not formally to recognize the ministry of the Chabad rabbi was Thomas Mullelly, the Catholic Aquinas Institute chaplain. Chaplain Mullelly pointed out that the university had recognized a variety of evangelical groups that presented their particularistic views of Christianity and that while agreeing to abide by the rules and guidelines set by the dean of religious life, they were often somewhat separatist in their teaching and activities, stressing their distinctiveness. Tom Mullelly might have added, "as do Catholics," for I surmised that despite the size of the Catholic presence at Princeton, he had some sense of what it could feel like to be marginalized and thought to be separatist in one's religious beliefs and practices. Perhaps more to the point, I knew that he had had to make his own considerable efforts to negotiate a place for the more conservative Catholics on campus and their pressures for yet more distinctiveness and stress on their understandings of Catholic teaching and morality. Opus Dei had been active in Princeton for over twenty-five years and had its own house and clergy. Tom had worked to give them a role in Catholic services and ministries in the chapel. Thus, as far as Chabad was concerned, fair-mindedness and wisdom about relationships meant, as Chaplain Mullelly put it, "better in than out."

I was also impressed with a small group of students who came to discuss the matter with me. One was a son of alumnus Michael Scharf, whose founding gift had been important for the beginnings of the Center for Jewish Life but who had then felt some sense of disillusion when the religious use of the facility was placed under the sole supervision of Hillel.[11] I particularly remember Arthur Ewenczyk (class of 2009 and later the student president of Chabad), who politely but firmly held that Chabad was being singled out for reasons that did not apply to other religious groups on campus. I listened and tried to explain but had trouble refuting his contentions regarding the distinctiveness of other religious programs and Ewenczyk's pointing out that there was a group of students who appreciated the ministries of Chabad and that this was a major criterion for the recognition of other chaplaincies at Princeton. I reminded Arthur that no one was forbidding a student Chabad group to have recognition on campus. It was, however, then that I learned that even the Chabad student group had had to struggle for an official recognition that is usually rather readily granted. Rabbi Webb had come to Princeton in late 2002, but it was not until late in 2006 that the student group received recognition, and only then, several interested observers told me, after the university had given campus status to the evangelical Faith and Action, which had also earlier been denied recognition as a student group but had threatened a lawsuit.[12]

I began to think that I had not given President Tilghman the best counsel on the matter—that I had not researched the issues and personalities sufficiently thoroughly, including noting the recent reception of Chabad at other universities. Those feelings were later confirmed when I was able to share a kosher luncheon and conversation with Eitan Webb. We began as he led us in the blessing over the food: *Baruch ata Adonai Eloheinu Melekh ha-olam, ha-motzi lehem min ha-aretz.* He then expounded on how the blessing presented four different ways of referring to and thinking about God, "who brings forth bread from the earth"—"You, Lord, God, King of the universe." I told him that I had learned to translate his word "King" as "Sovereign," and he said that was all right for some, but he politely reiterated "King."

Firmly dedicated and devout in Chabad's beliefs and practices, Rabbi Webb seemed remarkably irenic toward other Jews as well as those of different religions. Only when it came to the promised land of Israel did I hear unyielding resolve, although certainly more from a biblical and

---

[11] Scharf gifts to the Chabad ministry have been significant. It is now officially the Scharf Family Chabad House at Princeton University.

[12] Faith in Action had evidently been denied recognition largely because of its links with the Christian Union organization, publisher of the *Ivy League Christian Observer*, and its being a strong critic of the lack of vital Christian faith and witness in the elite Ivies, with its leadership not seeking the form of campus ministry that official recognition would entail.

theological determinism than any political alignment with the present state of Israel. A careful teacher, so well educated in his religion, he offered me thoughtful explanations of Chabad's messianic beliefs and views on education. The essentials of Chabad's Judaism, he explained, taught that every Jew was called to be a messenger of God's goodness and love in the world. Some Jews could best do this by dedicating themselves to the practices of Chabad's orthodoxy. Other followers of God, he assured me, could become such messengers in their own ways. The delay in Princeton's formal recognition of Chabad had been, he thought, unnecessary, but he did not disagree with the proposition that it may have brought about a more appreciated welcome in the university.

Indeed, it now is the case that the Princeton Chabad Student Group is listed as one of the recognized student organizations, and on the website of the Office of Religious Life and in its official brochure, one finds Rabbi Eitan Webb among the recognized chaplains, along with notice of the Shabbat dinners and the Thursday challah baking and coffee. When Alison Boden came to Princeton from her position as dean of Rockefeller Chapel at Chicago, she brought with her an experience of Chabad's ministry at the University of Chicago and awareness of its presence on other campuses. In the spring of 2008 she attended a Shabbat dinner in the Chabad house on Edwards Place next to the campus, as then did President Tilghman, along with nearly a hundred students who were there to witness to their appreciation of the Chabad ministry. A manner of live-and-let-live modus vivendi was adapted between Chabad and the Center for Jewish Life, and a still greater diversity between and among religions at Princeton was given official recognition.

As the number of Muslim students at Princeton has grown, so has the ministry. The Muslim Student Association was formally organized in 1995, and now in Murray-Dodge there is a Muslim Prayer Room set aside as a *Musalah*, or little mosque, with foot washing stations for use before prayer. On Fridays at around 1 p.m. some eighty undergraduate and graduate students come to Friday prayers in the West Room of Murray-Dodge. Halal meat is served on Fridays at the Frist Student Center and at other dining facilities. During Ramadan the food services of the university seek to accommodate the special meal hours for Muslims. In the 2007–8 academic year, through the Office of Religious Life Princeton hired its first coordinator of Muslim life. (The designation "chaplain" is only sometimes used, in part because it is felt that it is not that well understood among Muslim students and "coordinator" seemed a better description of the ministry.) News of the appointment brought several letters of protest to my office in the time I was interim dean, but the other chaplains either accepted or welcomed Khalid Latif's half-time ministry until he went on to be the Muslim chaplain at New York University and the city's Police Department. Now Sohaib Sultan is the university's first full-time coordinator of Muslim life. Born in North Carolina of a Pakistani father and a mother from India, he grew up and was educated in Indianapolis, at an English school in Saudi Arabia, and in Charlottesville, Virginia. He majored in journalism and political science at Indiana University in Bloomington and then had a short career as an independent journalist in Chicago, where he was asked to write *The Koran for Dummies*,[13] which, on my reading, seems like a book for intelligent people trying to learn about Islam. He then earned a master of arts in Islamic studies and Christian-Muslim relations at the Hartford Theological Seminary and further prepared for his present ministry by serving a part-time chaplaincy at Trinity College and then two half-time ministries at Trinity and Wesleyan. It is, of course, interesting that Sohaib Sultan was born and largely grew up and was educated in the United States and so represents a generation and, in this sense, generations to come of United States citizens whose Muslim faith is now also a significant part of religious life in this country. He tells me that he was raised in a devout family but was skeptical in college, while searching, before he found a faith he could call his own. In that he is, of course, not unlike a number of his peers of several faiths.

Sohaib Sultan is Sunni Muslim, and I asked him how those who were Shias were able to relate to him and participate with the others. He told me that for the present there is no problem. The Shias are smaller in number and once a month he asks one of them to lead the prayer services. If and when their numbers grow, he realized, there could be a desire to have their own worship, not dissimilar to the separate practices of different Christian denominations. From that perspective I was amused as he told me how the Sunnis and Shias negotiate the fifteen-minute difference in the method they use to calculate the end of Ramadan. I could only think of the weeks of difference that often separates Orthodox and other Christian observances of Easter. One of the first lessons I had to learn about

---

[13] Sohaib Sultan, *The Koran for Dummies* (Hoboken, NJ: Wiley Publishing, 2004).

religions in theological seminary is the differences caused by reckoning between solar or lunar or otherwise varying calendars.

I asked Sohaib Sultan about relationships between Muslim students from the United States and those from abroad—whether they had, for instance, stereotypes of each other. Perhaps students from strongly Islamic countries were unsure whether those in the United States fully practiced their faith. Maybe American Muslims wondered about the tolerance and theological sophistication of Muslims from abroad. "Stereotypes do exist," he knew from experience. It helps, he explained, that the Muslim faith is so diverse, making it more difficult for Muslims at Princeton to see their own or any version as the truest or most authentic. They do learn by meeting and praying together, he said, and they are curious. Sometimes they are surprised to recognize each other's depth of understanding of Muslim faith and the strength of their commitments.

He tells me that while his main ministry is with Muslim students, others come to talk to him, sometimes out of intellectual curiosity or because they have an academic question from one of their classes. "I hope," I laughed with him, "that you give them a copy of *The Koran for Dummies*." He also meets with other students when he engages in Jewish-Muslim dialogue, for which he and Rabbi Julie Roth recently received a significant grant, enabling them to further the programs and conversations. Often these conversations are held over meals where students can talk about some of their favorite foods and common dietary concerns. "We are," as one of them recently commented, "in many ways cousins with our faiths coming from the same part of the world." There are occasional Hindu-Muslim dinners as well, and a dialogue with Catholics also takes place.

The Princeton Buddhist group offers programs that include meditation, instruction, and discussions. Murray-Dodge has an interfaith meditation room available to Buddhists and others seeking space for quiet meditation. There is also a small student Bahá'í Club that brings back to my memory the important role that Mehrdad Baghai played in the early days of the Interfaith Council, hardly surprising as Bahá'í teachings stress the spiritual unity and equality of all humankind and the unity of all religions. It is sad and ironic to know the history of the persecution of Bahá'í followers in their Middle Eastern homeland, and one is pleased that they have communities and centers in North America and other countries now, as well as a small presence at Princeton where they can share stories of their faith and vision.

More numerous are Hindu students, who now also have a four-fifths-time coordinator of Hindu life on the staff of the Office of Religious Life, with an office, too, in Murray-Dodge Hall. Vineet Chander's parents came from New Delhi. He was born in New York City and was educated at its public schools before going to Carnegie Mellon, where he was a writing major. Graduating from college in 2000, he chose the George Washington Law School for his law degree and then worked in the Queen's District Attorney's office. Although not brought up in a particularly devout home, he found himself more and more interested in religion, attracted to a tradition of Vaishnavism that he describes as monotheistic and devotional, and, I noted, that also has been characterized as panentheistic; that is, a faith in the Divine Life indwelling all of creation that is also part of the belief of some Christians. It was, he suggested, in some ways comparable to the Sufi tradition of Islam or the devotion of Franciscans, and we were now, I realized, engaged in a comparative religion discussion as he taught me about his faith. While working as a communications officer for the International Society for Krishna Consciousness, Vineet Chander heard of the opportunity at Princeton. He began in the post half time in the 2008–9 academic year and then agreed to take on the ministry on a nearly full-time basis.

Ministry among Hindu students is challenging because of the extraordinary diversity of Hindu life. "Hindu" itself is a word that has come to be used to try to encompass many groups that are sometimes as much culturally Hindu as religious in a Western sense of the word. Vineet Chander offers opportunities for devotional music and fellowship and study of the Bhagavad Gita. Sometimes he guides students in meditation. He recounts with considerable enthusiasm the high point of the year when over two hundred Hindu students, Sikhs, Jains, and others, come together with other students for the celebration of Diwali in the University Chapel. It is, as he tells of it, an evening of devotional music and art, sacred readings, and classical Indian dance that is at its heart a worship service. On those evenings Hindu students think of the chapel as Princeton's "sacred space"—hallowed by the prayers and worship of many.

Vineet Chander converses with students from other religious backgrounds who come to him with questions, and he serves as a spokesperson and resource for the understanding of Hindu beliefs and practices. He notes the particular dietary needs of some Hindus and offers sensitivity training sessions for members of the university's dining services in this regard.

Some sense of the contemporary diversity of faith practice and opportunities for learning and sharing at Princeton can be garnered from reading through the calendar of holy days and holidays for the 2011–12 academic year, which is published by the Office of Religious Life in its brochure and on its website.

Princeton Religious Life Office Holy Days and Holidays Calendar, 2011–12

September 2011
    September 28–October 5: Navaratri begins (Hindu)
    September 29–30: Rosh Hashanah (Jewish)

October 2011
    October 6: Dashehra (Hindu)
    October 8: Yom Kippur (Jewish)
    October: Sharada Purnima, Lakshmi Puja (Hindu)
    October 13–19: Sukkot (Jewish)
    October 20: Sh'mini Atzeret (Jewish)
    October 21: Simchat Torah (Jewish)
    October 26: Diwali (Hindu, Sikh, Jain)
    October 20: Birth of the B'ab (Bahá'í)
    October 31: Tulsi Vivaha (Hindu)

November 2011
    November 1: All Saints Day (Christian)
    November 10: Guru Nanak's Birthday (Sikh)
    November 6: Eid al-Adha (Islam)
    November 12: Birth of Bahá'u'lláh (Bahá'í)
    November 4–7: Hajj, Pilgrimage (Islam)
    November 24: Thanksgiving—Interfaith
    November 24: Gita Jayanti (Hindu)
    November 27: First Sunday of Advent (Christian)

December 2011
    December 5: Ashura (Islam)
    December 8: Bodhi Day/Rohatsu (Buddhist)
    December 21–28: Hanukkah (Jewish)
    December 25: Christmas (Christian)
    December 26–January 1: Kwanzaa (Interfaith)

January 2012
    January 1: New Year
    January 6: Epiphany (Christian)
    January 7: Orthodox Christmas (Eastern Orthodox)
    January 23: Chinese New Year (Confucian/Daoist/Buddhist)
    January 28: Vasant Panchami (Hindu)

(continued)

(*continued*)

February 2012
　February 3: Shivaratri (Hindu)
　February 4: Mawlid an Nabi (Islam)
　February 15: Nirvana Day (Buddhist)
　February 27: Clean Monday—Lent begins (Eastern Orthodox)
　February 22: Ash Wednesday, start of Lent (Christian)

March 2012
　March 8: Purim (Jewish)
　March 8: Holi (Hindu)
　March: Vaisakhi (Hindu)
　March 21: Naw Ruz (New Year's Day) (Bahá'í/Zoroastrian)

April 2012
　April 1: Ram Navami (Hindu)
　April 1: Palm/Passion Sunday (Christian)
　April 6: Mahavira Jayanti (Jain)
　April 6: Good Friday (Christian)
　April 7–14: Pesach (Passover) (Jewish)
　April 8: Easter (Christian)
　Palm Sunday (Eastern Orthodox)
　April 13: Holy Friday (Eastern Orthodox)
　April 14: Vaisakhi (Sikh)
　April 15: Pascha/Easter (Eastern Orthodox)
　April 21: Ridvan (Bahá'í

May 2012
　May 6: Buddha Day—Visakha Puja (Buddhist)
　May 27–28: Shavuot (Jewish)
　May 27: Pentecost (Christian)
　May 29: Ascension of Bahá'u'lláh (Bahá'í)

Religious Studies

Princeton's Religion Department has continued to widen and develop its offerings to include the study of a number of religions. While it does so from predominantly historical and analytical perspectives, the fifteen full-time faculty feel freer now than they might have some years ago to examine with an in-depth understanding the beliefs and practices of religious believers past and present. Several faculty are believers—others agnostics, nontheists, or atheists. Students have opportunities to study specific aspects of particular religions in courses like The Early Christian Movement, Muslim South Asia, God and Creation in Ancient Judaism, African American Religious History, and Mind and Meditation in the Buddhist Tradition. Other courses such as Religion and Existentialism, Religion and Medicine, and courses on nonviolence, ethics, fiction, movies, and religion and politics often deal with several religions and have cross-disciplinary dimensions. Dean of Religious Life Alison Boden has taught a course that looks at Women, Religion, and Human Rights in Islam, Hinduism, and Christianity. During their junior and senior years some forty students have their major concentration in the Religion Department, but many hundreds of Princeton undergraduates will take at least one course in religious studies while at the university. The department also has eight or so graduate students who will sometimes interact with undergraduates while working as teaching assistants. Two of its more well-known professors, Elaine Pagels and associate faculty member Cornel West, are among the most widely read religious scholars in the world. The offerings of the Religion Department are augmented by the Program in Judaic Studies (begun in 1996) with courses enabling students to gain an interdisciplinary perspective on the history, religion, and culture of Judaism from biblical times to the present. With its film series, conferences, and exhibitions the program also serves as a resource for programs of the Center for Jewish Life and the Center for the Study of Religion.

Princeton's Center for the Study of Religion, with its faculty associates and seminars for graduate students from different departments, was begun in 1999 to foster yet more interdepartmental study of religion and its practice. Graduate students from English, history, anthropology, religion, sociology, comparative literature, classics, Near Eastern studies, and politics meet and study together in seminars such as Religion and Public Life and Religion and Culture. Postdoctoral fellows may join in the Buddhist Study Workshop and the program in Christian Thought and Practice. Directed by the foremost sociologist of religion and student of religious pluralism in America, Robert Wuthnow, the center also offers a number of public symposia and lectures for university students, faculty, and a wider audience. These symposia deal with religious understandings and beliefs as well as customs and practices—from prayer and meditation to economics and politics and the relation of religion to science and medicine.

Center associate and professor of religion Jeffrey Stout, for example, presented through center programs the themes of his book, *Democracy and Tradition*, which envisions opportunity for appropriate use of a variety of religious as well as secular points of view in public discourse. And then he discussed his *Blessed Are the Organized*, which describes how through grassroots democracy local community and church groups have organized to help some of the most challenged members of American society.[14] David Miller heads up the center's Faith and Work Initiative and teaches an undergraduate course called "Business Ethics and Modern Religious Thought." While Princeton has come a long way since "theology" taught as biblical studies, philosophy of religion and ethics could together be called the "queen of sciences" and seen as a central integrating subject for knowledge and human understanding, the significance of the study of religion in academia has yet reestablished itself. As President Harold Shapiro noted at the center's inauguration, "It is quite extraordinary to realize that, while millions, even billions of people view so many different concerns through the lens of their religious faith, this crucial subject remains one of the most understudied social phenomenon of the twentieth century. We are determined to change that for the twenty-first century."[15] When full funding for the permanent endowment of the center proved difficult to obtain, the university backed up its words with money from general funds. The interfaith character and purposes of the center were underscored by Bob Wuthnow when discussing his study of faith-based social services in America: "Our rhetoric about respecting religious diversity rings false if we don't really understand those other faiths. . . . This is a place where colleges and universities have a major role to play in promoting those conversations among the diverse people on campus and in communities."[16]

The allied Center for Human Values continues to probe a variety of ethical issues both in public and private life and will, from time to time, include more specifically religious questions and perspectives in its purview. Some years ago I attended an intriguing and yet at times amusingly unfocused (due largely to Buckley) seminar, "Mind, Faith, Spirit" with James Forbes, William F. Buckley Jr., and Laura Geller, hosted by Bill Moyers. In a society and university that no longer holds common values based in the same religious teachings, the center can be regarded as an ongoing experiment for exploring resources in humanistic, utilitarian, and other forms of philosophical and applied ethics. The election of Peter Singer to a distinguished professorship in bioethics in the Center for

[14] Jeffrey Stout, *Democracy and Tradition* (Princeton, NJ: Princeton University Press, 2004) and *Blessed Are the Organized: Grassroots Democracy in America* (Princeton, NJ: Princeton University Press, 2010).

[15] Shapiro at the inauguration of Center for the Study of Religion. Quotation in the center's 2001–2 brochure.

[16] Wuthnow in "Princeton Scholars Examine Intersection of Politics and Religion," *PWB*, May 31, 2004, 6. His book is *Saving America? Faith-Based Services and the Future of Society* (Princeton, NJ: Princeton University Press, 2004).

Human Values at Princeton in 1999 was a significant sign of Princeton's willingness to be open to this exploration. It did, however, cause a fellow trustee at the time (then campaigning for president of the United States) so to object to several of Singer's ethical positions that he temporarily withdrew his donations to the university. I was pleased to learn that the then dean of religious life, Joseph Williamson, promptly invited Singer to speak to a faculty group to continue the exploration and to see what values and virtues might be found in common.

Note should also be taken today of the role of the Princeton Theological Seminary in the larger community and in relation to the university. It has been well over a century since the seminary might have been seen as any kind of competitor or a locus of theological or sectarian controversy for the university. With an endowment larger than that of many institutions of higher education, the seminary is able to carry on its own mission apart from the university and yet offer useful ways of cooperation in terms of the working together of libraries, language courses, some cross-registration and faculty assistance for graduate students from both institutions (I once taught several courses at the seminary), and sharing special lecturers and speakers. Seminary faculty and students take advantage of lectures and symposia at the university, and several seminary faculty and visitors are often worshippers and sometimes participants in the Sunday chapel services. Two seminarians continue to be chosen each year to be chapel assistants and sometimes to offer informal short courses for students.

OFFICE OF RELIGIOUS LIFE

When Joseph Williamson became dean (1990–2001) the title had been changed to dean of religious life and the chapel better to reflect the expanded oversight and roles of the dean and also to signal the possibility that one day a dean of religious life might not also assume the duties of a dean of the chapel. Sue Anne Morrow continued to serve as associate dean until 2003, providing a remarkable twenty-two years of continuity and leadership as the many programs and activities of the office continued forward and developed. She took these experiences and skills with her to a multifaith ministry as school chaplain at the nearby Lawrence-ville School.

The myriad multidenominational and interfaith activities of the Office of Religious Life are now presided over by Dean Alison Boden, who came to Princeton in 2007 bringing with her twelve years of experience as dean of Rockefeller Memorial Chapel at the University of Chicago and previous to that as university chaplain at Bucknell University. The office describes its ministries in these terms:

> The Office of Religious Life promotes Princeton University's care and support for the many religious communities that flourish on its campus. We seek to support all religious traditions in the practice and expression of their faith, and we strongly encourage interfaith dialogue and cooperation. We also seek through our own programs and in collaboration with others to provide opportunities for community service, cross-cultural understanding, and constructive social action.

While the work and programs of the office are campuswide, the concourse for much of the activity continues to be Murray-Dodge Hall. The crowded third floor houses shared offices for the Catholic, Episcopal, Baptist, Lutheran, Presbyterian, Methodist, Manna, PEF, and Faculty Commons chaplains alongside those of the Hindu coordinator of religious life, with the Muslim Prayer Room and the Interfaith Meditation Room just up the hall. On the floor below are the offices of the dean, the coordinator of Muslim life, and the associate deans—Deborah Blanks having been at Princeton for fourteen years and Paul Raushenbush, who has now become the religion editor for the *Huffington Post*, leaving Princeton after eight years of ministry. Just to walk into Murray-Dodge during late afternoons or early evenings can be a revelation about religious diversity, dress, and practice. It is true even in daytime hours as students from different faith traditions cannot help but see and encounter one another. As they are all Princetonians and share a common language, it is easy to strike up or overhear a conversation: "Do you eat any particular food at the end of Ramadan?" "Why do you take your shoes off?" "What does it mean to make the sign of the cross?" Sometimes it is simple curiosity that leads to learning about another's faith practice and perhaps to new friendship.

Paul Raushenbush is a great-grandson of both Supreme Court Justice Louis Brandeis, that crusader for social and economic justice who was

appointed by Woodrow Wilson as the first Jewish justice, and Walter
Rauschenbusch, the leading figure of the Social Gospel movement of the
late nineteenth and early twentieth centuries. In 2007, on the hundredth
anniversary of the publication of Walter Rauschenbusch's *Christianity
and the Social Crisis*, great-grandson Raushenbush edited a new publication of the book along with chapters of commentary and reflection by
contemporary religious social justice advocates such as James Wallis and
Princeton's Cornel West.[17] Ordained an American Baptist minister, and
having been an part-time editor for Beliefnet.com and the *Huffington
Post* and author of a multifaith advice and guide book for young people
on spirituality and religious issues,[18] Paul Raushenbush has in recent
years also been codirector of the Program of Religion, Diplomacy, and
International Relations at the Liechtenstein Institute on Self-Determination
at Princeton. The director of the institute, Wolfgang Danspeckgruber, is a
lecturer at the Woodrow Wilson School and a member of the chapel ecumenical congregation. Dean Raushenbush has been especially helpful to
Danspeckgruber in the selection of fifteen students who become Fellows
on Religion studying the "multiple intersections of religion, diplomacy
and international relations."

One of Paul Raushenbush's major ministries has been with the Religious Life Council (RLC), a continuation of the earlier Interfaith Council.
Revived and renamed in 2001, the council consists of some twenty-five to
thirty students and meets on a weekly basis, usually over a vegetarian
meal. The purpose of the meetings is to learn from one another, to encourage spiritual understanding and growth, and to plan various programs for the university. While about half of the members represent
Christian and Jewish groups, there are, as well, Muslims, Hindus, and,
regularly during the school year, one or more Sikhs, Buddhists, Unitarians, Mormons, Zoroastrians, and representatives of the Jain and Bahá'í
faiths. There have been Quaker members and regularly there are also
"seekers," or those describing themselves as "unaffiliated" (and sometimes "secular humanists," "agnostics," and "atheists") who often ask the
best of questions. About half of the weekly meetings are "open" when
other students are invited to come and share in the topic of the day. One
of their more entertaining but also informative sessions is called "Speed

[17] Paul B. Raushenbush, with the original 1907 text of Walter Rauschenbusch, (New
York: HarperCollins, 2007).

[18] *Teen Spirit: One World Many Paths; Your Guide to Spirituality and Religion* (Deer-
field Beach, FL: Health Communications, 2004).

Faithing: The Worlds Religions—Each in 5 Minutes," when students display both their knowledge and their craftiness in pouring forth the attributes of their faiths. With funding from an anonymous donor, the RLC holds an annual retreat, alternating between urban and more rural sites, where the group has time for extended discussions and opportunities to share their spiritual autobiographies, meals, and time for quiet reflection. Members encourage their respective religious groups to offer "Open Houses," when other students are invited to their worship and for conversation and hospitality. In a sense, all this culminates in an evening of "Performing the Sacred," when religious groups come together in the chapel to offer music and other aspects of worship from their traditions. The RLC also sponsors an Interfaith Day of Service in which other students can join them in such activities as cleaning up a park in Trenton or meeting and sharing with a local group of teenage leaders.

"What Matters to Me and Why?" has been continued under the auspices of the RLC. As in the past, the "why?" often proves to be the more challenging part of that assignment. Among speakers in recent years have been President Tilghman; Dean of Admissions Janet Rapelye; and Nobel Prize winners Eric Wieschaus, professor in molecular biology, and professor of psychology and public affairs Daniel Kahneman. Another important ministry has been a panel for the upper-class residential council advisors on interfaith awareness, providing insights and understanding they can share with incoming students.

Council members also have the opportunity to meet with their counterparts on other campuses. In 2005 the Princeton Religious Life Council sponsored a "Coming Together" conference of representatives of multifaith councils from some thirty-five universities and colleges. At this first now-annual gathering (since held at Johns Hopkins, the University of Southern California, the University of Puget Sound, and again at Princeton), programming ideas to promote conversation and cooperation among religious group were discussed. Other subjects were the planning of interfaith prayer services, the joys and challenges of being religious students on campus, and a sacred text study on war and peace issues and questions. The RLC at Princeton sent representatives to the 2009 Parliament for the World's Religions held in Melbourne. In addition, Dean Raushenbush has led a form of pilgrimage for small groups of students to India and other countries. They have met with the Dalai Lama and other religious leaders. One can imagine the interest of the other students when these representatives return and report on their pilgrimages and their meetings of the Parliament for the World's Religion and with representatives of multifaith councils from other universities.

Funding for the RLC has meant that each member of the council can apply for a one-time fellowship to pursue activities they believe will enhance their spiritual growth. Often this opportunity involves a trip to a spiritual homeland, meeting there with others of their faith and then bringing these experiences back to share with friends at Princeton. At one of the annual retreats and again at a recent evening meeting I was invited to participate and hear of some of these trips and activities. I related stories from old Interfaith Council days, and they reported that they continued to discuss "Big Questions." The list of topics they presented was daunting: Sin. Conversion. Truth. Peace. Conflict. Creation. Prayer. Worship. Gratitude. Modesty. Faith. Reason. Food. Service. Fasting. Angels. Skepticism. Hope. Death Penalty. Interfaith Relationships. Contemplative Practice. Prayer. Scripture and Literalism. Forgiveness. Salvation. Race. Sin. Death. Academics. Music. Sexuality. The puckish side of me wanted to ask why they had left out sports, but I contented myself with a question that did interest me. "How," I asked, "do you think the Internet has changed the way you relate, communicate with one another, and gain information about people's different religions and practice in comparison, say, with students of even just ten years ago?" They guessed that some things had changed a good deal. They could go through search engines to various websites and sources to learn about other religions. Through Facebook and other social networks they could share some of their thoughts and experiences with one another and readily put out information about meetings and programs. They found that valuable but, while exchanging eye contact and smiles, they maintained that there was no substitute for personal experiences and coming to know one another.[19]

With the assistance of her administrative staff, Dean Boden helps coordinate, guide, and inspire all this activity and conversation. Decisions have to be made about money, especially now after the deep recession and loss of a significant percentage of university endowment. There are occasional

[19] The importance of coming personally to know those of other faiths and beliefs (not least through intermarriage) is frequently noted by Robert Putnam and David Campbell in *American Grace* as the "grace" that is able to bridge religious differences. See 516–50.

disputes to settle. Not long ago several Mormon students had to be reminded of the agreement that campus groups are only to solicit and hand out information at select locations on campus between the hours of 9 a.m. and 5 p.m. Alison Boden is the chief reminder of the need for civility, care, and empathy in discussions about religious issues and differences. She finds this empathy particularly valuable in her teaching about women's issues, rights, and challenges in the different faith traditions—a set of core religious and cultural concerns that she and many others see as of primary importance in the improvement of educational standards and economic and social development in every part of the world. She shares these and other multireligious and cross-cultural interests with students in class, conversation, and by means of field trips. These trips have included study visits she led to meet and talk with religious leaders and activists in Bolivia and Venezuela; a forthcoming trip to Cambodia will look at religious responses to issues of human trafficking.

The days are past when a dean of the chapel might be seen as acting for the president of the university in the religious, moral, and ethical life of the college, and in so doing reporting directly to the president and sitting on the highest councils of the administration. It was perhaps inevitable that as the modern university continued to grow in size and complexity, new presidents would want to streamline reporting roles. In this regard Princeton now more resembles its peer institutions in which institutional support for religious life on campus is viewed as among the several important extracurricular programs and services the university provides for those who want and need them. Dean Boden reports to and has frequent meetings with the vice president for campus life. She finds the vice president is highly supportive of her ministry, and the meetings help keep her plugged in to what is going on in the university.[20] On a relatively contained residential campus, she remains a visible and well-known figure who, she tells me, has the ear of the president and other administrative leaders whenever she feels she needs it, and when death or other tragedy strikes the campus these leaders will often act together with her in a pastoral role to the community. She meets regularly with peer officers in student services, including the director of athletics, the dean for undergraduate students, and the head of health services; she finds that she is

---

[20] Janet Dickerson (vice president for campus life, 2000–2010) was instrumental in helping the Office of Religious Life expand to include the coordinators of Muslim and Hindu life.

often consulted in important issues regarding the emotional and physical as well as spiritual health of students. In recent years, she notes, she has had to devote considerable time to pastoral relationships with university staff and faculty who are experiencing various forms of stress due to the financial pressures felt within the institution.

Indeed, the counsel of the dean of religious life is available to members of the university community for any number of issues, such as emotional, academic, spiritual, and moral health—issues small and large but always of moment to someone. Dean Boden and I discussed a conversation I had had with Professor Robert George, who has a well-earned Princeton and national reputation as a distinguished professor of jurisprudence and for defending conservative principles in ethical and theological as well as political matters. A Roman Catholic and advisor to the Anscombe Society, "Robby" George was, I quickly learned, both as outgoing and as trenchant and careful a thinker as I had been led to believe. I suspected we could have reached agreement on several matters and disagreement on others, while wanting to believe that we could find some common ground regarding the emotional and spiritual health of persons seeking faithful sexual relationships. George particularly wanted me to know how disturbed some freshmen women of several faiths had been when required to participate in student-led orientation sessions with the name "Sex on a Saturday Night." They felt, he told me, that the sessions had the "aura" of condoning if not even commending a measure of sexual permissiveness as a form of sexual liberation—to the extent of also making jokes about chastity. I felt there was probably a measure of truth in what he was telling me, while my queries to university personnel about the need for such a required orientation session were met with responses such as: most of the orientation sessions were thoughtful and dealt with important issues of sexual and relational responsibility. In any case, it was added, most freshmen at Princeton in this day and age were experienced and wise enough to deal with occasional efforts at attention-getting humor and some healthy kidding around on the subject of sexual relations. Still, I wondered if it was not legitimate to ask whether there were better ways to help "orient" young women or other sensitive souls from, say, a conservative Muslim, Christian, or Jewish home to student life at Princeton.

Another matter that had come up in the spring of 2007 was the future of the Student Volunteers Council and a planned change in its supervisory encouragement. From a historical perspective, it is interesting to note that the SVC now no longer operates under the general advocacy and protection of the Office of the Dean of Religious Life. It and Community House (begun in 1969 when students mobilized by their ideals lived and worked in the John Witherspoon Street neighborhood of Princeton) are now administered by the Pace Center, a promising effort of the university "to provide a center source for civic engagement" and "to use existing faculty and curricular resources to study and understand problems of social and public concern as well as to take action to alleviate them." In my short tenure as interim dean of the chapel I had registered my concern that while the Pace Center might better link the SVC with faculty and curricular resources and perhaps help provide longer-term strategies for dealing with societal issues and problems the SVC volunteers were trying to ameliorate, there might also result a sense that the SVC activities were less student initiatives and more official programs of the university.

On the other side of that equation, the forthcoming move of the SVC to the Frist Student Center could give it a good new central place in that hub of student activities and will free up much needed space in Murray-Dodge for the many religious activities there. From my conversations I know that the deans of the chapel and other chaplains will continue to work with the Pace Center and support the work and spirit of the Student Volunteers Council while encouraging new initiatives in volunteer services.

Concern as well as hope for the future of the SVC is but one example of the issues that are discussed, thought about, and prayed about in Murray-Dodge Hall today. Recently I was invited to one of the meetings of the chaplains at Princeton, now called Princeton Affiliated Chaplains (PAC), convened by the dean of religious life. Sitting side by side were the coordinators of Muslim life and of Hindu life and the Hillel rabbi. Rabbi Julie Roth described the company she found at these meetings now that she had non-Christian colleagues. She also nodded across the room to Chabad Rabbi Eitan Webb, and I told the group the story of Catholic chaplain Tom Mullelly's concerns when Chabad had earlier not been granted status as a recognized chaplaincy. Sitting next to me, Tom Mullelly warmed to the subject of the full accommodation Catholics as well as others had been given on campus—particularly in the free use of the chapel, lecture halls, and Murray-Dodge. In turn, the deans appreciated the difference it made for the chapel and the campus that much of Catholic worship and programming took place in the university.

Peter French, an Australian and the relatively new Episcopal chaplain, introduced himself, and I met again the Manna chaplain, Blake Altman, and Scott Luley of the Faculty Commons. Longtime staff members were present as well: Deans Blanks and Raushenbush and the Baptist and Athletes in Action chaplain David Buschman have been at Princeton for a number of years. The Wesley Foundation and Intervarsity Christian Fellowship chaplain, Keith Brewer, a fellow New Testament scholar, has been at Princeton for eighteen years, and Princeton Evangelical Fellowship's Bill Boyce has ministered on campus for a quarter century. Soon to be retiring Orthodox Father Dan Skivir began his ministry as assistant to his father-in-law, when I was dean of the chapel, and we recalled the days when the Orthodox shared worship space in Murray-Dodge with the Jewish group—their Torah scrolls stowed away in a cabinet when not in use.

There was opportunity also to try to take in the whole picture. In a world of political, cultural, and religious differences and challenges, it is not easy to know how better understanding and sharing among religions and spiritualities can happen. But here in the contemporary university some of it was happening. Princeton and a number of other universities have become rare and special places where future American and world citizens can learn of the possibilities of dialogue and something of the depths and diversity of their own and other faiths.[21] Here there can be not only interreligious meetings between faiths but also intrareligious conversations among, say, evangelicals and Catholics; Sunni and Shia and other Muslim groups (some discriminated against in their homeland countries); and Orthodox, liberal, and conservative Jews. Among these chaplains there was a sense of camaraderie and a shared ministry to the campus. Dean Boden observed, "I have never seen a campus with this much religious activity and interest in religion and spirituality."

As I left the chaplains' meeting, I found myself crossing Firestone Plaza and by habit entering the quiet of the chapel. Except for the work-study

---

[21] As a further testimony to and plea for the values of this education and discourse, see Robert J. Nash, *Religious Pluralism in the Academy: Opening the Dialogue* (New York: Peter Lang, 2001).

student reading in the narthex, the building appeared empty of all but memories. As I wandered up the center aisle, I became aware of a couple sitting toward the front in one of the pews—pews made from the wood for Civil War gun carriages. Heads close together, they were whispering with one another, perhaps thinking they might one day be married here. Now I also noticed a little group of three—probably visitors—making their tour of the chapel, and, far forward, sacristan Bernie La Fleur was polishing one of the saints of Western civilization carved into a pew post in the sanctuary. There the late afternoon sun was casting through stained glass pastel patches on the wall next to the great east window, enshrining God's love for the world and Jesus's words, "Love one another as I have loved you." I sat halfway up the nave, sliding over near one of the massive pillars. I became aware that I was not far from the memorial inscriptions engraved into the stone wall for Robert Goheen, John Witherspoon, and Benjamin Rush. I thought of Fred Fox and other alumni with their names there—some who had died in wars. Before and all around me were other names commemorated in the wood of the pews. Perhaps, I thought, my name might be carved here "someday."

I grew further nostalgic and heard Judge Medina again extolling Woodrow Wilson's baccalaureate address: "be transformed by the renewing of your mind that ye may approve what is that good and acceptable and perfect will of God." I could imagine cadences of Martin Luther King Jr. ("Hate cannot drive out hate: only love can do that") from that same pulpit and thought of students, faculty, and deans who had prayed and worshipped here—many inspired by the words, the passion, and spirit of Jesus. All life and change involves loss, I reflected, thinking back to the years when this faith seemed more at the heart and inspiration of the university. I thought of colleagues who perhaps wished they believed in God but could not, and the many who had passed through Princeton on their own pilgrimages hoping for some lasting meaning in life's adventure—some of whom had at times ventured that hope or prayer in this building, as first, many years past, I had done.

A young man walked up the far side aisle and entered the Chapel of the Blessed Sacrament. Perhaps in a few minutes university organist Eric Plutz would begin his practice. I looked again into the sanctuary to the interfaith banner of the burning bush—the tree of life—and in my mind's eye could see it being carried in procession, kites swirling above, and the chapel full of freshmen, and, on another day, graduating students of different faiths with all their questions, doubts, and aspirations. "And now faith, hope, and love abide, these three; and the greatest of these is love," reads one of the students. "To do justice, to love kindness, and to walk humbly with your God," "in the name of God, Most Gracious, Most Merciful," "I have a dream . . ." continue others.

But a few weeks earlier I had been here for "Performing the Sacred," presented by the Religious Life Council in cosponsorship with the Departments of Music, French and Italian, Art and Archaeology, and the Lewis Center for the Arts. Poet and professor Paul Muldoon read a poem by a ninth-century monk. Conducted by the gifted Penna Rose, the splendid Chapel Choir sang a paschal hymn to the Mother of God from the rear balcony of the darkened chapel. There was classical Indian dance and a Sufi composition played on the sitar by Hidayat Khan and on the tabla by Manjul Bhargava, professor of mathematics—the two sitting before the altar with its gold and white Easter frontal in a chapel become temple with the great columns lit as though from within. A Jewish a cappella group sang "Shalom Rav" ("Abundance of Peace"), followed by a small Orthodox choir with "Holy God, Holy Mighty One, Holy Immortal One, Have Mercy on Us." There was a lyrical Islamic devotional poem and a duet danced by two members of the American Repertory Ballet based on a text from the book of Job. "Performing the Sacred" continued, concluding the night with the combined choir and glee club singing "Steal Away . . . Steal Away, Steal Away to Jesus . . . Steal Away Home." All who were present were invited to think of the chapel as a spiritual home. Who could not be grateful for such poetry, dance, and song—the rich resources of multifaith students and faculty?

I found myself thinking, too, of programs now taking place at other universities with their interfaith councils and different worship, conversations, classes, meetings, and prayers. I wondered what all this might mean for the future of religions, for faith and hope—for better understanding, compassion, forgiveness—for peace, for salaam and shalom, and I realized I was praying for that future.

ACKNOWLEDGMENTS

In addition to the scholars of American religion and higher education who are cited in this study, I am grateful to former colleagues and friends old and new who have aided me through conversation and by reading portions or the entirety of this manuscript. While the views expressed and any errors herein are certainly mine, these readers have been generous with their time and insights. Indeed, a number of them play a role or are heard from in the book, and I want to record my special thanks to Paul Kemeny, Robert Wuthnow, William Bowen, Neil Rudenstine, Sheldon Hackney, George Rupp, John Wilson, Thomas Wright, Robert Durkee, Eugene Lowe, Stanley Katz, Alison Boden, Paul Raushenbush, Deborah Blanks, Sue Anne Morrow, Keith Brewer, Carl Reimers, Charles Bennison, Patricia Karlin-Neumann, Susan Laemmle, Sharon Kugler, Robert Gregg, Harry Adams, Edward Feld, Elizabeth Davenport, Jay Demerath and Arthur Bellinzoni. Several of these friends have also assisted in major ways in the overviews of other universities as I have noted in that chapter.

I wish to acknowledge as well the friendship and assistance of Daniel Linke and staff at Princeton's Mudd Manuscript Library and the counsel and encouragement of Peter Dougherty and his colleagues at the Princeton University Press along with the skilled editorial assistance of Dawn Hall. My thanks, too, to Barbara Borsch, my partner and participant in one way or another in a number of these Princeton stories (ask her about the night of the plane crash), for her perspective on all this and patience in listening to portions read aloud while trying to correct some of my infelicities.

INDEX